support. Keep live music alive

CHOICES

W. Granville Brown

9 May 09

First published by Dog Ear Publishing
4010 W. 86th Street, Ste H
Indianapolis, IN 46268
www.dogearpublishing.net

ISBN: 978-159858-906-1

This book is printed on acid-free paper.

This book is a work of Fiction. Places, events, and situations in this book are purely Fictional and any resemblance to actual persons, living or dead, is coincidental.

Printed in the United States of America

DEDICATION

I would like to dedicate this book to my children; Shania, Kevin and Tifanie. I pray with seeing your 46 year old father accomplish a life-long dream, you guys will continue to have your own dreams and believe that age is not an excuse to give up simply because a dream hasn't come to fruition.

To my mother Sallie McDowell all I can say is thank you. Whether you know it or not, you have been an example of strength and determination. Two qualities I needed in completing this labor-of- love.

To my editor LauraMaery Gold I extend my hand of friendship and gratitude. I've thanked you enough and still I feel that isn't enough.

My heart-felt thanks go out to everyone at Dog Ear Publishing. Your professionalism was second to none.

I also want to take the time to thank my numerous family members and friends especially, Ty Dangerfield and Lyndell Ends for giving me your ear, your time and more importantly your support.

And lastly but certainly not least, none of this would've been possible if it wasn't for my blessing who entered my life at its lowest point—my beautiful and awesome wife, Isabella. Without your love, belief and support it's very possible that none of this would be any thing more than a dream-deferred. I thank God every day for blessing me with a love like yours. One year and counting! I love you 4-ever & ever & always!

Prologue

The meeting took place in an out-of-the-way nondescript motel so deep in no-man's land, the ancient woman who checked them in quickly forgot doing so.

"Are you kidding me? Why are we meeting in a dump like this?"

"A place is more than its appearance."

"Well this place appears to be a dump."

"You have always failed to appreciate the beauty of what I've created."

"Ha ha. Let's not forget you also created the flip side where I prosper."

"There once was a man who threw a gold coin into the air with the intention of allowing the side it landed on determine his fate."

"What in the..."

"Patience my son."

Immediately a sense of peace and light filled the dim, dingy lit room.

"My fault, please continue."

"Momentarily he was distracted and took his eyes off the descending gold coin. It bounced off his outstretched palm and rolled through a crack in the floor, lost forever."

"So what happened?"

"I don't know. Someone changed the channel."

"Oh so you got jokes. And people think you don't have a sense of humor."

"Laughter is medicine for the soul, my son."

"Yes it is. Where I reside we laugh often at how easy our job has become. In days gone by it was a little more difficult to get someone to denounce you; now let them miss the last digit on a lottery ticket after they prayed for a winner and bam. I have a new convert."

"You have always underestimated the faith of my children."

"With all due respect, I think you overestimate the faith of your children."

"An argument for another time. I see you have been quite busy lately."

"We all have our cross to bear. No pun intended."

"No offense taken, my son. Now have you considered my faithful servants?"

"Ah, yes the young married couple in Philadelphia. I've been keeping track of them for some time, especially since the husband has stopped attending church regularly. I feel that they are ripe for the picking though you have blessed them greatly. However, as I am notorious for saying, remove your

hedge of protection from them and they will surely curse you."

"Behold all they have in is your power. Only do not touch them."

"Including their relationship?"

"Yes."

"Why am I dealing with them as one?"

"Because what I have put together let no man divide."

"Consider it done. I will prove to you that the faith you have in your people is far greater than the faith they have in you."

CHAPTER ONE

Tonight there'd be no squealing of his woman, no squeaking of bedsprings. None of the sounds that was jazz to Trey Edwards' ears. Quiet were the noises that filled him with pride at his sexual prowess. The band wasn't in town tonight as he laid flat on his back looking at the slow moving ceiling fan overhead.

"Drea," he said nudging the slumbering body lying beside him in the four-poster bed. "You 'sleep?"

He rolled over on his side and blew warm air into her ear. In return he received a hand to the face, pushing him away.

"What's wrong with you Trey? Can't you see I'm trying to sleep?"

"Come on baby; sleep is overrated."

"Look at the time. You know I have to get up early in the morning. Now go to sleep," she commanded.

"Put me to sleep," he pleaded.

"Hand me a brick."

Trey silently cursed under his breath as he bumped against her until she finally had enough and jumped out of bed.

"See you're awake. Let's make love."

"Start without me while I go to the bathroom," she said smartly over her shoulder. "Just be finished before I get back."

"That's cold, woman. You do know it's been awhile since we had sex don't you?"

"You keep waking me up in the middle of the night it's going to be a lot longer," was her response.

Trey watched his wife, salivating at the sight of her nude body in the moonlight from the bedroom window. Even after fourteen years of marriage and two children, her body still aroused him. It drove him crazy that she slept in the raw especially on the nights she rejected his advances of affection; which according to his want-some-loving-bad-meter registered six weeks, fours days, seventeen hours and about nineteen seconds. If any more time went by he could re-qualify as a virgin.

Quickly, before she returned, Trey hopped out of bed and reached into his nightstand. Tiptoeing across the room like a cat on cotton, he lit the scented candle on top of the dresser. Instantly the flickering candlelight played shadows along the walls. He pushed the play button on the CD player, filling the room with the mellow voice of Barry White singing about practicing what you preach. With the mood set Trey, squirted himself with a dab of cologne, and then replaced his cotton boxers with a pair of silk pajama pants.

Three songs played all the way through before Andrea exited the bathroom to find Trey standing by the bed illuminated by the light of the candle moving seductively to the beat of the music.

"Trey," she said weakly, "not tonight."

"Tonight is as good a time as any, Drea. Come on girl. I miss making love to my baby."

"I'm too tired. Don't be selfish."

Annoyance started to set up shop, but Trey simply refused entry. "Is it selfish for a man to want to make love to his woman?" He halted her reply with a wagging finger. "Is it selfish for a man to lust after his wife and not another woman although his wife rejects him like some chump from the club at last call?"

"May I speak now?" Andrea said bitterly then caught herself. "Maybe selfish was the wrong word; I'm sorry. I meant to say try and understand that I'm simply tired and not in the mood."

"For over a month?" Trey shot back.

"I'm not fighting with you tonight," she said walking toward the bed. "Good night, Trey."

His eyes were glued to her full bosom, licking his lips he admired how well her body had held up over the years. Though she was a little loose around the mid-section, the rest of her figure was tight and firm from constant battles of diet and grinding exercise. Trey turned around to look at her tempting bottom.

"Fifteen minutes," he heard her say.

"You can't time the magic," he said excitedly wiggling out of the silk pants.

"Fifteen minutes," she repeated sliding into bed.

One hour later Trey wiped the pouring sweat from his face with a hand towel. "Whoa, now that's what I've been missing."

Breathing rapidly Andrea scolded him for exceeding the time limit.

"Don't blame me," he teased. "You the one kept saying don't stop."

"Go to sleep, fool." Andrea kissed Trey and rolled over onto her side.

Trey accepted the kiss and got up to blow out the candle and cut off the music. As he returned to bed he smiled feeling content that although he was the one doing the squealing at least the bedsprings made some noise.

****

Sunday morning Trey was awakened by banging sounds coming from down-stairs. He peeked out from under the covers, careful not to reveal too much of his face in case Andrea was still in the room. His excuse bucket was getting empty and he knew if she and the kids hadn't left for church, she would demand he attend service like he'd promised he would the previous Sunday. He sat up in the bed as the noise from below became louder. Trey decided to go investigate its cause.

Trey leapfrogged down the steps and entered the kitchen to find Ian Gregory, his best friend since second grade, rummaging through the kitchen cabinets. Without bothering to turn around he asked, "Where's the Cap'n Crunch?"

"Yo, free-loader since when you start paying rent?" he asked. "And where's Andrea and the kids?"

"Stop whining."

"I'm not whining."

Facing Trey, Ian said, "Go put some pants on. You're not my type."

Playfully Trey swung at Ian's head missing him by a hair. "Answer my question," he said as he walked away to put something over his boxer briefs.

"They were leaving to go to church— where I might add, you should spend a little time yourself— as I was coming in. And you can kiss my butt on the rent."

Trey laughed as he went upstairs to dress truly happy to see his friend. When he re-entered the kitchen he put on a pot of coffee even though he never touched the stuff. "Why are you here this early on a Sunday morning?"

"Don't trip; you know you take great joy in basking in my presence." Ian finger snapped to emphasize his point. He poured cereal and milk into the largest bowl in Trey's cupboard. Walking to the glass-topped kitchen table, he delicately set the bowl down, not spilling a drop.

"Your bowl runneth over I see," Trey joked amused that though Ian consumed twice the normal serving of food anytime he ate, his weight stayed the same. "How do you eat so much and not gain an ounce? Oh I know— free food has no calories."

Ian rolled his eyes so far back in his head it looked as though he'd passed out, but he continued to slurp and chomp his cereal gleefully. "Pray tell, why you so evil this morning?"

Trey tossed him a napkin motioning where milk had dripped onto Ian's chin. "I'm feeling a little disconnected from Drea lately."

Ian shook his head while wiping his chin. "You back on that trip again? I keep telling you that watching the Huxtables, don't make you them."

Trey stretched his arms above his head and let out a loud moan full groan. "Man, I ain't trying to be no doggone TV family; I'm just trying to be happy with the one I got."

"So what happened this time?"

"You think I'm tripping again?" Trey accused watching his eyes for conformation.

Not one to back down Ian returned Trey's glare. "Can't answer that one since I don't know what you might be tripping about."

"Okay," Trey stated flatly. "First off we barely have sex anymore. Last night was the first time in months and I had to darn near beg for that."

"Urg." Ian made a face. "Married folks having sex. Now that's just sick."

"You done? I'm serious. This is serious."

"It must be you said it twice." Ian was having fun.

Trey got up to fix Ian a cup of coffee. Placing the finished product in front of him, Trey continued, "Sex and finances break up more marriages than anything else."

"You're having money troubles too?"

"No."

"Then what does that have to do with you guys?"

"I'm making a point."

"About what?"

Getting frustrated, Trey sank his head into his hands and inhaled and exhaled deeply. He cracked his neck by twisting his head to the left then the right. The popping sound was loud.

"You going to break your neck one of these days doing that," Ian said making another face. "All right, Trey, what's really up? Maybe you guys need some alone time. No kids; just the two of you go somewhere and wear each other out. I know! Go to a casino hotel. That way you can take care of the finances *and* the sex. I'll bill you later."

"Yeah." Trey didn't sound too sure. "Maybe you right. We have both been going full speed working and running the kids here there and everywhere."

"Of course I'm right. You think too much."

"I just don't feel settled in my spirit."

"Maybe you should have gone to church with your family."

Without responding Trey walked over to the expensive stainless- steel fridge that Andrea had begged for until he agreed to purchase it during one of her remodelling kicks. Although a couple thousand was way too much to spend on a stupid refrigerator, Andrea had ways of getting what she truly wanted from him. She'd wait until he was engrossed in a sporting event on television and then present her case. So during the Super Bowl, she did just that and he kind of said yes. Two days later, when he had run into the kitchen for a bite to eat, there sat a brand new stainless-steel fridge, fully loaded.

Taking a gulp of orange juice directly from the carton, Trey asked, "Hey tell me, how're things on your end?" Trey didn't miss Ian's grin, knowing he hadn't fooled him with his sudden change of subject.

Ian obliged him. "I got a new bass player. The boy has played behind darn near everybody. I'm talking about Miss Diva Patti, Luther, you name them. His bass lines drive the groove big time."

Trey was happy to hear the rebirth of energy in Ian's voice as he shared the latest updates about his music career. Ever since high school Ian had performed all over Philadelphia and had built up quite a local following. But after two self-produced and self-financed CD's hadn't gotten him a recording contract with a major label, his buddy's dream of stardom was dimming. "Is this going to be a steady band?" Trey asked as he wiped his mouth before putting the carton back into the hated fridge. He sat back down as Ian got up and strolled over to the stainless steel double sink. Placing the bowl down gently on the Italian- marble countertop Ian spun around answering hopefully, "From your mouth to the music god's ear. I need one, man I've gotta take my music to the next level or get a real nine- to- five. I'm not twenty anymore."

"I know you're…"

"Shut your mouth," Ian interrupted.

"I'm only talking about…"

"You better be talking about Shaft," he retorted. He leaned back against the sink, cutting eyes at Trey hooting with laughter. Age wasn't a subject open for discussion with Ian at any time.

Through his laughter Trey asked, "When you going back into the studio?"

"Studio time is costly. Bunk that! That's exactly why I'm not dealing any more with cats that ain't for real about music."

Trey readily agreed, then asked, "What about getting a manager? A real one this time." He couldn't help recalling the joke of a manager Ian had had two years ago.

Beaming from ear to ear Ian crossed his arms over his narrow chest. Keeping the suspense going for as long as he could, which was about three seconds, he blurted out, "That's why I'm here so early on a Sunday morning, besides the free grub. I'm going to the jazz brunch on City Line Avenue and meeting…" He paused for dramatic affect, "Taylor Daniels."

"Who?" Trey was puzzled and clueless.

"Did you ask, who? You must get out more. Taylor Daniels is the baddest manager in the business. Not only is she fine, if that's your thing, but she is the chick that got Johnny Fisher his deal with Too Fat Records."

"Thanks for clearing that up."

Trey's utter ignorance of who was what in the music business apparently exasperated Ian. In order to school him, Ian sat back down and for the next ten minutes explained to Trey how Taylor Daniels at only twenty years of age had become a senior vice-president with Upworld Records, until they merged with either Sony or Warner, and yes she got that high-powered position because she was reportedly sleeping with the CEO. In her time at the label three acts that she had found put out recordings that went double platinum, proving that giving it up or not, the girl knew her stuff. After the merger the network of good ole' boys squeezed her out and she moved to Philly, started her own management firm and quickly served notice that she was looking for talent. Everybody in the city that thought they sounded good in the shower auditioned for her. No one stood out until— as the story went— she was taking the subway somewhere and Johnny Fisher, a young boy from West Philly, was singing on the subway ramp for loose change. Within three days she'd talked his mother into letting her manage his career, had him in the studio and signed him to a two-album deal with Too Fat Records.

"Now that's what I'm talking about! She came to the club last night, heard me do my thing and I must add, I was simply fabulous. She asked me how come she hadn't heard of me and then she said that was ok because she definitely knew who I was now." Ian stopped long enough to catch his breath and started examining his fingernails.

Caught up in Ian's excitement Trey impatiently waited for him to continue but Ian was milking it. "Go on, man."

With all the nonchalance and arrogance he could muster Ian said, "She invited me to brunch today so we could talk about her handling my career."

Their shouts bounced off the striped walls of the kitchen. Ian's dream had been on life support. This put the plug back in and they both knew it as they rejoiced, screaming at the top of their lungs and jumping into each other's arms.

"This is it, man! You're on your way!"

Tears began to flow freely from Ian's eyes, clouding his vision. They embraced without any display of self consciousness. "Thanks man, I love you."

Trey squeezed even tighter as he tried to blink back his own tears. "Back at ya."

Looking at the clock on the black flat-top stove to see how much time he had left Ian insisted Trey continue their previous conversation. Trey shrugged his shoulders and told him that all was cool; Ian was right about him over-reacting to nothing. After pushing Ian out the door, wishing him good luck, Trey ran down into the finished basement of his house to do his Sunday morning workout. Lying back across the weight bench he hoisted the bar with over two hundred pounds of barbells from the rack. Lifting the barbells into the air he effortlessly brought it to his heaving chest then raised it up again in an attempt to work his muscles to exertion so as to tire out his body and give his brain something else to focus on other than the nagging notion that somehow his marriage was in trouble.

Sitting up he said aloud, "Lord in your mighty name, help us."

****

"Ok listen up. The big guy has removed his hedge of protection from Trey and Andrea Edwards. We have permission to wreak havoc on them. Only I can't touch them. We are to treat them as one person. We'll start with their relationship. Nothing works better than exploiting trouble areas in a marriage. And like most, they have some. Now remember the wife is a praying, church-going woman, so she has potential to be a tougher nut to crack. However the husband has removed himself from the gathering of other like-minded people and is becoming more and more frustrated with the lack of intimacy between them. Let's throw some temptation his way. To bring down this union we'll start with an oldie but goodie: infidelity."

CHAPTER TWO

"Mom," Brett called out from the back seat of Andrea's 2004 Lexus, "Mom I know you hear me."

"Boy can't see you I'm trying to drive here?" she scolded him, cutting eyes at her husband's spitting image through the rear view mirror. Driving back home after a powerful church service her concentration was split between handling the car and thinking about other matters.

"And that stops you from answering me?"

"Boy do you want to live to see eleven? Don't get popped in your mouth. Last time I checked I was the parent and the one driving this car. Yes Brett. I'll stop at Wadsworth Pizza. Now leave me be."

"Yeah boy, that's what I'm talking bout, a big cheese steak. Hey big head," he hollered as he plucked his little sister in the back of the head. "Wake up. We going to Wadsworth Pizza."

"Stop! Mom tell him to leave me alone. You better keep your hands to yourself." Brittany turned around and swung at her brother, but he was too fast for her. Before she could duck he grabbed her nose and squeezed lightly. Their excited giggles filled the car until Andrea complained about the ruckus.

"Don't make me pull this car over." She couldn't contain her own laughter when Brittany and Brett mocked her. They settled down quickly when she threatened to drive right by the pizza shop.

As normal the traffic on Wadsworth Avenue resembled a parade, bumper to bumper. Where once the Mt. Airy section of Philadelphia was the haven for the well-to-do German and Jewish families, during the 60's and early 70's there began a migration of Blacks moving uptown. Immediately, White families sold out, not caring whether they made a profit or not. Fortunately for many Blacks they were then able to move into twin or double-style homes and the lucky few grabbed up the limited number of single-family homes in the area like the house Trey's parents owned.

Soon, though, the drug dealing started – as it did in so many cities—and Mt. Airy was no exception. Parents who'd moved uptown to escape the "ghetto mentality," gave birth to children who embraced it, as if doing so allowed them to- keep it real. In clear view, Andrea witnessed three drug transactions as she drove along with the slow-moving traffic.

"Right there, Mom that bad ride is leaving!" Brett shouted from the backseat. "That's what I'm talking bout. I'm getting me one of those when I grow up."

Andrea hit her flashers to signal her intention to park and waited for the braided-haired woman driving the huge SUV struggle to get out of the tight squeeze two smaller cars had left her in. For what appeared to be the longest time the woman inched forward and then backward in an attempt to maneuver the massive automobile. With a mighty grunt that Andrea and the kids heard, she finally escaped and rocketed away as she narrowly missed hitting a car in the opposite lane.

Andrea expertly parallel parked in front of a barber shop packed with men of various ages and hair styles. "Ok, watch your sister and bring me back all my change," she instructed, giving Brett twenty dollars.

The kids exited the car and ran into the pizza shop two stores down from the barber shop where she'd parked. As she replaced her wallet she felt a vibration. Scrambling through her purse she found her pink cell phone. "Hey girl." She recognized the number displayed on the caller ID. "I was just getting ready to call you." Her head bobbed as she listened to the caller. "I heard that. Look I'm right around the corner from your place. The kids are just leaving the pizza joint. I'm on my way. Explain when I get there."

Half an hour later as Andrea knocked on the storm door minus the screen, she was certain she heard raised voices and the sound of what sounded like skin hitting skin.

"Mom, do we gotta go in there? Can't we wait in the car?"

"Shush boy. I'm trying to hear." She banged harder on the door not bothering to ring the doorbell since in the five years of knowing Tina Jenkins it hadn't worked. "Tina!" Andrea shouted to be heard. She was sure the hollering voice she was hearing belonged to Tina. Turning the doorknob, Andrea found it unlocked, so she twisted the knob and stepped through the door to find Tina beating the crap out of her seventeen-year old daughter. Andrea felt her mouth open and knew she was screaming for her to stop. It took a couple of seconds for her to realize the screaming she heard was in her own head.

"Stupid behind!" She heard Tina shout. "Didn't I tell you I ain't putting up with your crap no more?" With every word she threw a punch or a kick at the balled-up figure on the floor.

Brett pushed past Andrea and Brittany to get an upfront view of the one-sided fight. "Dang! She is whuppin that."

"Shut your mouth, boy," Andrea said, snatching him by his collar and pulling him back from the fray. "Tina!" She shouted trying to get Tina's attention. "Tina! What are you doing?"

Tina was too busy hitting and trying to get through her daughter's guard to turn around so she said between blows, "Whuppin this fool's behind again!"

The defenseless girl was trying her best to block as many punches and kicks as she could. Her nose was bleeding and her left eye was starting to swell.

"Oh, Sweet Jesus." Andrea's hands covered her mouth. With a strength she didn't know she possessed she pulled Tina away from her whimpering daughter. "Tina, you can't keep beating on that girl like that. Get up Rochelle." Andrea bent down to help her up off the dirty tiled floor.

Rochelle kept her head down as she worked her way up onto her knees and accepted Andrea's hand.

"Now take your ho'ing behind upstairs before I knock you out. You lucky Drea saved your butt!" Without missing a beat Tina turned and smiled at Andrea and grabbed her into a tight hug. "Listening to those religious tapes has really helped me with all that cussing I used to do." Then she looked at the kids. "Don't y'all look nice in your church clothes. Come give your Aunt Tina a hug."

Brett nudged Brittany to go first then held his breath as she pulled him into her large breast.

"Boy, you as fine as your daddy and girl ain't you sumthin. Drea, that girl done worked my last nerve." Tina acted like it was a normal event for guests to find her beating the snot out of her oldest child.

Andrea told the kids to go watch TV in the living room. "Uh, ummm, what in the world was that about?"

Tina didn't answer her as she led the way into the kitchen area of the rented three-bedroom home that she shared with her three daughters. It was obvious that Tina had once been quite a looker and still could be if she cared. But, living hard and fast does take a toll. Two hundred pounds was too much for her five foot, two inch frame to carry, so she'd stopped worrying about it and said men love the big ones anyway. Her once dancing eyes no longer heard the music.

"Want some beer?"

"I just came from church."

"They drink wine up in there."

"Girl, you crazy." Andrea swatted at a roach that refused to move off the torn cushioned chair before she sat down. "You need to come to church with me. Listening to sermons on tape is all well and good, but getting the word up close and personal is so much better. Now what was that about?"

Tina flopped down across the table from Andrea while screwing the top off a forty-ounce beer bottle. Taking a big swig from the bottle, she burped and said, "One step at a time, girl. "You ain't gonna believe this sh…I mean crap. I came home from copping some weed. You wanna get high?" She didn't give Andrea a chance to respond before she answered her own question. "Of course you don't Miss Thang; I know you don't get down like that. Anywho as I was saying I left this house for one-two hour's tops and when I got back that little heifer had some roughneck all up in my house, drinking my shit. Oops, I owe you one Lord. And on top of that when I came through the door she was on her knees in front of the fool."

Andrea was confused how that warranted Tina beating her daughter up. "Did you tell her not to have any company?"

"Did you hear me? She was on her knees in front of him and I think his zipper was undone."

"Whoa, you didn't say all that."

"I said she was on her knees. You ain't that high and mighty, church- going or not. I'm the only one up in here getting down like that. And for real girl, I ain't trying to be nobody's grandmother at only thirty-four."

Andrea empathised with Tina. She knew from watching some of her other girlfriends that being a single parent wasn't easy, but when you threw in lack of education, no job and no man to help out either financially, or otherwise as was Tina's situation it only made matters worse. However, she didn't help her own plight by having her first child at seventeen, and then having one child a year for the next two. To compound her troubles all three girls had different fathers, ranging from a convicted drug dealer to a wanna-be-pimp to a married man who flat out denied being the father.

Andrea first met Tina when she applied for a job opening at the prestigious law firm where Andrea worked as a paralegal. Tina had showed up for the interview in the shortest, tightest skirt she could possibly squeeze into and still have the ability to breath. At the time Tina hadn't gained the weight she now carried. Needless to say, she didn't get the job, but she and Andrea met outside of the office building on Broad Street and over coffee at Starbucks a friendship was born. Despite the fact that the two were as different as winter and summer. Andrea was a product of the South, growing up in a little eastern North Carolina town that made Mayberry seem like a big-time city and Tina was borne and bred on the mean streets of North Philly. She dropped out of school in the ninth grade and received her formal education in crack houses and gambling joints. The one thing they did have in common, though, and which bonded them was: trust. From their initial conversation five years ago till now they trusted and confided in each other like sisters. There wasn't anything Andrea couldn't tell to Tina and vice versa. Try as she might— and for the length of their relationship she tried— Andrea wasn't able to make Tina believe in herself and put any effort into being anything more than a welfare queen. At least she started listening to the taped sermons that Andrea had given her over a year ago.

"I hear you and I feel you, but you still have to find another way to discipline Rochelle other than kicking her behind," Andrea reasoned with Tina.

When it came to her girls, Andrea knew that Tina was a warrior. She made certain they were well-fed, went to school and didn't run the streets. She confided many times to Andrea, she simply refused to allow her daughters to suffer the same hand she'd dealt herself. So if it took beating one of them down to keep them on the straight and narrow, it was her duty as a mother to do just that.

As Tina lit into the beer, tears began to flow down her ruddy cheeks. It truly did break her heart any time she hit one of her kids and sometimes her temper combined with a heavy dose of fear took over. Rochelle had tried to explain to her that nothing was happening when she barged in and the boy had used the bathroom and she didn't know whether his pants were zipped or not. "She said she was just sitting between his legs looking at the TV."

"And you didn't believe her?"

"No. Dammit I know what I saw," she said slamming the bottle down onto the wobbly table.

Andrea took hold of Tina's hand that wasn't holding onto the bottle. It broke her heart knowing her girlfriend was in turmoil and so much pain. "You want to ask God for guidance?"

"Girl, He gave up on me a long time ago." She paused. "I didn't mean to hit her so hard, Drea." The tears were beginning to pour from her eyes. "I can't have my girls messing up their lives like I did running behind some no-good ass man!"

"Your life is not over, Tina. You are a good mother doing the best you can by yourself. Besides all three are doing well in school. But beating the hell out of your child ain't gonna do nothing but turn them against you one of these days. Honey, you can't let your fears rule you. God didn't give us the spirit of fear. Don't I keep telling you that?"

"Yeah," she said rubbing her eyes roughly. "But you don't understand. You got a man, a house and a job."

"The grass ain't always greener," was Andrea's cryptic retort.

Sniffing loudly and wiping the tears from her eyes Tina looked closely at her friend for the first time since Andrea and the kids entered her home. "You trying to tell me something?"

Another roach attempted to take up residence on the chair Andrea was sitting in. Her skin began to crawl from the nasty insect being so close to her and the thought that more would come out made her stomach ache. Pushing the chair back from the table Andrea stood up and went over to the sink which was full of food-caked dishes. Trying not to touch another roach she turned on the water to wash her hands. "Tina, will you please get an exterminator up in here."

"Girl, they want too much. If those lazy heifers of mine would clean up behind themselves they would go away."

Girl, I'm calling Tony's Pest Control in the morning for you. I'll pay for it. You gonna be here tomorrow?"

"Where else I'm gonna be?"

Andrea dried her hands on the last piece of paper towel making a mental note to leave Tina with a couple dollars to tide her over until the first of the month.

"Wanna talk about that grass?" Tina asked, having fully composed herself. Now it was her turn to look out for her friend. That's the way it worked with them. Andrea would lecture Tina on a better way of life, how she needed to stop drinking and smoking weed, go to church, and Tina would listen to Andrea complain about her marriage, raising two kids while working a high-stress job and how hard it was playing the role of superwoman.

Andrea pointed toward the living room. Quietly she walked to the opening of the kitchen to peer into the room to check on the kids. The last thing she wanted was one or both of them listening in on grown folk conversation. Adding to her mental list she reminded herself to warn the kids to not mention what they saw today to their father. Brittany was fast asleep on the imitation leather sofa and Brett was busy practicing his remote control skills. Andrea smiled looking at her two precious children, proud of the job she and Trey were doing as parents. At least they got that right.

"Now this is between you and me," she said sitting back down.

"That goes without saying." Tina sucked the last drop from the bottle and burped loudly. "Damn, that was my last forty and I ain't got no ends. Sorry girl, go on I'm listening."

"Trey wants sex all the time and I'm just so tired at the end of the day," she blurted out. "I don't understand why he can't understand that."

"I wish I had your problem," Tina said. "Drea, do you have any ideal how many women out here, would sell their soul to the devil for your life?"

"You don't get it," she answered sharply.

"Would you rather he be out in the street getting it from someone else?"

"No," she weakly said. "But still I'm beginning to feel like a masturbation tool."

"What woman doesn't at some point in time? Excuse me, but ain't you the one who told me about abundance? So if your man is giving you more than enough, consider that a blessing from God."

"That's blasphemy," Andrea scolded.

"Sorry. I'm just saying, here you are where I want to be and…"

Andrea interrupted her. "Don't get me wrong. I thank God every day for my family. I guess I'm just stressing. Look here, girl let me get out of here. Trey is probably wondering where we are. Before I go let me loan you some money to help you out until the first."

Tina played her role by saying, "Oh no girl. I still owe you from the last time and you gonna pay to get rid of these filthy roaches."

It was a weak protest. Andrea grabbed her purse, praying she wasn't taking any roaches home with her and handed Tina three twenty dollar bills. "If you need more than this let me know." She made Tina promise she wouldn't buy beer or weed with the funds. "I'm serious, girl don't let me down."

Tina kissed her cheek and told her – meaning it this time— not to worry; she would indeed be responsible with the money. As usual Andrea insisted they say a prayer prior to her leaving.

Ten minutes after Andrea and the kids pulled away from the curb, Tina grabbed her shoes and walked around the corner to buy more beer.

Later that evening Trey set the stage for a repeat performance from the previous night. When he bounced into the bedroom after tucking his eight-year old daughter into her pink canopy bed, he discovered all the candles he'd lit extinguished and the music no longer playing. Andrea was buried deep under the covers and playing a lullaby from her throat.

Trey pounded his pillow in disgust and pulled on the covers in an attempt to wake her up. It didn't work, Andrea didn't budge nor did she change her tune.

CHAPTER THREE

For Trey, driving to work on Monday morning was an adventure as always. Lincoln Drive was once again transformed into a race track with all drivers ready to cross the finish line at the same time. Although the posted speed limit was 25 MPH, no one drove less than forty or fifty, or even sixty if traffic allowed. The funny thing to most users of this twisting and winding road was the fact that there clearly stood for all to see a police station that cars sped by every day. Trey was right in the middle of the pack, wheeling his C240 Benz, releasing his "inner Richard Petty," enroute to work. As usual the car's radio was set to his favourite station: 105.3 WDAS. He needed his early-morning fix of old- school R&B classics to set the mood for a long hard day of selling high-end vehicles. Trey simply refused to see himself as just a regular car salesman; the dealership he was employed with sold only Benz, BMW and other expensive high-end automobiles. That set him apart from the other hawkers of cars as he saw it. The music and the nice breeze coming through the open sunroof of the car soothed Trey and allowed him to free his mind of any negative thoughts.

He didn't want to contemplate his marriage; if he started, he knew it would ruin his entire day and take him off his game. But he couldn't believe how selfish Andrea was becoming by withholding affection and rationing it out like he was a two-year- old begging for cookies. Stopping himself before his thoughts became muddled, he chose to reflect back on the irony that was now his chosen career.

After his discharged from the Army after seven years of service, Trey went back to college and finished his four-year degree at Temple University. When he married Andrea, he took night classes and started to work side jobs just to pay the bills. The money wasn't good enough so he looked into other options. Never one to fear taking risk, he made the decision that it was better to pay himself than to have someone else pay him whatever they thought his time, talent and effort were worth. There were only two ways to make that happen: either start his own business or work on commission. Since he and Andrea didn't have enough funds in savings to buy a fast-food kids meal, the business thing would have to wait.

One day while hanging out at the Gallery Mall, he ran into a classmate from school. Trey couldn't remember the guy's name or the class they shared, but the conversation put him on the path to bigger paydays.

"Yeah, man. That's how I paid for my education," the guy had said.

"Selling insurance? You were able to pay for school and drive that Camry?"

That was enough for Trey. Within two weeks he had completed the weekend insurance class, taken and passed the test and started selling insurance for Washington Insurance Company. During the next seven years Trey built a client base that allowed him the financial freedom and flexibility he thirsted for. Brett and Brittany were born; they bought their current home in Mt. Airy and had all the trappings of success. Like most successful men, after getting to the top of his chosen mountain, Trey began to lose interest in the insurance industry. He vividly recalled telling Andrea how he was thinking about looking into doing something, anything else. He chuckled as he maneuvered his Benz along the snakelike turns of the road, remembering the hissy fit Andrea threw after he told her his plan.

He could still see the fire in her eyes and the heat that came from her mouth when she asked him, if he had lost his entire mind. It took all of his charm, salesmanship and a lot of begging and pleading to even get her to the point of further dialogue about what she considered his way-too-early midlife crisis.

Now five years later, he was the number-one salesmen at the largest Black-owned dealership in the tri-state area. And if all went as planned his dream of owning a dealership was less than six months away.

As Trey reminisced, he couldn't help from wondering why, after all this time; it appeared that Andrea still hadn't forgiven him for leaving the insurance business.

Parking in the parking spot reserved for the top producer—his for the past five years—he stepped out to survey what had become his passion. The dealership was owned by Dexter Fortune, a man whom Trey admired and looked up to as a father figure, though he was only five years older than Trey. The massive lighted sign that hovered over the entrance to the huge car lot was lit up like it was competing with the sun. It read, "Fortune Motors, Ltd: For the driver of fine cars who doesn't want to spend a fortune." Trey still thought the sign was a little cheesy, but how could you argue with a business that employed over 150 people and had an impeccable reputation known throughout the city? It was as Dexter was fond of telling Trey and anyone else in earshot, "A motto for a business has to state exactly what the business does and how it applies to the consumer." Since he practiced what he preached and had the success to show it, Trey listened and took notes whenever the great man spoke.

Wiping some non-existent lint form his black Armani slacks, Trey breathed in deeply and said a silent prayer before hitting the remote on his keychain to lock his pride and joy.

"Look at the man, styling as always. Boy, that's a bad suit."

"What up, Tony?" Trey answered eyeing the short guy walking toward him in an off-the-rack suit.

"Chillin.' Yo man, this month you're giving up the parking spot. I hope you know that," Tony smiled, revealing the whitest teeth this side of a shark.

Trey laughed. Tony had made the same prediction every month since he started working at the dealership two years ago.

"I hear you, Tony. First you gotta sell a car."

"Oh snap, a brotha' want to sound on me. I'm serious as a fat woman tryin' to get in a thong. This is my month; check the board, big man. I'll holler. I see my next satisfied customer." Tony strolled off to intercept a leather-clad man admiring a grey BMW.

Inside the dealership Trey walked to the company break room to view the leader board that tracked the number of cars sold by each salesperson.

"That's right Slick," said Paula, the receptionist.

Spinning around at the annoying shrill of her voice, Trey caught a glimpse of her inviting and always exposed cleavage.

"Tony is up one. He got one last night after you left and one first thing this morning. Oh yeah, Mr. Fortune said for you to come see him when you got in."

"Mmmmmm, nice top, it highlights your eyes."

"Yeah like you or any other dude around here notices my eyes," she said sarcastically, though Trey knew full well she enjoyed the attention and especially from him.

"I do," he defended himself, and added, "I'm a married man."

"But not a dead one. Quick," she challenged, "What color are my eyes?"

"Your eyes are light brown size thirty-eight D."

"Uh, huh, just like I thought. Married man my behind. All men are just alike, married or not. You all like to look and most love to touch."

"Here we go again. Ain't no harm in looking and it's not like you don't have them puppies in the window."

"Boy, you so crazy. You betta' hurry up; you know your Daddy waiting," Paula teased, pointing toward the back of the dealership that housed the offices. She leaned over the counter to watch Trey as he walked away in that sexy strut of his that made her almost want to forget her religion and lay hands all over the man. "Light-skin is back in. That man can have me anytime, married or not. Forgive me Lord. I have sinned."

The booming voice of Dexter Fortune rang out when Trey knocked on the mahogany hand-carved door. "You wanted to see me, Dex?" Trey asked. The inner sanctum of power gave Trey a rush every time he stepped into the huge office with its expensive artwork and furniture that cost more than most people spent furnishing their entire home.

Dexter was ensconced in a high-backed burgundy leather chair behind a desk he'd picked up from an antique shop in Italy. The desk was made of thick mahogany with lion heads engraved into the legs and the front trim. It was an open desk and Trey observed that Dexter was without his shoes, as was his habit when sitting.

"Yes, Trey, have a seat," he said. At forty-five years of age Dexter had accomplished more than most men given similar background and experience. He'd grown up in the projects of Johnson Homes in North Philly. Like Trey, he'd started off selling cars and learned the business from top to bottom under the stern guidance of his own mentor, Douglas Kingsley, who before his death amassed an empire of dealerships in Philadelphia, New Jersey, Delaware and New York.

Trey noticed Dexter's eyes nearly well up as he stole a glance at the picture he kept on his desk of Douglas and him standing in front of his first car lot during the grand opening ten years ago. Now here he sat, the owner of the largest Black-owned (the Black thing bothered him greatly) automobile dealership in the tri-state area. Just as Douglas saw something in Dexter and took him under his wing, Dexter chose to give back by being equally generous with Trey. Ever since Trey started and showed that he had an aptitude for the car business Dexter had made it a point to teach him everything he knew. Having no sons of his own, he almost considered Trey family of sorts. "I still get emotional every time I look at that picture. One of these days you'll have a picture of us on you desk."

"From your mouth to the car god's ear."

"There is only one God, Trey. Pray to Him and all things are possible; leave Him out and watch out."

"Just a saying," Trey assured him.

"There is power in the tongue. Life and death are in the tongue. Never put any false gods in front of the only One. Not even the car gods."

"I hear you." Trey felt like sliding out the chair and under the door. Once Dexter started talking about the goodness of God, he could go on for awhile.

"I tell you, Trey, before I gave my life to the Lord; all I thought about was money and honeys. But one Wednesday I was at the lowest of lows. I had more money than I could spend and more women than I could...well you know what I mean."

"Right," Trey said, just to appear interested. He'd heard this testimony a million times over the past four years.

"I know I've told you this before, but it deserves to be repeated. One day, Trey you will have a true testimony to share. Trust me; God has plans for you, outside of the car business. I've told you before; you have a calling on your life."

Not this again, Trey thought. *This is a place of business, not church. The only wisdom I'm interested in, Dexter, is what you did to get you to where you are.* But he smiled and leaned forward to give the impression of being enraptured with Dexter's oft repeated story.

"As I was saying, one Wednesday night about four years ago I was down and out. The devil was on my butt like he was a bee and I was covered in honey. Well I was on my way to pick up some woman, whose name I can't recall. I stopped at the red light and heard all this ruckus coming from this little storefront. Something took over my body and next thing I knew I was parked and walking through the door. Trey, there was only ten people in there, but I tell you they sounded like a hundred. It turned out that this was a church and they were having Bible study.

Trey interrupted him, filling in the rest of the story he now knew by heart. "And that's how you got saved and since that night your life has never been the same."

Dexter's smile was warm and friendly around the mouth. When he was annoyed, though, the smile didn't reach his eyes. They went almost black in color and when he caught someone in his sights; it was as if he could read the brand of underwear they wore.

Being under the spotlight of Dexter's stare had stopped making Trey nervous a long time ago, but this morning he felt a slight wetness under his arms. "Uh, no disrespect, Dexter. I just got caught up in the story."

"Testimony," he corrected Trey, steepling his hands. "Well, let's get down to business, shall we? I see Tony is taking it to you this month."

"He's definitely on top of his game," Trey replied, happy to be on a subject he felt comfortable talking about. "If he beats me it will be because he outsold me."

"That's normally what it means."

Trey wasn't the least bit concerned with being outdone by Tony. From the first month after he was trained and released to sell cars without a trainer, he had been the top dog. Salespeople had come and gone, but in five years no one had ever dethroned him. "We still have two days left and I have an appointment coming in at eleven and one at two-thirty. It's cool," Trey assured him.

"Okay, because Jerry thinks you're ripe for the taking."

Jerry was Trey's manager, a job Trey had turned down too many times to count over the years. "Jerry thinks Tony can beat me?" He was flabbergasted. Ever since Jerry's promotion three months ago, he'd made no secret of the fact that he wanted to see someone else's name at the top the leader board. Being Trey's superior wasn't easy. Trey hadn't answered to anyone other than Dexter the whole time he'd worked for Fortune Motors. Everyone knew it and most resented it. "One good month since he's been here and Jerry thinks Tony is as good as me."

"He has been consistent with his sales."

"And I haven't been?"

"There is more to life than being number one on the leader board, Trey. Don't forget to give God some credit for all your success. Yes, you have talent; just remember it was placed in you." Dexter laughed in his loud cackling way, "I'm just having some fun with you. Nothing is better for the sales staff than some friendly competition. Jerry wants to make a big deal if he does beat you; he thinks it would motivate the others to try harder to do the same and show them that even the great, Trey Edwards can be beat."

"And?"

"I must admit, you've been on top since you started and it may be a boost to the other's confidence if Tony is given a little recognition for being the first to top you."

"I'm a team player," Trey said none too convincingly.

"I know you are. How are things on your end? Have you heard from the bank?"

"Not yet."

"Just keep praying and asking God for his blessings. Everything in His time."

"Yeah," Trey said getting up to leave. Dexter's transformation over the years was beginning to wear thin. He had nothing against religion, but being preached to every day was getting on his nerves. It seemed that lately Dexter talked more about that than business.

CHAPTER FOUR

Morning time for Andrea was the worst time of the day. She dreaded getting out of her comfortable bed, hassling with the kids, (especially Brett) and fighting the traffic. Driving into downtown Philadelphia was never fun, and this morning was no different. It seemed to her that she caught every red light as she crawled along. Even though taking the expressway would save her time on her way to work, she preferred driving what Trey called, "the scenic route," straight down Broad Street. As a child Andrea hated getting up in the morning. Crawling out of a warm bed at five o'clock every morning, rain or shine to feed the chickens and slop the hogs had filled her with distaste for the mornings. Try as she might it was something she couldn't shake. And to her chagrin, Brett had inherited his early-morning blues from her. This morning in particular almost drove her to give her son a swift kick in the butt. That boy rode a nerve like it was a horse. There was no doubt he was his daddy's son.

Stopping at another light, she switched CD tracks until her favorite Whitney song filled the car. Andrea ran her hands through her hair, reminding herself to call Stacey and set an appointment for a retouch. As the light switched to green she immediately regretted looking out of her passenger side window. A dark-skinned guy with enough gold teeth in his mouth to pay the rent was grinning and motioning at her to roll down the window.

"Oh please," she muttered as she sped off without acknowledging his weak attempt at getting her attention. "Like I don't have enough problems."

Her thoughts wandered back to her morning, when she had woken to find Trey standing over her with her favorite coffee, made just how she liked it, two creams and one packet of artificial sweetener. He kissed her lips softly and walked away without uttering a word. Sipping the warm liquid pick-me-up, she savored the flavor till the end. She got out of bed to go check on the kids, only to find that Brittany was up and dressed as usual, while Brett was barricaded under the pillows and comforter. It took multiple shouts, coming back into the room, threatening and finally literally pushing his little behind onto the floor to arouse him. When she was able to get herself dressed and came downstairs, Brittany told her Trey had fixed breakfast and left it in the microwave oven for her and Brett.

"Your daddy left already?"

"Yep, he said bye," Brittany said jumping down from the counter stool.

The school bus pulled up in front of the house and blew its horn once. The kids quickly kissed Andrea, grabbed their lunch bags and book bags and shot out of the front door. She watched the bus roll off and waited until it turned the corner before she stepped back into the house. Trey's preparing breakfast and fixing the kid's lunch was a welcome surprise since he hardly ever helped out on a weekday morning. As she dug into the eggs, also made to her taste—over easy with the yolk not broken—she thought about coming home and returning this surprise with one of her own. Maybe she was being a little selfish in the lovemaking department.

A honking horn snapped her back to the present. The gold-tooth guy was alongside of her car pounding on his horn. With the loud music playing in her car, she couldn't make out what he was saying, but his intentions were clearly demonstrated as he licked his lips in the worst LL Cool J impersonation she'd ever seen. Andrea reached for the Bible she kept in the car and raised it up to the car window. Lover-boy made an ugly face, shook his head, and drove right through a red light. Andrea laughed all the way to her office.

Forty-five minutes late for work, Andrea flopped down at her desk and buried her head on her arms.

"You must have hit the lottery, showing up for work nearly an hour late."

Andrea slowly lifted her head. Standing in her office doorway was her supervisor and best work friend, Kathy Wiggins. She wore her short-cropped hair in the natural style, refusing to conform to what she considered society's way of saying an African-American woman couldn't be attractive unless she wore her hair flat and straight with enough weave to quilt a rug. She dressed in the finest designer clothes—easily affordable on her nearly six-figure salary—and went to the gym with a vengeance to keep her body in the dancer's shape she carried deep into her forties. Her mannerisms and sophistication gave her a regal bearing that belied her background. The relationship between the two of them was formed over their shared love of shoe shopping and the Lord. Though they never associated with each other outside of work hours they still had a bond and on occasion gave each other a glimpse into their personal lives.

"I wish, but I guess I would have to play first. Sorry, traffic was a killer, it won't happen again," Andrea said upset with herself for getting caught as if she was napping.

"I saw you yesterday," Kathy said with a smirk.

"Where?"

"Your church," she responded. "I was at the morning service."

"I didn't see you there."

"I came in right before the pastor started his sermon."

"He's new; our old pastor retired."

"That man can preach his booty off," Kathy gushed. "Not to mention he's quite good-looking."

"Yes he can," Andrea agreed.

"And he's fine."

"I hadn't really noticed," Andrea lied feeling her face get hot.

"Sweetie, Stevie Wonder could see that."

Changing the subject and trying to hide her discomfort, Andrea asked what made her visit her church and why didn't she let her know she was doing so.

"Last-minute thing. My church was visiting our sister church in West Philly and I got up to late, but I can't go a Sunday without finding a house of worship."

"I know what you mean."

"I have something to share with you."

"Okay," Andrea said nervously half expecting Kathy to pull magically from the air more files to go with the thirty on her desk.

"It's actually great news." She paused, waiting to see if Andrea had anything to say. When Andrea looked at her expectantly, she continued, "Mary was promoted this morning. You missed the announcement coming in late. But anyway, just wanted to let you know that." Again she paused, "You're getting her old office and if the Board approves it, you might just get promoted yourself."

Andrea was speechless. Just in case she misheard Kathy, she insisted that she repeat everything.

"You heard me. Pack up your stuff so you can get out of this tiny space. Take your time, but finish up before lunch if you can. I'll see you later." And with that she opened the door and cat-walked out, leaving Andrea with her thoughts and a racing heart. Kathy wouldn't have mentioned the promotion at all if she didn't think the Board would rubber-stamp it. Swiftly she closed her office door and got down on her knees in the center of her office. Picking herself up, she grabbed her make-up case from inside her purse. Her mascara was running down her face from the tears she'd shed while giving thanks. Before Kathy or the Board could change their minds, she busied herself with moving her belongings to Mary's old office. Stopping mid-way through packing up the boxes she'd gotten from the mailroom, Andrea called almost everyone on her friends and family list to share the- didn't-happen-yet-but-any day-now-news. It wasn't until later that day she realized she hadn't called her husband.

CHAPTER FIVE

Waking up in strange hotel rooms wasn't exactly the norm for Ian, so it took him a moment to collect himself. Wiping the sleep from his eyes he delicately rolled back the covers so as not to disturb his snoring bedmate. He sneaked a peek back to make certain the mission was accomplished. Walking into the spacious bathroom of the suite, the tiled floor of the bathroom was very cold to his feet. He turned on the shower and set the water to the proper temperature. Since he was already in the buff, he stepped right into the hot stream of water. He lifted his face to meet the water and ran his hands over his face and through his hair.

He couldn't wait to call Trey and tell him the great news. And boy would he be shocked to hear that Ian had slept with a woman.

Unlike Trey in his single days, having intercourse with a bunch of different women didn't make Ian's top-ten list of signs of success. When Ian found it profitable, sex made the list – but only temporarily. He believed that if women could benefit from sleeping with men, then what was good for the goose was better for his gender. So he slept with females only when it served his purpose and his purpose last night was to advance his passion.

Turning off the shower and opening the curtain he was startled to find Taylor Daniels sitting on the commode. *How disgusting*, he thought. Keeping his voice steady he asked, "I didn't wake you did I?"

"No I reached for you and you weren't there," she answered without any display of discomfort or shame.

Ian didn't know whether to step out of the shower or close the curtain to give her the privacy she obviously didn't seem to require. He started to feel extremely uncomfortable and the odor in the bathroom wasn't helping him feel any better. You gotta be kidding; she couldn't wait until I was finished in here? Trying his best to avoid eye contact with Taylor, he reached for one of the pristine white terrycloth towels and wrapped it around his slim mid-section, hitting the fan button before exiting the steamy, smelly bathroom.

Ian looked around at the elegant surroundings of the presidential suite of the Grandville hotel. Known the world over for its luxurious rooms and impeccable service, he found it hard to believe he was here, in the middle of all of this opulence, after a night of bed-rocking, sheet-wetting sex with the one person he felt had the connections to take him straight to the top of the music industry. He slowly walked over to the polished oak coffee table that stood in front of a butter soft leather sofa.

On the leather was the signed contract he and Taylor had executed the previous evening over a bottle of Moet and some nasty-tasting caviar and stale crackers. He picked it up and read for the hundredth time, his heart pounding against his chest. He wanted to make certain that none of the words had changed and that their signatures were still affixed at the bottom of the last page. His instinct screamed for him to consult an attorney prior to signing, but his ambition and fear that time was running out on him prevailed. To the best of his limited knowledge, it appeared to be a standard managerial contract, stating that Taylor would serve as his personal manager and agent, with the responsibility of making him a star. She'd told Ian she saw him filling the void caused by Luther's death; that he was made for all the lovers of strong male singers that could really deliver a song from the heart with pure, strong vocals. They disagreed briefly on the amount of her compensation and the length of the contract, but by the time he'd emptied the entire bottle of champagne himself, the oppulance, and Taylor rubbing his thigh, encouraged him to trust her. He took the pen from her hand, signed his name and planted a big, tongue-filled kiss on her. That kiss led them to move into the bedroom and really seal the deal.

It wasn't often that women got to Ian, unless they were taking him on a big-time shopping spree. If memory served him correctly the last female he'd given the privilege of his affections was Donna— the chick from the northeast section of the city— with the dirty blond hair, a little too much weight, and a never-ending flow of cash. He giggled as he flashed back to how that came about. After not speaking for months she'd called him and forced him to let her buy him the new spring line of Kenneth Cole. Oh well, he thought, what's a man to do? Of course he was indebted to throw her a mercy… sex was only for profit and if the woman got off, it was none of his concern. His preferences lay elsewhere.

Thoughts for another time, he reckoned, reading the contract again. Taylor's cut still bothered him sober, as it had with alcohol flowing through his system. Panicking he fought the urge to tear it up and continue what he'd been doing for the past twenty years. "Look where that got you," he said, looking around to make certain Taylor hadn't popped into the room unannounced. "Lord, you know you and I don't speak much, but if you could guide me on this one I sure would appreciate it."

Growing up his grandmother took Ian to church with her almost seven days a week. If praying was an Olympic sport she surely would have won gold.

When she took ill during his senior year of high school, the entire congregation came to the hospital and held prayer vigils. The pastor of the church declared her healed: she died. On that day, Ian's belief in a higher power was replaced by anger toward God. It was something he never spoke about, not even with Trey. So for him to say even the little prayer he'd spoken made him feel terribly awkward. Quickly he reasoned that he was owed one so he said, "Today I'm Ian Gerald, little-known singing sensation. Tomorrow, I'm simply Ian, Grammy winner and number-one- CD selling recording artist. Lord hear my plea" Then as an afterthought he said, "Amen."

The paper he currently held in his hands was realistically his last shot at making the one dream that had dominated his waking and sleeping days since he was five years old. Forty-year old singers didn't become over-night successes, not in the music industry. Well, if Taylor Daniels wanted a larger percentage then what was the industry standard, and she had the wherewithal to get him to the top, so be it.

The telephone rang out announcing the automated wake-up call he'd requested when they checked in. Feeling the need to share his exciting news with his boy he dialed ten numbers. "Hello, may I speak with Trey Edwards? Nodding his head at what the person on the other end told him, he sighed and swallowed his disappointment. "Okay, just tell him Ian called and I need him to hit me on my cell as soon as possible." He listened some more. "Nah, he has the number, thank you." Hanging up the phone, he searched for his clothing. It worked better for him if he could sneak out of the room before Taylor came out of the bathroom. Dressing quickly, he knocked on the door and softly told Taylor he would call her later that afternoon. Without hearing or waiting for a reply, Ian practically ran out of the suite.

CHAPTER SIX

Taylor listened at the bathroom door, hoping he would hurry up and leave. She sighed a sigh of relief when she heard the suite door click into place signaling that Ian had left. One thing she hated doing was rehashing the night before. If he was like most men she'd broken some off to, he would want to talk about it and ask that dumb question they all seemed to need answered, "Was it good for you too, baby?" Why couldn't men understand that sometimes a girl just wanted to get hers without any strings attached, just like them? No attachment, no name calling and no will you respect me in the morning? Just wham, bam thank you sir. Even her last fling turned out to be clueless. He thought because she gave in to his weak advances and made what he considered-"love to her"-that constituted them being in a monogamous relationship. Once the simpleton discovered that not to be the case, he used his power in the record company to get her terminated. Like so many before, he was stupid enough to underestimate her. Sure she used her womanly charms, beautiful face, creamy coffee-toned skin and a well-toned body to give her a foot up in the good-ole' boy network. So what? Didn't men use anything and anybody at their disposal to get ahead? Damn the double standards!

In spite of her previous success in the business, Ian held the key to her staying power. Taylor had no illusions about what had to be done to come out on top this time. She'd made up her mind that there wasn't anyway that she was letting this one get away. All that hard work she'd put into getting that hood-rat of a boy from the subway a record deal, only to have his uncle come out of the woodwork and push her aside. How could she have been so careless as to get him a deal without having a signed and delivered contract protecting her rights? It all happened so fast it caught her unprepared. In three short days she'd had the ungrateful little bastard in the studio and without even a finished demo had him signed to a deal. Sure it cost her a little dignity having to sleep with the president of Too Fat Records to make it happen, but at the time it seemed worth it. What did she have to show for all her hard work? A lousy roll on the desk and ten thousand dollars the slimy uncle gave her in a torn brown paper bag— and the fool gave her mostly five and ten dollar bills. That Fisher boy; had the stuff to out-do Usher and it was her, Taylor Daniels, who'd discovered him and taken a chance. Ten years in the rough and tumble recording industry and she had made one of the worst mistakes a person could make. Not having paper to back up the words. Hell to the no, not this time. That's why she made her lawyers design iron-clad contracts like the one Ian had just signed, contracts that made certain she wouldn't get screwed again. Never again would a man get the best of her, not without the fight of his life. Oh yeah, ten years had taught her a lot. It might be a man's world today, but boys better watch out because ladies are doing it for themselves.

Taylor located her Louis Vuitton handbag lying on the thick carpet next to the bed. It contained her copy of the contract. This time, she mused, she'd do this her way, with no man telling her what, how or when, and with nobody getting annoyed because she had the audacity to ask why. Never again would she get shown the door and then blackballed.

Management was the way to go. Find the talent, develop the talent, get paid off the talent and when the talent ran its course, start all over again. Singers were a dime a dozen, and for a shot at fame and fortune, even a nickel a bushel. Her rarely sober mother was right when she instructed, "Making money is easy, if a girl understood the power of the booty." And from a young age Taylor was very much aware of the effect she had on the male species. Ian was no exception. So if it took bedding him down on the regular to keep him in line, so be it.

Smiling broadly, Taylor threw herself across the king-size bed, grabbed the phone and ordered breakfast of steak and eggs. Figuring out how to promote a no-name, forty-year old singer was the least of her worries. How to come up with the fifty thousand- dollar advance she promised Ian topped the 'worry list.' "*Oh well,*" she thought, "*it won't be the last time I've made a deal with the devil,*" and with that she picked up the phone and dialed, "Hi D-Jay," she said coyly into the receiver. "I have missed you so much. I'll be in LA tomorrow. Let's do lunch."

****

"Who was that?" the voice under the covers asked, "And how you gonna answer the phone while I'm down here?"

"What I tell you 'bout being up in my bizness?" D-Jay forced his voice to be rough to hide the giant grin spread across his ordinary-looking face. *The chickens always come home to roost*, he laughed to himself, not minding the interruption at all. "Stop, stop, I said. I got things to do." He pushed the woman away and jumped out of the bed.

If eyes were laser beams, the blond woman's eyes would be burning a hole into D-Jay's back big enough to walk through. "That bitch! I know it was."

She retrieved the phone from the nightstand beside the bed and hit star-six-nine. On the fourth ring the phone switched to voice-mail. Before she could change her mind and hang up she blurted out, “You know who this is. Leave my man alone. Your day has passed.” Then to emphasize her point she said through clenched teeth, “Bitch!”

CHAPTER SEVEN

"Darn man. Gotta bow down to you," Tony extended his hand to Trey.

Beaming, Trey shook his hand firmly, "You put up a good fight." It took until the last day of the month for Trey to get the sale he needed to keep his regular spot at the top of the sales leader board. This was the closest he'd come to losing it.

"You know, man, if I hadn't run into some folks with bad credit, I'd have beaten ya," Tony boasted as they walked toward the parking lot.

Trey rolled his eyes and laughed. "Yeah, all right, whatever you say."

Tony shot back, "October is another month and trust me, brotha, you going down."

Trey politely turned down Tony's offer of stopping by a local bar for a nightcap. Tony hopped into his black-on-black BMW, blew his horn and sped off at the same time Trey slid into his Benz and flipped open his cell phone.

"Hey baby girl, tell your moms I'm on my way home."

"Mom," Brittany hollered on the other end of the phone, "Daddy's on his way home." After a beat he heard Brett's voice on the line. "Hey Dad, stop and get some ice cream, butter pecan or rocky road."

"No Daddy, we had that last time. Get some strawberry shortcake."

"Hang up the phone, girl. Daddy look out for your boy."

Listening to his kids go back and forth, all he could do was shake his head and smile. The two of them picked on each other constantly, but whenever he or Andrea fussed at one of them, one would always take up for the other. Starting the car, he backed out of the parking space, holding the phone with one hand while driving with the other. "Listen up, Ike and Tina," he said, "how 'bout I get both?"

They shouted agreement and Brittany hung up, leaving Brett on the line. "Dad, you want to talk to Mom?"

"Uh… not right now. I'll be home in a bit. Talk to you later." Trey disconnected the call, wishing he had spoken with Andrea. It bothered him so much he started to dial his home, but changed his mind. He had so much to tell her and longed to just shoot the breeze about everything and nothing, like the way they used to. He needed to tell her about Ian's great news, how he was once again top producer for the month and would receive another huge bonus and most important of all (Lord willing, and he prayed He was) if all went well he would soon become the owner of his own dealership.

He chastised himself for not keeping her fully in the loop from the beginning. He didn't want to speak too soon, especially since it could fall apart. Having Andrea say "I told you so," if it didn't come to fruition, really wasn't something he was trying to hear, especially since she let it be known she thought his desire to own a car lot was a pipe dream and would once again jeopardize the family's financial and long-term security. Every pay period, although he bought home six figures every year he'd sold cars, she still asked him how much he made and insisted that they save twenty-five percent of his income just in case roller skates replaced cars. It worked out well because Andrea made over fifty-thousand dollars a year; they lived below their means and were practically debt-free. But she could never get past the fact that when he left the insurance industry to sell cars he'd made a life-changing decision without first consulting. Even though they had gotten past that singular issue in their marriage, it still came up periodically during disagreements. It was like a stain on the sofa cushion; you turned it over and it disappeared until it came time to flip the cushion back over and lo and behold, it would reappear. Trey found the whole thing a non-issue. Since when had it become a crime for a man to do anything he could to further the progress of his family? He certainly wasn't sitting on his hump, working some dead-end job bringing home only enough money for a coke and a smile. He went to work every day and let her handle the money; she knew more about their finances than he did. Hell, he thought, she got half the money and all the control over when they have sex. And he couldn't get that when he wanted it. Gone were the days and nights of adventurous and spontaneous love-making. Like always when he thought about his marriage, the lack of intimacy between them came to mind. Andrea often complained that they could have sex "twenty-four seven" and he would still ask for more. Smiling to himself, he had to admit he was somewhat of a horny kind of guy, but what full-blooded man wasn't? At least he wasn't out chasing tail in the streets. Did she appreciate that? No!

Tonight they were going to relight the flame of passion in their marriage, he decided. Satisfied that his internal venting period was over, he turned up the music in the car to help block out any further negative thoughts. Trey took the words to a Teddy Pendergrass song as advice directed at him. "Turn off the lights and light a candle. Tonight I'm in a romantic mood." Trey wholeheartedly agreed, having forgotten that he'd tried that before to no prevail. Being a salesman meant never taking no as a definitive answer; he determined that tonight would be different.

CHAPTER EIGHT

While Trey was stopping at the 24- hour mini-mart for some ice cream, Brett was in his room as usual playing a video game, Brittany was in the kitchen finishing up her homework and Andrea was in the master bedroom on her cell phone, giggling like she was back in high school. "Oh no, Pastor. No problem at all. I'll be happy to help out with the plans for the women's group," she said. The pastor's mellow baritone voice comforted her in more ways than one. Andrea hadn't stopped blushing and giggling since the conversation began. His original purpose for calling her had been to ask her about heading up the new women's group he wanted to start at the church. Without a moments thought or hesitation, she'd agreed. "Thank you for calling, Pastor. Okay if you insist, Raymond."

Andrea hung up the phone feeling flush and winded. The man's rich, mellow baritone voice still rang in her ears. Whether she wanted to admit it or not, she was very much attracted to him. The very thought of that, unnerved her to her core. Not only was she a married woman, a happily married woman, but he was a man of God, the leader of the church. You didn't go around thinking in a physical way about the person responsible for your soul.

It wasn't as though she'd never noticed good-looking men before during her marriage. In a major city like Philly; they were everywhere. And considering she worked in Center City at one of the largest law firms, not only did she see the attractive ones; she worked with rich and powerful men. So why did the new pastor have such an effect on her? Sure, he was tall, dark and too fine to be in the pulpit, but that didn't explain why every time he glanced her way, her face got hot and her innards jumped as if she'd received a taser shot. Trey wasn't exactly chopped-liver. He kept himself in excellent condition and didn't look older than twenty-five, twenty-six— even though he would turn forty-one on his next birthday. When they were out and about, she noticed woman ogling him. Not that she minded; it made her feel good to have a good-looking man on her arm. And with Trey's curly hair, smoldering dark brown eyes and that cleft in his chin, her husband had it going on. So again she questioned herself, why did this particular man captivate her so? She concluded that the response to that query needed to remain unanswered.

Meanwhile down in the kitchen, Brittany lifted her head up, slightly bewildered after falling asleep before completing the math assignment that her third-grade teacher, Miss Henry insisted upon heaping on her accelerated pupils. After shaking the cobwebs in her head and wiping the sleep from her light-green eyes, she hopped down from the kitchen stool and bounced up the steps. Barging into her older brother's room against his strict orders for her to never enter his private domain without a signed decree from heaven, Brittany jumped onto his unmade bed knocking some comic books to the floor.

Without taking his eyes off the TV screen, he scolded her for entering his room. "Go away."

"I'm lonely," she whined. "Yaw left me downstairs by myself."

"Where's Mom?"

"In her room."

"Go bother her."

"I'm not bothering you."

"Go!"

"No!"

Brett put down the video game control and began to stand up. "You have to the count of five to get out."

"Are Mommy and Daddy mad at each other?"

"What?" He stopped in mid-stride. "What are you talking about?"

"Mommy and Daddy."

"What about them?"

"They don't play around like they use too anymore. Remember they use to always laugh and talk all the time and we would jump on Daddy and tickle him. We don't do that anymore." Her eyes began to leak.

"What made you think of that?"

"I had a dream that we were in the park. And Daddy wasn't with us."

Brett sat down beside his little sister and pulled her close. He gently wiped her weeping eyes and ensured her that everything would be all right. "Here take this joystick; I'll teach you how to play."

They played together until Brittany heard a sound coming from downstairs. Springing to her feet she squealed, "Daddy's home! Come on! Let's go get some ice cream!"

"Right behind you," Brett told her. He ran and knocked on his parent's bedroom door. "Mom," he called out, "Daddy's home and he bought ice cream."

"I'll be down shortly," he heard her say through the door.

The kids' thoroughly enjoyed spending time with both of their parents so when Andrea breezed into the kitchen they exchanged secretive glances and without warning they jumped on Trey, calling out for Andrea to join in tickling him.

CHAPTER NINE

Together they got the kids ready for bed. Trey read Brittany her nightly bedtime story and Andrea helped Brett pick out his clothes for the school portraits being taken on Friday.

"Tonight was fun, Daddy," Brittany excitedly told Trey as he tucked her in under the pink blankets of her canopy bed. "Can we go to the zoo on Saturday?"

"Yes it was and yes we can. Now go to sleep. It's way past your bedtime." Trey kissed his baby girl with their special goodnight kiss he called "the four-point kiss." One kiss on the forehead, one on each cheek and ending with a kiss to the lips. "Goodnight baby girl," he said turning on her nightlight. "Love ya."

"Love ya too, Daddy." She closed her eyes and after she was certain he was gone hopped out of the bed and kneeled on the floor beside her bed and began to pray. "Please Lord; make my Mommy and Daddy play together like we did tonight. Amen"

Trey's nighttime assignment was a snap compared to Andrea's. She and Brett were going at it over his choice; of attire for the school picture. "Boy, you are not wearing any doggone Sean John sweatsuit for your class picture." She was getting extremely agitated with him.

"But Mom…"

"No buts; the only butt is yours, which I'm about to spank. You're getting on my last nerve."

"For what? I just wanna wear what I want to wear."

Andrea almost gave in, then decided to try reverse psychology. "Okay, you want to look like some kind of hip-hop fool while the other boys in your class look like little gentlemen, then you go right ahead."

It failed to work on Brett. He shouted, "Yeah boy, that's what I'm talking 'bout. Thanks Mom, you're the best."

The agony of defeat came and went quickly. Andrea kissed her son, shook her head and left him alone to finish getting ready for bed.

"He won, huh?" Trey asked Andrea when she entered the bedroom.

"Like always. I don't know what has gotten into that boy."

"TV, radio, BET—we let him leave the house— take your pick." Trey continued to undress as he eagle-eyed every move Andrea made. He found himself hoping she would take her clothes off in the room and not go into the bathroom to change into her nightgown. The urge to make love to her outweighed his fear of rejection. Full of apprehension he approached her from behind and nuzzled her neck. "Is there any chance a loving, caring and downright needy man can spend some quality time with his wife?"

"Of course," she surprised him by saying. "Let me freshen up and I'll join you in a minute. Light the candles and turn on some music." She leaned her head back against his broad shoulders, enjoying the warmth and smell of his body. After a beat she wiggled out of his embrace and peeled off her clothes slowly as she sauntered into the bathroom, leaving a panting and gawking Trey in her wake.

Just as Trey was ready to drift off to sleep, waiting for her to return, Andrea stood in the bathroom doorway with a blue terry cloth towel wrapped around her voluptuous body. He admired her smooth caramel skin glistening, still damp from the shower. Her naturally wavy auburn hair cascaded down onto her shoulders the way Trey loved it. Andrea was truly a beautiful woman. He noticed other men checking his wife out when they were out and about. He didn't mind. It filled him with pride to be seen with a fine woman on his arm.

Following instructions, the room was set for romance. Knowing Andrea's penchant for making love by firelight, he'd placed candles around the room. All of the candles were set with care and great attention to detail so that their glow would cast a simmering light over the bed. One was placed on each nightstand beside the bed, while the others were set on the dresser opposite the bed. The flickering flame illuminated a painting mounted on the wall above the dresser. The artwork was a gift Andrea had given to Trey for his fortieth birthday. It depicted a nude man lovingly carrying an equally nude female across the sands of a moonlit beach. The melodic sound of a saxophone declaring love through notes played oh-so- lovingly by Kenny G. could be heard softly in the background.

"You like?" he asked, seeking her approval.

"I like," she responded, clearly touched.

"I know things have been a little weird between us lately."

"Don't talk," she said as she allowed the towel to drop almost in slow-motion from her body. "Just make love to me." She suddenly joined him on the bed and off she went.

Andrea attacked Trey's body like a lioness on the hunt. Trey snuck open an eye to peek up at her distorted face. Between screams and facial calisthenics, she reminded him of a death scene in an old Kung-Fu flick. Finally, she hollered as if shot in the butt with a dart, then proceeded to plop face down onto Trey's chest. Their shared heavy breathing soon replaced the noisy bed-springs as a musical backdrop to their lovemaking.

Blowing air through his parched mouth Trey almost felt like rolling over and sticking his thumb in his mouth. He reasoned to himself that if it was possible for a wife to molest her husband, then he had just been molested.

Her light snoring, which he knew would get louder as she fell deeper into sleep, was his cue that she'd drifted off lying on his chest. Gently he rolled her off his body, careful not to disturb her too much. He didn't; she way past gone.

Getting out of bed he covered her with the comforter that had wound up on the floor. He quickly located his silk pajama pants, slipped into them and quietly left the room. Going downstairs he was reminded of all the times one of the kids tripped the home security system off by wandering downstairs in the middle of the night, forgetting that the motion detector in the living room could sense body heat and would sound the alarm if it wasn't deactivated within thirty-seconds. He scooted over to the panel by the front door and punched in the four-digit code. A beeping sound alerted him that the interior system was shut down.

Trey went into the kitchen and opened up his arch-enemy, the stainless steel fridge, and grabbed a can of organic ginger ale. Going into the well furnished living room of their three-bedroom home, he settled into his favorite leather recliner by the fireplace they never used and proudly surveyed his surroundings.

The large living room was the only room in the house for which Andrea had allowed him any say in picking out furniture. His choice of cream-colored leather met her high standards, even if he did lose the TV battle. Andrea simply vetoed his vote to have a television in the living room. As a consolation, she didn't fuss too much when the delivery men showed up at the door with a 52-inch flat screen TV that he'd picked out during a lunch break right after Christmas. It now sat in the finished basement which was considered the family-room. Wait until they deliver the pool table I saw yesterday, he chuckled to himself. This is a man's world and his home is castle. Yeah right, until a man got married and his world consisted of a basement room with a toilet for a throne. The basement was the only space in the entire three- bedroom, two and a-half bathroom, two-story home where Trey had any say in choosing colors, furniture or artwork. They discussed such things when Andrea grew tired with the décor and wanted to make changes (which happened every two or three years) and somehow his suggestions never showed up in the finished product. Married life had taught him one important rule: know when to pick your battles. So if Andrea wanted complete control over the house, he willingly gave it to her. Besides, her taste was impeccable. Due to her flair for elegance and class, the Edwards lived in one of the best-kept homes in the neighborhood. He took great pleasure in coming home to an immaculately clean house after working the long hours. Giving credit where due, he admitted she deserved the title of "Superwoman," working nine-to-five, taking care of him and two kids, and cleaning the house herself. She'd even shot down his brilliant idea of hiring a maid to help out around the house. Everyone was required to pitch in and help, of course. Brittany and Brett had dish night and Trey was responsible for the trash and cleaning the bathrooms. He had to confess though, that with late nights and weekend work, sometimes he fell short. Since God blessed him with a wife that never complained about picking up the slack. He pretended to overlook her need to redecorate all the time.

At two o'clock in the morning the house was still and quiet. Trey actually took solace in being alone. He cherished being by himself to reflect, plan and sometimes— even pray. It wasn't unusual for Trey to wake up in the wee hours of the morning, while the family was fast asleep, come downstairs to sit in the recliner, especially when his over-active brain wouldn't shut down.

This morning he had a lot on his mind. He was baffled by his wife's uncharacteristic sexual aggression, and he was distressed at not having heard from the bank about his loan application. He determined that he would concentrate on Andrea a little later; for now the fact that the deal could go either way filled him with fear. He stood to lose a ton of money if the bank declined the loan. Maybe it wasn't such a good idea to put up a non-refundable cash deposit on the deal. Snap out of it, Trey, he scolded himself. Think positive. The fact it's taking so long is a good sign; it means they're really looking at this thing fully. Na, Na. It's nothing. Edwards' Motors is coming into existence. No weapon formed against me can prosper. God didn't give me the spirit of fear. He began to pray. "Please Father; let the bank approve my loan. That's all I need."

He was grateful that his boss Dexter had offered him financial backing. Dexter was giving him the chance to become an equal partner, but he wanted the opportunity to be his own boss for a change. Dexter mentoring him for over the past five years had given Trey an in-depth knowledge of every aspect of the car business, and the confidence he needed to make his dream come true. While Dexter wanted him to become an extension of his empire, Trey wanted an empire of his own. That's why he did all the due diligence. He had searched for a vacant lot or car lot going out of business and when he found an owner that was selling out, he jumped at the chance. It was a perfect location, right off Roosevelt Boulevard in the northeast section of Philly. The previous owner was well known in the area and had been in business for over thirty years from the same location. The lot would hold over one hundred cars, there was a service department, it already had a sales force and there was plenty of room for expansion— not to mention the built-in client base. If…no…*when* the bank signed off on the loan, he would take ownership no later than March of next year. *Yeah boy*, he thought, *next year is gonna be my year! What is this, October? Yeah just two months to go. We'll talk after the money comes through*. He had no doubt that Andrea would understand his keeping her unaware once everything was finalized. He sat deep in thought until sleep refused to be ignored any longer.

He returned to bed trying his best not to wake up Andrea. Once he was settled under the covers Andrea rolled over to face him and asked, "You okay?"

"Yep. Couldn't sleep," he said then he kissed her and pulled her into his body.

"Goodnight, Drea."

"Goodnight, Trey." An unwelcome tear trickled down her cheek and fell onto his chest. His light snoring indicated to her that Trey was fast asleep and was unaware she was crying in his arms.

****

"I see that you have been quite busy in the world."

"I must admit, sometimes your people credit me for things I had nothing to do with."

"They will learn."

"With all due respect, you have parted seas, flooded the earth destroying all except one family, started over again, come to earth in the flesh, died for their sins… I can go on and on. And yet you still believe they will learn."

"I have placed wisdom in them all. Wisdom is what they seek and through wisdom they will learn to not lean on their own understanding. With wisdom, they will learn to use the power that I have given each and every believer. You dwell in darkness; I live in light. My light will forever shine and those who come to me shall see the light and no longer fear the darkness, which is you."

"Well, that sounds good, but must of your people go through life with blinders on. Like the Edwards."

"I'm listening."

"The foundation has been laid for their demise."

"Infidelity."

"Works like a charm. Put a little dissatisfaction in the mix, then add in temptation and then stand back and watch the power of suggestion take over."

"I don't approve of you using one of my shepards. However I have given you permission to operate freely. But I heed my word; do not touch them."

"Sometimes I obey you more than those who call your name."

CHAPTER TEN

The moonlight sneaking past the vertical window blinds cast a soft glow of light around the bedroom. The alarm clock on Andrea's nightstand told her if she closed her eyes and went back to sleep she could get in another three hours of much needed shut-eye. Turning her head slightly to the left she observed Trey shifting into a higher gear; soon he'd be snoring too loud for her to drift off if she didn't make him turn off his back. He looked so peaceful and content; his handsome face showed the hint of facial stubble that he wouldn't ever let grow out to the full-grown beard Andrea wanted him to wear. She gently traced her fingers over each of his eyebrows and down his face. Then she kissed him fully letting her tongue snake across his lips. So deep in sleep, Trey didn't move at all.

There were times the love Andrea felt for her husband filled her heart with so much joy she could hardly contain herself, as she was now experiencing watching him sleep. Alongside love there was pain and discontentment. Being married wasn't easy in today's world and staying together was even harder. With that as a reality, she did take pride in the fact her marriage was entering its fifteenth year. Not one of her girlfriends from high school came close; in actuality some were working on their second and third marriages and at least two had never gotten hitched at all. But having kids, now that was a different story. All of them had children and one of her best friends combined multiple kids with different fathers to match the multiple marriages. Maybe her own situation wasn't so difficult she thought. She was wide awake now looking up at the ceiling. Being married to Trey wasn't all that bad, although he acted like she should be able to have sex anytime and anywhere like when they were teenagers making out in her basement while her parents were upstairs watching TV. She wasn't happy about him making decisions that affected her without giving her the respect of talking to her first. That was really the thorn in the side for her. For some reason, she couldn't bring herself to forgive him for selling the insurance agency, even after he'd achieved success selling cars. She remembered the day he informed her that he was getting out of the insurance field to become a *car salesman*. After she got over the shock of hearing such foolishness, fear had griped her heart like a vise. All she saw was the crumbling security of her world. She'd prayed to God that Trey would come to his senses and stay put; when he didn't, she lost a little faith in her prayers being answered. Fortunately Trey's belief in him paid off. They were pretty well set financially and even had a safe, secure, high-performing retirement account. Not many people could say they could safely retire and continue to live their current lifestyle like she and Trey could. Thank God, he'd stopped talking about opening up a car dealership. No way was she ever going to agree to take that type of risk. One roll of the dice was enough for her. It's like her granddaddy used to say: "Gamble with a dollar, lose a buck, gamble with your livelihood and lose your life." They had too much to lose at this stage of their lives. In her vision for their lives, Brett was going to Harvard and Brittany was attending Spelman and that took money. Again she thanked God that at least this time her prayer got through and was answered since Trey knew how she felt about risking everything on a pipe dream. Andrea simply wanted him to remain satisfied with being top dog at the dealership. As far as she was concerned that should be enough.

Sleep set in as Andrea prodded Trey's shoulder so he would roll off his back, then she turned on her side. Before she drifted back to sleep, the image of the pastor entered her mind and guilt instantly set up shop in her heart. She silently asked for forgiveness of her sin. The entire time she and Trey were making love, she'd fantasized about Pastor Raymond Douglas.

CHAPTER ELEVEN

Saturday morning before the rooster crowed, Brittany burst through their bedroom door, threw herself across the still- prone bodies lying in deep slumber and shouted, "Get up! Get up! It's time to go to the zoo! Daddy promised."

Trey sprung up from under the covers startled and groggy. Andrea didn't move. "Baby girl, what time…" He looked at the alarm clock. "Britt, it's only five o'clock. The zoo ain't open yet."

"We should get there early so we can watch the animals eat breakfast," was her innocent reply.

Trey grabbed his precious daughter in a tight bear hug and rubbed his knuckles against the top of her head. "Knucklehead," he said, "It's too early, and the animals don't wake up until, at least twelve o'clock."

She gave that some thought before responding, "Okay, Daddy."

He removed Brittany from the bed and carried her back to her bedroom. She made him pinky-swear and cross his heart with the fear of having a needle in his eye if they didn't actually go to the zoo, before he was able to settle her down and return to his own bed. In all that time Andrea hadn't moved a muscle in any direction. She was in the same position, lying on her right side with the covers up over her head. From under the covers he heard her say, "Whatever you do Trey, don't let her down this time."

Without needing to elaborate, he knew what she was talking about. The last two times he'd committed to take the kids to the zoo, he had canceled for his job. In the car business, evenings and weekends were normal working hours. Getting home before nine or ten o'clock on most nights was a treat and Saturdays were the busiest day of the week for foot traffic. They'd agreed to get away or do something as a family every fifth Saturday. Trey cleared that promise with Dexter shortly after being hired, though it didn't always happen. Trey found it too difficult to step away if he was on a roll or in a slump. He regularly assured both Andrea and the kids he would make it up to them. Sometimes he forgot his promise and at times a deal he was working took longer to close than he expected. But this Saturday would be different. He would simply go into work at seven-thirty for his eight o'clock appointment, which should take about two hours top, return home by ten-thirty, he hoped and they'd reach the zoo by eleven— twelve at the latest.

"You hear me, Trey?" she asked with the slightest hint of annoyance in her voice.

"It's cool. I got everything under control," he assured her. Then he said a silent prayer that everything be under God's control. "I won't disappoint anyone today, I promise."

Under her breath, Andrea said, "That would be a first."

Whether she wanted him to hear her words or not, he had and it hurt him deeply to know that she felt that he would ever intentionally let his family down. Biting his tongue, he wondered if Andrea fully appreciated the sacrifice he made for them. A man had an obligation and responsibility to make the most money he could to support his family. And if that meant not always being able to make every baseball game and dance recital, the wife should understand and be more supportive. Right? Staring up at the textured ceiling, Trey worried about Andrea's tone of voice and the real meaning behind her words. Sure he'd missed some parent-teacher stuff and a few things over the years. But that doesn't make me an absentee father, he thought. It takes money to live like we do. If she wanted to, she could stay home and not work. I told her to stop working a couple of years ago and no, she refused. We're a team and I shouldn't have to feel guilty because I'm out doing the best I can for my family. Just wait; after the bank signs off, she'll see. We'll spend so much time together they'll beg me to go back to work. He offered up another prayer for guidance. *Maybe I'll go to church with them tomorrow*, he thought. Feeling wide awake he decided to jump into the shower and fix himself a bowl of his favorite cereal. Maybe he should wake up Brett and spend some alone-time with him. Kids grew up so fast. Where had the years gone? It felt like only yesterday that he and Drea were changing Brittany's diapers and potty training Brett.

The sound of running water coming from behind the bathroom door confirmed to Andrea that Trey was not coming back to bed. She almost cursed herself for being too hard on him, until the VCR of her mind played back the many times he'd failed to live up to his words. That never happened when he sold insurance.

To her Trey was a great father and provider. It was in other areas where he fell short. He simply believed that as long as he kept them in the finer things of life, that he was doing his job. That was the problem. He viewed the family as a job—something he never did when he sold insurance. Back then, we spent plenty of time together because he controlled his own time. Not like now. I think he worked harder selling insurance than selling cars. But to Trey it's all about the money. Thank God he's stopped that foolishness about owning a car dealership. I would love for things to go back to the way they used to be. If they were, maybe I wouldn't be thinking about…She stopped herself in mid-thought and peeled the covers back to free her arms. She stretched her legs, then knelt down beside the bed.

That's how Trey found her when he came into the room. Andrea was on her knees in front of the bed with tears streaming down her face and babbling in an unknown tongue.

Standing over top of his wife, he gently placed a hand on her heaving shoulder. The tears and people jabbering in foreign languages always made him nervous when it happened in church. It was one of the main reasons he stopped going every Sunday. Religion just didn't make sense. Now to watch his wife do it in their bedroom made him want to turn tail and run. Normally when folks got what they called "the Holy Ghost," they would wail like Andrea was bawling now, like she was hurting pretty bad. He resigned himself that he wouldn't leave her side unless she told him to. Secretly he wished she would.

CHAPTER TWELVE

Rochelle was sneaking back to her mother's house just before dawn. She put her key into the lock as quietly as possible. The door opened with a creak that was a little too loud for in her nervous state. With all the curtains drawn shut the house was pitch black even though the sun was starting to show outside. She prayed that Tina, her mother, was sleep, drunk, high, or had stayed out all night herself. Experience had taught Rochelle many things when it came to dealing with her mother, the most important of which was that her mother was crazy. Staying out all night was a definite wrong on her part, but time just got away from her, and no way would Tina understand or even give her a chance to explain. Stepping like a mouse past a cat, she entered the house, half expecting to feel her mother's fist connecting with her head.

Her hunched-over form made its way toward the steps that led to her bedroom. As soon as her foot hovered over the first step, she looked up to see Tina standing at the top of the staircase.

"Mom," was the only thing she could think to say ready to dial 911.

Tina deliberately took her time coming down the steps taking one at a time. Rochelle was frozen in place; it was if she had lost complete control of her extremities. She stared at her mother, dreading what was to come. Then their eyes met and Rochelle backed up slowly. She tripped over her feet and landed flat on her behind. Tina finally finished her slow march down the stairs and now stood over her fallen daughter.

With an inbred fear that came from many beatings over the years she took hold of Tina's outstretch hand as she helped her to her feet. Rochelle thought she was having an out-of-body experience. For all the years Tina had knocked her down, never had she ever helped her back up. Without speaking Tina turned and walked into the kitchen and put on the coffee pot that sat on the counter. Rochelle saw herself following behind her mother like she was having an out-of-body-experience. Tina motioned for her to sit down and she did. Her eyes never left Tina as she calmly went through the task of taking two mugs from the cabinet and pouring hot coffee. Then she scooped two spoonfuls of sugar into each and added cream from the fridge. Tina gently placed one cup in front of a speechless Rochelle and took a seat before placing her own cup down.

That's how Rachel, Tina's second oldest child found them sitting when she entered the kitchen two hours later.

"Get out," was all Tina said. Rachel took one look at her mother and oldest sister sitting across from each other and turned on her heels quickly. She knew to avoid Tina's wrath.

The third daughter, Robin, met her sister at the bottom of the steps and whispered, "What's happening in there?"

Rachel roughly snatched the younger girl by the arm and told her to shut up. Pulling her up the steps while Robin struggled to break loose, Rachel tighten her grip. She finally released her hold at the top and said harshly, "You want Mom to kick your butt after she done whuppin' up on Roe?"

"You didn't have to grab on me like that," Robin whined rubbing her arm. "I just wanted to know what was going on."

Rachel led the way into the small bedroom they shared. She flopped down on her twin-size bed; Robin copied her on her own twin-size bed that sat opposite. "I don't really know," Rachel started off saying. "All I know is Roe didn't come home last night and when I went into the kitchen her and Mom was just sitting at the table."

"Doin' what?"

"Nothing, just looking at each other."

"Looking at each other? You mean Mom wasn't hollering and slapping the bejesus out of her?

Rachel told her she was just as shocked.

"I hope she don't kill her this time." Robin worried and Rachel agreed as she pulled the frayed blanket over her body. They were afraid for their oldest sister but neither one would leave the room until whatever was going down in the kitchen between Tina and Rochelle was finished.

In Rachel's haste to exit the kitchen she failed to notice the tears streaking down her mother's cheek. Tina's actions were confusing Rochelle as much as they scared her. In all the time they sat at the table neither one had touched the cups of coffee or spoken a single word to the other. Tina simply cried and rocked in the chair letting out a sob every once in awhile; Rochelle sat motionless.

"Mom," she said finally gathering the courage to say, "can I explain what happened?" Her voice quavered as she choked back tears that threatened to burst free. "It's not what you think."

Reluctantly Tina looked at Rochelle without opening her mouth. The look that Rochelle saw in her mother's eyes released the floodgate of tears she'd tried to block. Both remembered the last physical encounter that happened between them. It still tore a hole in Tina's heart when she replayed that Sunday afternoon and saw how her fury ended up with Rochelle getting a black eye and swollen lips. By the grace of God, Andrea had shown up right on time. Lord knows she was mad enough to have killed her own child that day. *Why can't this child see that all I want for her is to not end up like me?* Tina envisioned holding her daughter lovingly in her arms and calmly telling how why she felt the way she did and why she reacted the way she often did when Rochelle stepped out of line. But Tina hadn't held one of her daughters in her arms since they were small children. Warm and tender moments were few and far between with her. If she wasn't hollering at one of the girls, she was going up side their heads in anger. How many times had she wondered if all of them, including her, wouldn't have had better lives if she had put them up for adoption? Tina honestly believed she was a lousy parent and an even worse role model. While these and other thoughts floated around from time to time, Tina would without hesitation have taken a bullet for any one of the three of them. Coming from an abusive and loveless environment as a child had conditioned her in ways she still didn't understand.

Catching Rochelle coming into the house after staying out all night had been an accident, since she thought Rochelle was asleep in her room. The floor almost got soaked when she noticed someone starting to come up her stairs. It wasn't until the person looked up that she recognized her oldest child sneaking into the house. To Tina the scary part was that if she hadn't gotten up to come downstairs for a cup of coffee for her hangover, Rochelle would have snuck in and she would've been none the wiser. The realization that her seventeen-year old daughter, had been out in those streets without her knowing scared the hell out of her. She saw images of her child being raped; doing drugs or getting pregnant by that lowlife she'd caught her with that day.

Tina longed to wipe the tears from Rochelle eyes but she simply couldn't bring herself to do so.

"Mom," she sobbed heavily. "It's not what you think."

Memories of past beatings flooded Tina's brain. Tina loved her daughter and couldn't help that she went off over any little thing. It wasn't as if Rochelle was a bad child. Her grades were decent and getting a 1250 on the SAT practically guaranteed her admission to a good college. Tina mumbled, "I can't take this anymore. You gonna wind up pregnant or dead running those damn streets and I just can't take it anymore."

"Pregnant? Mom I'm still a virgin," she gasped. "I keep trying to tell ya I ain't going out like that."

Composing herself while attempting to contain her temper Tina said, "You think I'm some kind of fool? I saw you remember?"

Rochelle exhaled deeply and wiped her eyes and wished for the thousandth time Tina would listen to her and believe in her. "Mom, you can take me to the doctor if you want. I'm telling the truth."

"Let me tell you something, Miss Thang, I've been out there and I know what goes on in those streets, so don't come up in here trying to hoodwink me."

"I'm not you."

Tina's pot boiled over and before Rochelle could pull the words back into her mouth, Tina's fist struck her square in the lips. "Don't sass me!" Then catching herself, Tina softened her voice and said, "Please don't sass me."

The sting of her lips failed to hurt as much as the stabbing pain shooting through her chest cavity. Rochelle put her head down and kept quiet to avoid any continued assault.

"Look at me Roe," Tina said guilt-ridden. "I'm so sorry. I shouldn't hit you." She added by way of explanation, "You know how I get."

"I was at church."

"What?"

"Church. I was at church and the guy you kicked out that day is a youth minister from the church." Rochelle went on to explain that the church had a late night prayer service that she had attended. Afterward she stayed behind to talk to the pastor and his wife and before they knew it, a new day had begun. They offered to come in and explain everything to Tina, but she didn't know what shape she would find her mother. Not wanting to embarrass her, she lied and told them Tina knew about the service.

"But you were between his legs," Tina exclaimed. "I saw you."

"We were praying and when I heard you come in, I made him get up."

"Why?"

"Because you don't believe in God."

"No girl. He don't believe in me," she sobbed.

"Yes he does, Mom and so do I." Rochelle stood up and walked around the table. Standing in front of Tina she bent down and embraced her mother. At first Tina tried to push her away, but Rochelle just held on tighter until Tina gave into the show of affection that was long overdue for both mother and daughter.

Robin silently crept into the kitchen and witnessed her mother and sister hugging and crying. She sprinted upstairs to wake Rachel and told her what she saw and together they went and stood at the doorway of the kitchen watching, not believing their own eyes.

After letting go Rochelle said, “I know, I’m grounded.” Then they laughed and the other girls started to laugh as well, though they were clueless about what they were laughing at. All they knew was that Rochelle wasn’t dead and their mother wasn’t going to jail…this time.

CHAPTER THIRTEEN

The drummer was too loud for Ian's taste and the lead guitarist continued to play a rock lick instead of the blues riff he wanted at the beginning of the song.

"Stop, stop. What the hell is wrong with you guys?" he shouted as he removed the headphones. "Come on, Junior tone it down. And Manny what happened to the blues-riff, man?" The practice session with the new guys still wasn't working for him, not even after two weeks of practice. Ian was preparing for a singing engagement Taylor had set up at the Blue Way. She'd put that into play before she jetted of to LA promising she be back in a couple of days. That was over a week ago and Ian hadn't heard from her since. His nerves were shot to hell dealing with all the details that his erstwhile manager should be taking care of. Here he was acting alone because Taylor was in the wind.

"That was blues, brotha'," Manny told him puffing out his narrow chest.

"Uh, brotha,'" Ian began, puffing out his equally narrow chest, "I know the difference between rock and blues. Now if you can't play what I want, the way I want, you can let the doorknob hit ya."

He looked over his shoulder just in time to catch Manny mimicking him. Before he could say anything Manny played the opening notes exactly as Ian called for.

"Now that's what's up," Ian said. He longed to fire the difficult musician and he would have last week if the boy wasn't so darn good. With the gig being so close, he knew he would have to suck it up and pray they came together before opening night. Musicians could be the biggest a-holes to work with. Everybody wanted to play like Jimmy or pull a Miles. If he could do the entire show a cappella he would do just that. Where in the world was his so-called manager, with his money and support?

Ian's earlier excitement of working with Taylor had passed, especially since she still owed him the money they'd agreed to when he signed with her. He was footing the bill for the practice sessions and had to pay for his own wardrobe for the gig. That was unheard of when one had a manager to handle all the little details. Thus far, other than booking him for three shows starting this Friday, Taylor hadn't done anything at all to promote his career.

He hoped that the Blue Way, located in the heart of Center City, would be packed every night so he could showcase his talent. He was the main attraction for three nights. If he was lucky the club might have conducted some advertising for their weekend venue.

"That heifer betta have her fine butt back here soon," he muttered, dialing her cell phone again. "And have my money. Dang, where are you?"

****

Taylor's cell phone ringing for the tenth time in less than an hour made it very difficult for her bedmate to concentrate on what she was doing to him. "Yo, don't ya wanna get that? It most be important, as much as the damn thing goes off."

"Just business, baby. You know I can take care of business," she purred sexily, then added, "in and out of the bed." Having sex with D-Jay hadn't changed over the years; he was still the most selfish man she'd ever met in her life. Doing so was a necessary evil. She fully believed in the golden rule: he that had the gold made the rules, and right now she was in desperate need of some of his gold.

"Damn, Taylor I have missed you. You know you need to bring your butt back to LA."

"I'm sure Blondie is taking good care of you," she said smartly.

"Forget her. I'm here with you ain't I?"

"Sneaking."

"What the hell ya mean? I ain't gotta sneak nowhere. You forgettin' who ya talking to." D-Jay got out of the bed and began picking up his scattered clothes.

"So now you're leaving?" Taylor put on her best little-wounded-girl impersonation. "I'm sorry, baby, I shouldn't have mentioned her."

"Nah, that's cool. I gotta meetin' cross town with some playas looking to make some money."

"Speaking of money. D-Jay, are you going to give me the money?"

D-Jay enjoyed the power his status and wealth gave him over women. He finished buttoning up his silk Armani shirt as he stepped into his Kenneth Cole shoes. "That's a lot of paper you tryin' to hit a brotha' up for. What's in it for me if you can't pay me back?" he wanted to know.

The image of running him over while driving a big truck played in her head. Two weeks of lying up with his trifling behind and once again, degrading herself for a man, made her sick to her stomach. Fighting back tears she blurted out, "All I'm asking you for is some upfront cash to help me out. Look my management firm is doing great. I signed…"

He cut her off. "I know everything that's goin' on in Philly. You signed the youn' boy and lost him to his uncle and now you workin' with some ole-ass nobody. Yep, things are wonderful." His cruel laugh told her that she had been played once again. He wasn't going to give her one red cent.

"You owe me," she mumbled weakly.

"I don't owe nobody nothing. Remember, I took you in and gave you a life and what did you do? You left me and ran off to the East Coast."

"What?" she screamed. "You kicked me out and moved that white bitch in! How dare you say I left you?"

"That's beside the point. You should have stayed in LA." As he pimp-walked to the door he said over his shoulder, "I'm gonna break you off the money, on one condition."

Her elation was short-lived. Taylor waited to hear his terms.

"If this ole' dude don't work out – or even if he does," he said, "you come back home and marry me." She gasped. He was out of the door, leaving her with her comeback stuck in her throat.

****

A blonde-haired woman sat across the street from the hotel watching the entrance. As the man emerged and handed something to a valet, she saw that her instinct had been dead on. She gripped the steering wheel and shook it hard. Leaning back against the headrest she pounded the roof of the Corvette. She looked up in time to see D-Jay hop into his black Jaguar, tip the valet and pull out into traffic. He sped past without noticing her. She put the car in gear and drove into the driveway of the hotel. A valet was at the driver's side door before the wheels stopped rolling. "Good afternoon, Miss. Welcome to the Potosi', Beverly Hills newest and grandest hotel."

"Don't touch my car. I'll be right back," she commanded as she stepped from her vehicle not caring that she exposed herself. Call it a gift. She paid no attention to the gawking men as she strode up to the reception counter.

"Excuse me; I'm D-Jay's personal assistant. He left his wallet in the room and asked me to come get it for him," she told the handsome desk clerk. "May I have a key to the room?"

"I'm sorry miss. I can't do that. Besides he didn't have a room. He was here visiting one of our guests."

"Oh wonderful; his sister is in town. I forgot."

The front desk clerk wasn't buying her act. He'd been in Hollywood too long to be fooled by amateur performances. "I can't give out information. Hotel policy. Is there anything else I can help you with?"

She flung her hair in his face as she stormed off and jumped into her car, racing the engine as she exited the driveway. She was fuming. "There is no way that ho is coming back into town and taking what I've worked my tail off to get. Not a chance."

****

Having lived the high-life with D-Jay, Taylor knew the only thing better than flying first class, was flying in a private jet. But for now that particular luxury was out of Taylor's reach. She leaned back into the butter-soft leather of a commercial flight and accepted a glass of champagne from the male flight attendant. Weighing down the ring finger on her left hand was a sparkling 4.5 carat diamond ring. She giggled as she savored the bubbly liquid and admired her hand. While the ring was nice, and unexpected, it was strictly her cash shortage that had compelled her to fly out to LA. She'd been prepared to do almost anything to get the money out of D-Jay, but marry him? Never! It was number one on her Don't Do This list. Making that a stipulation for giving her the money made absolutely no sense at all. *The fool never once told me he loved me in the whole time we were together.*

Hell would become a vacation destination before D-Jay convinced her to become his wife, and have the ability to use, abuse and discard her again.

To think that all this time he'd been keeping tabs infuriated her. Taylor removed the ring from her hand and stuffed it into her recently purchased purse. Knowing D-Jay, he had the ring insured, so if she sold it, after creating a believable story that she somehow lost it, well, no harm no foul. She estimated the value of the ring to be worth somewhere in the neighborhood of one hundred thousand dollars. Yeah, the ring, alongside the fifty-thousand dollar cashier's check in her possession, would help her cause out big time.

She reminded herself to call Ian from the airport, certain that when she put the cashier's check in his hand, any anger he harbored about being abandoned would dissipate. D-Jay actually came through for her. After all this time and the horrible way he'd treated her in the past, in the end he came through. Maybe she wouldn't sell the ring after all. Regardless of his actions, there wasn't the slimmest possibility of her accepting his crazy proposal of marriage. Taylor Daniels wasn't for sale and certainly not for a lousy fifty thou and a gaudy ring. On the other hand, the guy's net worth could keep her in designer clothes and living 'ghetto fabulous,' for quite some time. *Check yourself*, she thought. *He's is still the same D-Jay, whether he came through or not. Make your own gold then you can be the one making the rules.*

Taylor drifted off to sleep with a cat-ate-the-goldfish grin on her lovely face.

CHAPTER FOURTEEN

By the time Trey located a parking space three blocks away and entered the Blue Way, Ian's first set was just ending. Trey was wide-eyed as he stepped through the doors of the legendary nightspot. He remembered begging his parents as a teenager for a couple of dollars to come see stars and wannabees grace— or disgrace— its stage. Many people in Philly called it the other Apollo.

"My name is Trey Edwards, man. My boy, Ian put me on the list," Trey said to the large dude working the door.

"Look, brotha', the cover charge is twenty bucks with a two-drink minimum per set. That goes for you and everybody else tryin' to get up in here."

Another man walked up and stood directly behind Trey during the exchange. Trey felt hot smelly breath on the back of his neck. Turning to look over his shoulder, he blew air through his lips. The Black incredible hulk stood behind him. Squaring his shoulders Trey asked, "Is there a problem?"

"Nah little man. Just makin' sure ain't nothin' 'bout to jump off," the hulk responded, bored but ready to throw the pretty boy out of the club on his head if called for.

Trey was every bit of six feet tall, but the bouncer towered over him. Before things could take a turn for the worse, Trey reluctantly pulled out his money clip and paid the cover.

"Thank you very much. Enjoy the show, brotha.'"

"Yeah whatever," Trey answered, eyeballing the hulk to prove that he wasn't intimidated.

Ian was taking his bow and accepting thunderous applause from the jam-packed club. Every table was full and the bar area was packed with people; clearly the owner had disregarded the fire code for tonight's performance. Scantily clad barmaids roamed the club placing drinks in front of folks or taking their orders.

"What up, good brother? Thanks for coming out," Ian said to Trey after hopping down from the stage, slapping hands with other patrons as he passed them. "Where's Drea?"

They embraced and upon breaking the hold Trey responded, "She sends her love and best wishes, man, but a brotha's on his own tonight."

"You wearing a wire?" Ian joked.

"Nah, she had something at the church, some women's group stuff."

"On a Friday?"

Trey shrugged and shook his head, checking out the booty of one of the passing barmaids.

"Check it out," Ian said, trying to distract Trey's wandering eye. "You likes?" He spread his arms and twirled around to give Trey a full view.

"Sharp," Trey told him admiring the black silk suit with hidden buttons. "Hey man, the shoes are the bomb too."

"Right, right…you know a brotha' got to do what he do. Too bad you missed the first set. The boys were tight and thank God the sound system didn't mess up."

"Cool, well I'm here now."

"Come on man. I want you to meet Taylor. And I gotta change for the next set."

Trey trailed Ian past the crowded bar and stage down a flight of creaky stairs to the dressing room area. "So who you supposed to be, changing between sets, Miss Ross?"

"Hey don't go hating on Diana. It's what we do. Seriously T, can you believe I'm changing in the same dressing room that Jackie Wilson and Al Green used?"

"Hopefully they took theirs with 'em'."

"You know that's right," Ian laughed, knocking on the paint-peeled door.

"Come in."

Trey stepped into the room on Ian's heels. He looked around slightly disappointed. The room was closet-sized small and poorly lit, with ancient furniture that was past worn. Even the mirror had a spider crack in it.

Ian bumped Trey's leg to get his attention and introduced him to Taylor.

"Hi. I've heard a lot about you." She extended her hand.

Her voice washed over him like warm molasses dripping down the bark of a tree. She had the longest, sexiest legs he'd ever seen. Without thinking, Trey wiped a soft curl that had fallen onto her forehead. She caught hold of his hand and shook it.

"Good looking and fixes hair," she said winking at Ian, who was looking at Trey as though he'd lost his mind. Turning fully to face Trey she added, "Two traits I like in a man." Before Trey found his voice, Taylor smiled at him and excused herself, reminding Ian that the next set started in twenty minutes.

When the door closed behind her, Trey pounced on Ian. "Yo man, you didn't tell me she was that fine." He grinned. "Man did you see the body on her. All I can say is…damn."

Ian didn't say a word as he hung up his new black suit and changed into an all-black soft leather one-piece.

"That's tight, man. You got that Johnny Cash, Eddie Murphy thing happening." Shifting gears he said, "Now *back* to Taylor."

Ian adjusted himself in the front and walked over to the cracked mirror to make certain his hair was in place. "What about her?" he asked nonchalantly.

"How fine she is."

"As fine as your *wife*. Gotta go. My adoring fans await my return to the stage."

As they walked out of the dressing room Trey asked, "What the hell does that have to do with my wife?" Ian didn't respond.

Upstairs in the club, Trey felt lucky to find an empty table near the exit. He stretched out his legs and readied himself for what he knew would be a good show. It baffled him; why after so many years of doing music, Ian still hadn't made it big. Ever since high school, he'd been singing in clubs all over the city. Over the years Ian had become a local musical legend with an enormous following for his live shows.

Trey recalled asking Ian years ago why he thought he hadn't gotten signed to a major label and Ian named five other unknown singers that sounded better than singers heard on the radio every day. "What's your point?" Trey asked. Ian answered that it took more than a good voice to make it. It took luck, exposure, a great song and a machine behind the singer with long dough willing to spend on marketing, advertising and getting the song placed on a radio station's playlist.

Even without a record deal, or a hit song, Ian still found a way to make decent money taking gigs all over town and even doing some studio work singing background on other people's records. Trey watched his best friend take the stage to begin the second set. He was proud of his buddy and like Ian truly believed that one day his star would shine bright for the world to see. *I hope Taylor can do for my man like she did for that Fisher kid,* Trey speculated. Instantly a picture of Taylor popped into his mind and disturbingly she was removing the black dress she was wearing. Snapping out of his reverie, his eyes connected with hers at a table near by. He thought she blew him a kiss, but couldn't be certain because a big-butt barmaid blocked his view. When the barmaid moved, Taylor was facing front, applauding as Ian hit the stage to the sounds of an old James Brown number.

****

On stage Ian had the audience finger-popping, foot-stomping and completely wrapped around his pinky finger. He worked the crowd and drew them in deeper and deeper. At the end of every cover tune, the crowd whooped and shouted, "More…more! His forty-five minute set turned into Ian closing the joint down. When the bartender announced last call no one moved toward the bar. Even the barmaids were transfixed watching Ian as he lay flat on his back caressing the notes of a mournful song of lost love. When the band stopped playing and the applause rained down, he turned onto his side and sang a rendition of "A House is Not a Home" without the accompaniment of the band. It brought the house down.

The stage lights faded to black while the band performed solo instrumental pieces. Ian stood up with tears bubbling in his grey eyes and a huge face-stretching smile. He bowed dramatically soaking it all in. This is what made performing in front of a crowd so addictive, the adulation and appreciation of his talent. If he never made it outside of the "City of Brotherly Love," so be it. If he died right now God would get an earful.

He spotted Taylor bum-rushing her way through the crowd. "You were incredible!" she hollered. "You were simply incredible!"

"Thank you, Taylor. I tried for years to get up in here, but they stay booked. I don't know how you pulled it off, but thanks."

"We have work to do. Tomorrow we are in the studio putting together a demo. Please tell me you write songs."

"Gotta book full," he assured her. Looking past her, Ian called out for Trey.

"Congrats my brotha'. You tore it up. I ain't seen you throw down like that in awhile."

"Excuse us, Taylor," Ian said grabbing Trey by the elbow and steering him over to the bar.

"Why you acting like you never saw a pretty woman before?" he demanded of Trey as soon as they were out of earshot.

"What you talking 'bout?"

"Man, you gawking at Taylor like you just got released from prison."

"Man, please. I wasn't doing no such a thing."

Affectionately Ian touched Trey's shoulder then slapped him in the back of his head. "Get a grip, man. I know you. The worst time to start admiring other women is when the home fires are not getting lit."

"My home fires are a-blazing, okay. Well, maybe not forest fire; more like campfire."

"If anybody knows you, I do," Ian reminded him. "Go home; be with your family." Ian was dead serious. He knew Trey tried hard to stay faithful, and being a good-looking guy making plenty of money, the opportunities to cheat came his way often. To the best of his knowledge and from what Trey had shared with him he'd resisted temptation up to now. But the look he saw in Trey's eyes when he looked at Taylor made him nervous for his friend.

"I'm out," Trey said. "Again, bro, congratulations on tonight. Don't forget us little people on your way up."

"Never you. Now some of these other mutha's consider them forgotten."

****

Taylor saw the two men embrace and watched Trey walk out the door with mischief in her light brown eyes. Other than sleeping with Ian and D-Jay for financial gain, her love life was slacking. Married or not, she found Trey to be very much to her liking. His marital status was his business, not hers, and if the opportunity presented itself…it was on.

Strutting over to stand beside Ian she asked, "Where's your friend, what's-his-name going?"

"Home to his wife."

Ian failed to notice the sly smile that passed over her full lips. "So what does he do for a living?" she asked innocently.

"He sells cars."

"Oh, I think I might be in the market for a new ride. Do you have his card?"

CHAPTER FIFTEEN

The church was jammed pack with woman full of ideas about the women's group. Ironically most of the females seating in the pews hardly came to regular services. Amazing what a, handsome, single well built man could do for attendance. The meeting that started at eight o'clock had turned into a tug-of-war for power and positioning. And it was becoming a marathon as well. A simple hour-long meeting was still raging at two o'clock in the morning.

"Ladies, ladies," Pastor Raymond Douglas said into the microphone. "As much as I enjoy being in the house of the Lord, we really do have to wrap this up. Believe me when I tell you, I greatly appreciate all of you ladies coming out tonight and giving your input, but like I said, I asked Sister Edwards to be in charge. So we don't need to take another vote on leadership. Sister Edwards kindly accepted and is more than willing to give of her time and expertise. I suggest we give her our total support."

Andrea sat on the platform behind the podium not paying any attention to the other woman in the audience; she was completely absorbed in every word the pastor said. She had lost control of the meeting hours ago and was thankful when Pastor Douglas came back to lock the church up while they were still arguing back and forth over who should really be in charge.

One of the deacon's wives spoke up. "Pastor," she dripped syrup on her words, "I totally agree with your choice of Sister Edwards. She will do a fine job."

Andrea stifled a snicker since just prior to the pastor's arrival the woman had been one of her biggest critics. It wasn't that any of the women thought she couldn't do the job, or in truth wanted it themselves; they just wanted to work closely alongside the handsome newcomer to the congregation and the fact that he was the spiritual leader of the church went out the window when it came to single female hunters on the prowl for husbandly prey. Even the married ones were acting like they had forgotten their husbands were at home.

It had been that way since the old paster retired and appointed Pastor Douglas to take over. Once news got out that the new pastor was young, single and handsome, females who hadn't been to church since who-knew-when started filling the pews on Sundays. The man got enough dinner invitations to fill his calendar for the next year and a half.

"Ladies," his smooth baritone voice reverberated from the microphone through the loud speakers of the church, "there will be many disagreements even in God's house. It's okay to have them. However we must respect each others rights, and sometimes just agree to disagree. I would love this evening to have us all on the same accord for the good of this church. And I want peace from every last woman in this congregation and those who God leads to join this place of worship. So by a show of hands, do we all agree that Sister Edwards is an excellent choice to lead the women's group?"

Almost like people doing the "wave" at a sporting event, first the ones in the front pews raised their hands and then everyone else (whether they wanted to or not), joined until everyone's palms were in the air.

"Praise the Lord. It fills His heart with joy when his children come together in harmony for the good of each other showing love, honor and respect." Pastor Douglas was getting wind up. "I tell you, sisters, that the devil is an evil sort; he will attempt to get in where he fits in."

"Amen," someone shouted out.

"He will try to tear down whatever my God has built up."

"Preach, pastor," said another.

"But not in this House of the Lord; in this house we will seek Him first in all things."

"The devil is a liar," shouted another.

His voice washed over his captive audience like the calm before a storm. "We will tell the devil, Satan get ye behind me; there is no place for you here. I have come to serve the Lord and no weapon formed against me shall prosper. Can I get a witness?"

Most of the woman jumped to their feet and started clapping their hands ready to have church at two-twenty on a Saturday morning.

He raised his hands for silence and motioned for them to take their seats, inwardly smiling at the trance he seemed to have them under. Sometimes he secretly wondered whether, if he asked people to jump and down when he preached and bark like a dog, would they do it? "Sister Allen would you take us out with a song?" he asked the head deacon's wife. He sat down beside Andrea and patted her knee, allowing his hand to linger a beat longer on the last pat and move a tad bit past the knee.

The short woman with the wide body stood up and started blasting out a song of worship in a voice that deaf angels could hear. Soon the building was filled with handclapping and tambourine slapping.

While most of the women sang their hearts out, a few started gathering their things, sticking one finger in the air as they made their way toward the exit. A one verse song with call and response turned into a mini concert. Members of the church often joked that Sister Allen would sing her way into heaven. Not because she had the voice of an angel, but just to shut her up.

Standing up, Pastor Douglas slowly approached the podium. Clearing his throat he said a little louder than he meant to, "Yes, yes, thank you Sister Allen for leading us in that wonderful rendition." He was quickly finding out that the woman would go on and on until she wore the demons out, not to mention everyone else. "Ladies let us pray and thank God for this gathering and that He dispatch his angels to ride along with us as we journey home."

Afterward, Pastor Douglas walked Andrea to her car. "Thank you so much for taking on this challenging task."

"Not a problem. I'm just glad you came in when you did."

"I didn't do anything that you couldn't have," he complimented her. His hand was in the center of her back as they approached her car. "I take it that your husband and children won't be too worried about you?"

"Oh, no, my husband, Trey, went to see a friend of his sing at some club and my kids are spending the night with their friends."

"Are you okay with going home to an empty house?"

"Umm, huh, I'm sure Trey is home by now and I really must…" her cell phone vibrated in her small handbag. "Excuse me. It's my husband."

He backed off to give her some privacy after rubbing her lower back. He felt Andrea shiver from his touch. Stepping back further he admired her basketball-shaped bottom. Nothing got a man in trouble quicker than a big butt and a smile, he mused. Every man had a weakness he reasoned and for as long as he cared to remember his stood not ten feet away: accessible, sexually frustrated or repressed married women. Other than being able to reach inside people's very core and take them on a oral journey through preaching, his greatest gift was his ability to read the need, wants and desires of woman, especially the safe ones, those who were married.

"Well, umm…that was Trey, my husband," she said. "I told him the meeting got out of hand and that I was on my way." He noticed her hesitation. "I guess I'll get home. Thank you for walking me to my car."

"No problem, Sister Edwards. It's not often I get to play Sir Galahad to such a beautiful woman."

He smiled wickedly as she blushed and said goodnight. Moving forward he bent down and engulfed her in a hug, pressing himself against her fully. He brushed his lips against her cheek, inhaling her sweet scent. This time he was very certain she'd shivered and if he wasn't mistaken, maybe a little moan.

Releasing the hold, he backed up so she could enter her car. He waved and watched her pull off. Pastor Douglas didn't notice a figure squatting down, hidden behind the shrubbery alongside the parking lot as he walked past on the way to his own car.

As he peeled out of the driveway a woman stood up and dusted off. She took out a cell phone. "I found him," she said. "Yep, he's up to his ole tricks. No, no…don't worry. His time is coming."

****

Outside the wind raged with fury, bullying the huge trees and causing their limbs to shake violently. The leaves appeared to fly away escaping the torture. And with each howling wind, the night became darker and darker.

"Peace. Be still." Instantly the wind ceased and the trees stood still as floating leaves fluttered to the ground as softly as cotton. The moon shone forth with such brightness, people in the area would talk about it for years.

"Show-off."

"The same power that is in me is in my children."

"Fortunately for me they don't really believe that."

"When the final battle is waged, you will find out that my children have faith, trust and belief far past your ability to comprehend."

"Their faith, trust and belief start at their wishes and ends with their desires. If you don't fulfill either, they don't have any faith in you nor trust and as for belief that goes out the drain with the water."

"Your disdain for all that I have created will be your downfall."

"Like temptation will be for the Edwards."

"You relish bringing forth the weakness of man."

"I gotta make it do what it do, as your people say."

"You have been busy as of late."

"So many people so few hours in the day to deceive kill and destroy. For the Edwards, their inability to appreciate all that you have blessed them with is really the cornerstone of their demise. Now to go along with adultery, I thought it would truly be a show of their faith in you if I started to affect the other areas of their lives, such as their finances. Something your people hold so near and dear to their hearts."

"Behold everything they have is in your power, but do not touch them."

CHAPTER SIXTEEN

Andrea arrived home at half-past three o'clock in the morning to find Trey fast asleep in his favorite recliner, a book on his lap. Standing in the middle of the spacious living room she suddenly felt claustrophobic. Sweat built up under her armpits and her mouth begged out for wetness. Looking at her husband, guilt tiptoed across her heart. She struggled with wanting to wake him and talk or first jump in the shower to wash away the sins that tore at her spirit. The shower won out.

"You just going to leave a brotha' down here to wake up in the morning stiff as a board?"

Andrea slowly turned around hoping that her face didn't reveal her hidden shame. "You looked so peaceful. I was going to take a shower then come back and wake you up."

"Nah, I'm up now. I'll be up in a minute. So did everything turn out okay at the church?"

The church was the last subject she wanted to discuss. Quickly she changed directions. "How was Ian's show?"

"Oh baby, you should have seen him. The boy was on fire. Remember back in the day how he used to roll on the floor and all that stuff?"

"Yeah, he did that?"

"Baby the boy was on the floor. The only thing he didn't pull was a Pattie and kick off his shoes."

"Get out. Sorry I missed it. Next time I'll be front row. I'm gonna take that shower now."

"Okay, I'll get the lights." He stopped her in her tracks. "Hey baby, you know I love you right?"

Refusing to turn back around she sniffled, cleared her throat and said, "I know, and I love you too." She barely made it to the top of the stairs before the eye-dam broke and tears burst through.

Later they laid in bed each lost in their own private meditation. Trey slumbered, dreaming about the sexiest legs he'd ever seen and hoping he would get a chance to see them again. Andrea drifted off asking God for forgiveness as she imagined the pastor's lips moving from her cheek to her lips.

****

Sunday morning Trey purposely woke up before Andrea. He quietly rolled out of the bed onto the floor. Peering up over the edge of the bed, he made certain his movement hadn't disturbed her. He'd kept his promise to Brittany on

Saturday and made it back home in time to go to the zoo. Andrea had begged off citing a headache, so Trey and the kids went alone. He'd told Andrea that he would definitely make this Sunday's service. That wasn't happening today. Weighing his options he chose to take an ear-whupping for breaking his word rather than spending three hours sitting up in some church listening to somebody holler about the end is near. Like he really needed to hear some man tell him what not to do as he was probably doing that and more to half the chicks sitting up in there. Regardless, organized religion didn't work for him. He figured that as long as he believed that there was a God and he was a good person what more did he need to do? Prove it by going to church all the time? Nah, going on Easter and Christmas was more than enough. That way he showed homage on the Lord's birth and his death.

Sliding across the thick carpeted floor of the bedroom, Trey grabbed a sweatsuit he'd laid out before getting into bed and silently left the room. He threw water on his face in the hallway bathroom and ran down the steps, turned off the interior alarm, grabbed his car keys, scribbled a barely legible note to Andrea and went out the door, all in ninety seconds.

Andrea sat up in bed after Trey left, thankful that his predictability worked for her this time. She didn't want him to come to church this morning. Having the man she loved and the man she lusted for in the same place at the same time was something she couldn't deal with. *This is just a phases I'm going through, a test, nothing more. Get it together, girl. He is a man of God. Oh, Jesus I confess to you my sin. I have lusted in my heart and I repent of my sin and ask that it be thrown into the sea of forgetfulness. In your mighty name, Jesus. Amen.*

****

The praise and worship team had the entire congregation on its feet, making a joyful noise unto the Lord. Sister Allen stood in front of the assembly in all of her splendor, big hat with flowers around the brim, a two-piece sequined dress and huge diamond earrings that she swore were real. For over twenty years she'd been the leader of the praise team, and she took that position seriously. If a person hadn't followed Acts 2:38, and repented of their sins in Jesus' name and been baptized (fully submerged, no tipping a toe or sprinkling of the forehead for her) and filled with the Holy Ghost, they couldn't even think of being a part of the praise team. And if a member of the team backslid, she would kindly ask them to step down until they had gotten themselves back on track. Since she kept such a close watch over the lives of the team and stayed up in other's folk business, over the years there was never more than seven members at any given time.

Andrea ushered the kids to their usual pew, third row from the front on the left- hand side of the aisle. Brittany and Brett quickly took their seats and Andrea remained on her feet to join in with the singing. She wiggled her feet around in her high-heeled shoes hoping that the pastor wouldn't allow Sister Allen to go on so long that her dogs started barking. She silently prayed that she could enjoy the service and get out of the building without any contact with him.

At the conclusion of praise and worship, the ushers brought around the collection plates to allow all those who found it in their hearts to give unto the Lord the opportunity to do so.

Deacon Allen, the long-suffering husband of Sister Allen, grabbed a microphone and reminded the church that they were still short ten-thousand dollars on the building fund, "Remember, the Lord loves a cheerful giver. You can't expect a withdrawal from the Bank of God if you haven't made a deposit."

Mild grumbling could be heard throughout the church, but people dug a little deeper into their wallets and pocketbooks and put more money into the plates that came around for the second time.

Pastor Douglas slowly approached the podium as the organist played softly. "I was so glad when they said let us go into the house of the Lord," he stated. "Brothers and sisters, that means that an invitation went out and someone took it up. Today I stand before you, so glad in my spirit that you've decided to accept the invitation of the Lord and come into His house."

Church had officially begun. For the next hour and a half, Pastor Douglas preached, taught, hollered and shouted his sermon. By the end sweat poured down his brow and two women in the pews needed to be helped off the floor and placed back into their seats. Sister Allen caught the Holy Ghost and ran up and down the aisle knocking off hats and stepping on feet.

Andrea sat mesmerized till the end of the service and the preacher released the church with the same parting words the old pastor used to say; "What I say unto one I say unto all, watch."

"Mom, Brett fell asleep again," Brittany said. "Mom, you hear me?"
She did hear her daughter speaking, but her mind was pre- occupied. As if

in a trance, Andrea stood up, ordered Brittany to stay put and walked down the aisle toward the altar.

"Do you need prayer?" she heard a voice say. "No thank you. I'm fine," she answered a little too abruptly. "I mean, no thank you brother. I just need to speak with the pastor."

"He's in the back receiving prayer from the deacons. He sure did preach that word today, didn't he?"

"Yes he did," she agreed, although if anyone had asked her to repeat one word of it, all she could comment on was how fine he looked in his gray pin-stripe suit with a pink shirt and silk pink tie.

"If you need counseling, Sister, I can make an appointment for you."

"No thank you. I'll see him some other time."

"God bless you, sister."

"You too, Brother." Her swollen feet couldn't move fast enough to get her back to where she'd left the kids, but both of them were missing and nowhere to be found.

"Sister Allen, have you seen Brittany and Brett?" she asked.

"Who? Oh you mean your darling little ones. I think I saw them in the back. You know how Brother Joe loves to give the kids some candy they don't need."

"Thank you; see you at Bible study on Wednesday."

"I saw you up at the altar, are you in need of prayer or healing?"

"What…oh no, I needed to speak with Pastor about the women's group."

Sister Allen moved in close to Andrea and looked around before whispering, "Don't spend too much time with the women's group where it takes you away from your family. By the way, how is that handsome husband of yours, haven't seen him in church in a while?"

Andrea stepped back to get a close look at Sister Allen's face. The woman was always up in other folk's kool-aid, whether she knew the flavor or not. "I have my time under control and my husband is fine. Just busy at work."

"Well dear, you know, one should never be too busy to give some time to the Lord. Besides, a family that prays together stays together and that old pesky devil can't get in the gap."

Andrea smiled with her mouth and then picked up her Bible and walked away from the annoying woman before she said something she would regret.

She didn't hear Sister Allen's parting words. "Jesus send our Pastor a wife…and quick."

CHAPTER SEVENTEEN

The sales meeting was well under way by time Trey showed up. Jerry's fake smile barely concealed how much he loathed Trey's exalted status at the dealership. Jerry was in charge, and Trey came and went as he pleased without regard to Jerry's position as manager. "Welcome, Mr. Edwards to our mandatory sales meeting that started ten minutes ago. So nice of you to grace us with your presence."

Trey took an open seat in the back of the room, ignoring Jerry's jab and attempt at putting him in his place. Tony turned around and whispered at Trey, "Must be nice to not have to come on time to these things. When I grow up, I wanna be just like you."

Trey fired back, "Yeah, first you would have to grow a couple more inches, little man."

Tony grinned and turned back around but not before he pointed at the leader board. It showed Tony was number one with five units sold for the month and Trey was second with three.

"So as I was saying before I was rudely interrupted…" Jerry let his words linger for a beat then continued, "This is October and traditionally it's a solid month for our dealership. In reviewing last year's number we moved…," he flipped through the file he held and said, "Yeah we moved 235 cars. Now last year I wasn't in charge so needless to say I want us to beat that total and trust me, we will."

Tony waved his hand in the air to catch Jerry's attention. "Hey boss, who was the number one that month?" He already knew the answer as did everyone else in the room.

Jerry pretended to contemplate the question and went as far as to flip through the papers to find the answer. "Trey."

"Didn't he set a record for this dealership that month?" Tony was on a roll.

"Cut the bull, Tony. Don't worry 'bout what I did or am doing." Trey was tired of his junk. "Compete with yourself…Oh yeah…you already beatin' yourself." Trey jacked his slightly closed fist over his groin area to emphasize his point. He walked out of the meeting amid the laughter of the others in the room.

"All right…settle down." Jerry raised his voice to be heard. "I'm not done." He made a note to confront Trey later in the day for leaving his meeting without being dismissed. Boss's pet or not it was him, not Trey that ruled this roost.

"Why you bother to show up for one of his meetings if you just gonna walk out early?"

"What…," Trey spun around ready for a confrontation. "Oh, hey Paula. How you doing this morning?"

"Chillin', now what's up with you?"

Trey stepped over to her reception desk area and leaned on his elbows trying not to look at her over exposed cleavage. "Don't you ever cover them things up?" he teased wondering if they were real.

Paula bent over and said breathlessly, "And deprive you boys." She moved her hands seductively across her chest like a model displaying an item on a TV game show. "All this?"

"You wild girl."

Turning serious Paula beckoned for Trey to come closer, taking in the scent of his cologne. She almost fanned herself before saying, "What up with you lately? Your head has definitely not been in the game."

"What you talking 'bout? Please, darling. The month is early."

"I'm not talkin' about selling cars. I'm referring to you."

"Me?"

"Yes, you. You been moping round her for a while now all distracted and stuff."

Her observation was dead on and Trey's awareness of it made him uncomfortable that it was so obvious to others. "I'm cool, girl" he assured her stepping off. "I'm me, remember."

"Okay, you. Get your head in the game then."

Acting the part of getting his head back in the game, Trey sat at his desk pretending to work on some paperwork for over an hour. Every time any one came to his door to chat he quickly picked up the phone like he was in the middle of a conversation until they left.

"Trey, we need to talk," Jerry said entering his glass- lined office and closing the door.

"Can't it wait? I'm expecting a call back from a client."

Jerry ignored Trey's question and sat down on one of the chairs in front of his cluttered desk. "No it can't wait. We need to clear the air and I wanna do it now."

"Clear the air about what, man? Trust, I'm not in the mood for one of your power trips right now." Trey didn't realize his voice was loud and bouncing off the walls. The other sales reps milling around in the showroom stopped horsing around and directed their attention toward his office.

Jerry was caught off guard by Trey's outburst. He'd rehearsed his part to perfection and was totally unsure how to proceed. "There is no need for you to raise your voice at me," he said in an attempt to regain control. "I simply wanted to talk about you not attending meetings or showing up late. It doesn't send a positive message to the rest of the sales force."

With a tone full of finality Trey spat out, "Not now."

Deflated Jerry stood up, straightened his tie and smoothed down his trouser leg. He cleared his throat, then replied, "Very well. I can see you're busy. We will meet later."

"I'll let you know when," Trey added for spite. He had to admit it made him feel a little better watching Jerry shuffle from his office like it was his idea. The feeling faded as quickly as it came. Trey's concentration was focused on much more important items than Jerry's tiny ego.

Thus far he hadn't heard back from the bank on his loan request and the bank officer had failed to return any of his numerous calls. If this deal fell through he stood to lose more than a car dealership. To ensure that the seller dealt only with him, Trey had given him a non-refundable deposit. Moving fast, Trey worked an agreement that gave the owner a hundred- thousand-dollar down payment to sweeten the deal in his favor. At the time he truly believed that there wouldn't be any problems getting a bank loan, and he made the upfront money non-refundable while talking the owner into dropping the original asking price. That move took the dealership off the open market for six months. The timeframe gave the current owner time to finalize what he needed to take care of and afforded Trey the necessary time to come up with the rest of the money. To add to his troubles, he'd taken the money from their joint retirement account without Andrea's knowledge or consent. Not to mention, he'd forged her signature.

"Answer the damn phone, man." He dialed the bank for the tenth time in a five minute period. "Thank God, Mr. Davis. How are you this morning, sir? This is Trey Edwards…ummm…okay; I'll await your call. Thank you, sir." He slammed the receiver down hard.

****

Tony watched Trey from outside his office door and clapped his hands together. "Wonder what's up with ole' boy. That's right, Trey, stay off your game." Tony wanted to outshine Trey even more than he longed to get into Paula's pants…well almost. "Hey Paula, when you gonna let me take you out?" he asked, strolling up to her desk.

"Haven't you ever heard of sexual harassment, Tony?" She spat back.

"You can harass me sexually anytime," he shamelessly flirted.

"Jerry…," Paula called out, "don't you have something for your salesmen to do other than bother me?"

"Tony, take it outside. Cars don't sell themselves," Jerry ordered. At least he had control over the other salespeople. There was no way Dexter would make him general manager if he couldn't figure out a way to reel Trey in. He was aware that Trey turned down his job many times when asked to fill the slot after Dexter's younger brother moved to Atlanta. Since he kept his offices in Philadelphia this dealership was the only one Dexter owned without a general manager. In last month's management meeting, Dexter had informed them he was stepping down from the day- to- day operation and leaving his general managers in charge of his dealerships. Jerry could still see the look in Dexter's eyes when he stared straight at him and announced that the Philly dealership job was up for grabs. One of the other managers had the nerve to ask Dexter whether Trey was interested in the job. Dexter said something about Trey having other plans, what ever that meant. So as he figured it— if he stood a chance of becoming general manager— Trey either had to fall in line or get knocked out. Somehow, Tony or one of the other guys needed to out-perform the wonder boy. And the sales force had to move more units than last year. He had to find a way to show Dexter he was the man for the job.

Racking his brain an idea came to him. "Paula," he said into the phone. "Post a notice in the break room. It should read as follows: Anyone coming late for mandatory sales meetings will be sent home for the day and fined one-hundred dollars. That goes for everybody on the sales force…no exceptions."

Paula hung up the phone thinking that Jerry had just declared war against Trey. She was glad to have a front- row seat.

****

After a satisfying day of outselling Trey, Tony sat on the hood of his car smoking a cigarette in the parking lot. As Trey approached him he flicked the butt to the ground and stood up with a cheesy grin across his plain-looking face. "Tough day, huh…superstar?"

Normally, Tony's competitive childishness amused Trey, but today was not one of those amusing ones. "Nice work today, man. Be good," Trey said hoping to avoid any further conversation.

"Nice work today. You're funny. I'm all up in your booty and all you can say is… nice work."

"Tony," Trey patiently explained, "one day don't make a month and one month don't make a career."

Tony invaded Trey's personal space and spat out, "You know what, Trey? You full of crap. You don't wanna see nobody else on top but you and now that that I'm top dog you won't even give a brotha' no prop's."

Trey resisted the urge to push him away and instead leveled his voice to say, "Back up off me. I don't give a darn about the board, boy. You want props for doing your job? If you need someone to pat you on your butt, go see Jerry; he's the sales manager, not me." The itch to slug Tony overwhelmed him so much Trey had to stuff his right hand into his pants pocket to resist the temptation.

"You ain't right, Trey," Tony shouted, pouting and stomping off to his car. "You ain't right and next month the parking spot is mine."

"Get a life, chump," Trey advised him as Tony jumped into his car and squealed out of the lot.

"Heavy is the head," said Dexter stepping out of the shadows.

"He can have the crown."

"You tired of being king of the hill, Trey?"

"Nah, man just got other things on my mind."

"Let's go for a drink and talk about it. Your treat."

"We don't drink, and you invited me."

"See you at the pub," Dexter said over his shoulder.

The last thing Trey felt like doing tonight was hanging out with Dexter and being preached to. All he wanted to do was forget the day, go home, spend some time with Drea and the kids and go to bed. Instead he followed Dexter's steel-grey colored Bentley over to City Line Avenue for appetizers and sermonizing.

When they arrived the attractive hostess coolly greeted Dexter and immediately seated them although there was a long line of people waiting. The popular restaurant competed with the local clubs as a "meat market" for urban-dwelling professionals seeking to hook up. Even on a weeknight, the place was packed.

Looking around Trey began to feel out of place. "I feel like an old man," he told Dexter.

"No, you feel like an old married man."

"Don't remind me. I see that you come here often."

"What makes you think that?"

"The chick at the door. If looks could kill…I do own a black suit."

Dexter laughed and told him that was a story for another day.

Trey longed to hear it now; anything would work as long as it didn't bring forth a tirade about church. "Question for you. Haven't you ever wanted to share your success with someone?"

"I did, but the one I want…"Dexter's voice sadly trailed off.

"Special one got away?"

"Something like that," he responded without elaborating any further. Then switching course, he asked Trey about the confrontation with Tony. "That was a little beneath you don't you think." He said it more as a statement than a question.

"I know, Dex, I just got a lot on my mind lately," Trey said by way of explanation. "The bank hasn't gotten back with me yet and it's driving me crazy."

"Trey, it takes time. God's time most times," he counseled. "You are trying to borrow half a million bucks; don't go driving yourself crazy. Remember what I've always said. What God has for you is for you."

Trey nodded his head in reluctant agreement. "You right, man. I do need to chill out. All this pressure got me wind tight as a drum. It's affecting my sales."

Dexter accepted that and said, "Tony is all over you all the time because he wants your validation. The kid has made you his benchmark." Dexter schooled him, which wasn't uncommon since every chance he got he enjoyed dropping knowledge on Trey. "The boy is still wet behind the ears. Trey it's your turn to reach back. To whom much is given much is required."

Dexter made sense but Tony annoyed Trey to no end. He would rather have root canal than bother with his inflated ego. "I hear you."

"Hold up, before you talk about his bragging. Look in the mirror. When you first started you talked more trash than the law allowed. And you still do. You wanted to beat my brother every chance you got. It's funny that you now have your own stalker."

"All right, man you made your point, although I wasn't as cocky as…" He didn't bother to finish, already knowing Dexter's response.

After the impatient waitress stopped by their table for the third time they finally picked up their menus. They decided to share the house appetizer special.

They ate in silence until Dexter surprised Trey by asking whether he had accepted Jesus in his life.

"Where did that come from?" Trey asked almost choking on a chicken finger.

"Drink some water. You okay?"

Guzzling the water down, Trey looked around hoping the waitress would come back, his cell would ring, or even the fire alarm would go off.

"Does that question make you uncomfortable?"

"Nah, not at all," he fibbed.

"You didn't answer me," Dexter pressed. "Have you accepted Jesus Christ into your life as your Lord and Savior?"

"I go to church. My wife and kids, we go to church."

"I didn't ask you that."

"I know." An escape hatch revealed itself. "What is this rumor I hear about you stepping down?" Trey could tell Dexter saw straight through him, but he played along by saying, "Oh but for the grapevine. Yes, Trey I'm turning over the reins so I can fulfill a promise I made to myself."

"Which was?"

"Retiring at forty-five."

"Must be nice," Trey replied with a hint of envy.

CHAPTER EIGHTEEN

The month of October came and went so fast it left scud marks across the calendar. It was thirty-one days full of highs and lows.

For the first time since he'd been let loose alone on the sales floor at Fortune Motors, Trey Edwards' name wasn't on top of the leader board to end a month. Tony kicked it up a huge notch and keeping true to his boast outsold everyone— not just Trey— by double digits. The entire sales staff, service department and anyone else within earshot heard his razzing of Trey until even those who wanted to see Trey finally get beat, hoped he would turn it around and kick Tony's bragging behind in the end. It didn't happen. It took him two whole years but in the end Tony finally got the parking spot he's coveted.

Trey was too occupied with his own troubles to care. The bank officer still hadn't called him back. He had a growing fear that the entire deal was about to go up in smoke, along with his money. Selling cars seemed trivial in comparison. Even so, he still managed to finish a distant second.

The first day of the work week of November, Trey marched right up to Tony in full view of all and bowed at the waist as he congratulated him on a super month. Not only did he beat Trey, Tony had set a new record for cars sold in a month. It surprised Trey how much that small gesture meant to Tony. His competitive juices kicked in and he told Tony not to get too attached to his parking spot.

"A new sheriff is in town!" Tony shouted for the world to hear.

Nobody relished Trey's defeat more than Jerry. "Operation-knock-Trey-down-a-peg" was in full effect. He decided to call for a mandatory meeting tomorrow morning. Trey was bound to come late or not show up at all, since lately Jerry had been having more meetings than ever. He knew how much Trey hated his meetings.

****

Trey sat in his office staring at the phone as if watching it would make it ring. He was worrying his hair gray. Meanwhile his wife sat in her office with the door closed and locked, dealing with her own colors. Some days she was red with anger, white with fear of being caught in a lie, and blue with depression. As of yet, she hadn't told Trey about the promotion at work although it was effective the first day of the month. For the life of her, she didn't understand why, she just hadn't. It never came up in conversation at home and besides Trey was a little distant lately. Maybe he was withholding something from her. Boy was she grateful that his sex drive seemed to be in park since the last time they made love. She couldn't keep up the charade of making love to her husband with her eyes squeezed shut tightly to block out the image of Raymond Douglas. Andrea was beginning to live the lyric to that old O'Jays' song "Your body is here with me but your mind is on the other side of town." It didn't help that she was sneaking around talking on her cell phone late at night after Trey fell asleep. Sleep deprivation was threatening to send her over the nearest cliff. Just the sound of the man's voice made her heart skip beats, her palms sweat and her innards quaver. One could only pray that November bought some sanity to what was rapidly becoming a crazy daze called her life.

****

Ian woke up slowly from the recurring dream he'd been having lately. He'd be dressed in black from head to toe walking across a dark stage toward a light. The closer he'd get to the light the brighter it became and just as he was stepping into the light…he'd wake up. "Dammit I wanna walk into the light," he shouted to the empty room. Sitting up in bed he rubbed his eyes hoping to ease the early- morning pain that came with wearing contact lens. Even without the aid of contacts he could see the world clearly and it looked simply fabulous. Today Taylor had arranged studio time for him and the band to record some tracks for a demo tape. If that wasn't enough to keep his balloon in the air, last night after blowing the crowd away again at the Blue Way— where his original three-night gig had turned into him becoming the house performer— she blew him away with the news that this upcoming Friday three major labels were sending some executives to hear him sing. He had to admit, although he harbored some doubts about her, Taylor knew her stuff. Past hurts and disappointments in the music business were starting to be things of the past for him. Finally, a record deal with a major label and performing on the world's largest stages were clearly in sight.

****

Meanwhile in a Center City apartment over top of a drugstore, the one person who was changing Ian's life was gazing at her own reflection, not quite liking the image she saw. Taylor's hair looked as though she'd undergone electric shock treatment and her rheumy eyes were bloodshot as they looked back at her. A hangover headache knocked loudly inside her skull. Expensive vodka might make her feel alive going down, but the next day it left her pleading for a quick and merciful death. *My goodness, how many shots did I do last night convincing that fool to let me use the club on Friday for Ian's showcase? And come on, how long am I going to have to run around desk to be taken seriously as a businesswoman? Like I would actually sleep with that old goat. If he had rubbed my thigh one more time, I swear I would have split his wig.*

Turning the shower on, she stepped through the shower curtains and allowed the hot water to give her a "cascade moment." Thank God, Ian was turning the joint out and filling the place. Thus far Ian couldn't complain about her not doing her job as his manager. In a short period of time, Taylor had him in a position to demand more money than he'd ever made as a working singer. Ian was performing all over Philly and was the hottest act in town. Nobody could tell her that marketing, advertising and hustling big-time didn't pay off. Taylor had flyers with Ian's mug plastered on telephone poles from North Philly to South Philly to West Philly and even Northeast Philly. She had even gotten the old CD that Ian had self-produced ten years ago repackaged and re-released. To their surprise (though she wouldn't admit it shocked her), one single on the CD was getting played on the college jazz station. At last count over sixteen hundred units had sold in three weeks. She'd started selling them at all of his gigs and out of the back of her car. Who would've thunk it? A forty year- old vocalist making waves in an era where only the young made it, whether they had any real talent or not. If everything fell into place, come Friday he could actually get a record deal with a major label. And after that she would have aspiring acts, as well as already established ones banging down her door. Shoot-she could expand her management agency, move back to the West Coast and…she had to pump her brakes. She was getting too excited. Life was great!

Now if only D-Jay would stop harassing her and trying to force her to pick a wedding date. Especially she hadn't said yes in the first place. *That's alright, once I get Ian signed, I'll pay D-Jay back with interest.* On the other hand, no need to be hasty with her money. Taylor made a corporate decision.

She'd simply send him a check for the fifty grand and a bottle of champagne as thanks. With that settled, she popped out of the hot, soothing shower refreshed and back among the living.

The reflection smiling back at her was more familiar. Since things were going so well and she was making her own money, she needed a car that matched a woman of her status. Beaming, Taylor dried off and waltzed into the bedroom of her temporary one-bedroom apartment. She made up mind that today she would take care of two desires in one— buy a car and get laid.

CHAPTER NINETEEN

"Hold still," she ordered. Rochelle pulled her mother's head back between her legs.

"Ouch, girl. Do you have to be so rough?" Tina asked, looking over her shoulder. She was seated on the floor in front of her daughter agonizing, over the pain Rochelle was inflicting with the comb and on her frayed nerves.

"Mom when was the last time you ran a comb through this mess?" Rochelle asked, applying more grease to her mother's dry scalp. "I'm almost done. You are going to look so pretty."

Tina hoped so, Lord have mercy, whatever would help her get this job she was all for it. She silently thanked God for blessing her with another chance at becoming a better mother and for giving her the strength to call the number in the paper that advertised the "Welfare to Work" program the city's mayor had put into place. Ever since that morning in the kitchen with Rochelle, Tina was trying hard to wean herself off marijuana and alcohol. This time she was determined to get her life on track. *Hell, I owe my babies betta' then I've given them,* she thought. Saying amen, she timidly accepted the mirror from Rochelle.

"See Mom" I told you. Look how pretty you are," Rochelle gushed.

The woman staring back at Tina certainly was familiar, but she couldn't remember the last time she'd looked at herself and felt any pride. She welcomed the hug from her daughter. Then Tina uttered three words she hadn't spoken to another living soul since her own mother died when she was ten years old; "I love you."

****

Dexter counted out fifty crisp one-hundred dollar bills on top of his desk. Before the last bill touched the top, Jerry greedily scooped up the cash. Fanning himself with the money he cackled and pumped his fist in the air. "It's like I told you, Mr. Fortune, this team is more productive when everyone falls in line." He added, "including Trey."

Dexter sunk back into his high-backed leather chair. Inwardly he cringed, but on the outside he showed Jerry a cheesy grin. "October was a great month. Tony did a terrific job; outselling Trey is no easy feat. More importantly, great job pumping up the sales force and breaking the record."

"Thank you, sir." Jerry said. "Thank you very much." He floated out of the big man's office five grand richer and certain that the announcement of his appointment as general manager would be coming soon.

Before the office door shut fully, Dexter was on the phone calling his brother in Atlanta. "Lil Bro, what would it take for you to come back to Philly and take over?"

****

Pulling into the parking lot Trey instinctively maneuvered his car toward the space he normally occupied. It took a moment for it to register when he noticed another car in his spot. Tony's shiny black BMW gleamed from the sunlight beaming down on it. He had even gotten new personalized tags, they read: "1-2 beat."

Trey cracked up and found another place to park his car. He wondered if Dexter would forgive him for taking Tony with him when he left to run his own dealership.

****

Taylor swept into the car dealership as if she was on the runway. Heads turned, eyes got bigger and salesmen in the middle of working with potential customers lost their train of thought. Even the female customers checked her out either admiring her pumps or silently wishing they had her body.

"I'm looking for Trey Edwards," she announced to Paula.

Paula tossed her braids back, sighed deeply and stared Taylor in the eyes. With the slightest hint of sistatude she said, "Do you have an appointment?"

Taylor was having none of it, "Sweetie, I don't need an appointment."

"Taylor," they both heard Trey say. "Hi there. I thought that was you," he said as he approached the reception area and unknowingly prevented an all-out catfight.

She cut eyes at Paula and added salt by walking up to Trey and wrapping her arms around his neck. Not expecting a public display of affection he momentarily froze in place. He nervously returned the hug and quickly backed away. "Wha…um...what are you doing here?" he stammered.

"You do sell cars and I'm looking to buy one, so here I am."

Trey licked his suddenly dry lips, cleared his throat and attempted to jump back into salesmen mode. He ignored the hard stares from Paula and Tony, motioning through the outside window at him. He calmly asked Paula to show Taylor to his office and practically ran outside to Tony.

Tony met him just as he stepped through the glass doors. "Playa, you need me to ride shotgun on that one?"

"Nah man, I'm good."

"Not trying to get all up in your bizness, but ain't you married?"

"Friend of a friend, nothing more," Trey explained as he turned away and walked slowly back inside.

"Little Miss Thang is waitin' for you," Paula told him, not bothering to hide her disgust nor her jealousy.

"What?"

"Nothin'…your business."

"You heard her, she's here to buy a car just like everyone else who comes in here," Trey said defensively. "I've sold cars to women before."

Paula kind of snorted and shook her head. "I ain't seen no other woman throw herself at you like that. If you ax' me, she up in here looking for more than a car."

"Why you say that?" Trey asked not sure if Paula was tripping or maybe on to something. The hug was a little overboard since they had only met once.

"Woman's intuition," was all she said.

Trey waved his hand dismissively at Paula and briskly walked to his office checking his reflection in the mirrored glass to ensure his appearance was in order. "Well Miss Taylor," he said entering to find her holding the picture of Andrea and the kids that sat on his desk. A little rattled he said, "The family."
"Beautiful kids and your wife is gorgeous."

"Thank you," he said taking the picture out of her hand. Again his lips and mouth dried up. He almost pushed his chair out from under him as he sat down behind his desk. Embarrassed he was relieved to see Taylor had picked up a brochure off his desk and was flipping through it, missing his goof. For a second he forgot why she was in his office. "Umm…so you are in the market for a new car, huh?" *Nice job stating the obvious.*

Taylor coyly looked up. "Ian said that you were the man to see, so here I am." *This guy is cuter than I thought and charming in a haven't –been- with-another- woman- in- years kind of way.*

Trey soaked in her scent, beauty and the way the simply black dress she wore hugged her body showing off every curve to the fullest without being shameless. The neckline revealed just enough cleavage to make any breathing soul beg to see more. As she sat before him, he couldn't help but sneak a peek or two at her exposed thighs.

Taylor watched Trey's eyes narrow as he took her in from head to thigh. As she and Trey stole glances across his desk, Taylor chose to forget the images on the picture she admired earlier; his family was his concern, not hers. "I want a BMW, black on black." She finally decided, then inquired, "Do you have one on the lot I can test drive?"

Her voice went into his ears traveled down his chest, making a pit stop at his heart and ended up at his groin area. Just the sound of her speech moved him to Fantasy Island and Mr. Roarke and Tattoo was leading him to the bungalow where Taylor awaited his arrival…

Taylor patted the desk to get Trey's attention. From the expression on his face, it was apparent his mind had wandered off. "Trey, the car."

"What, oh yeah," he snickered. "Yeah, yeah, I believe we have one or two on the lot." He jumped up from his desk banging his knee and rapidly limped out of the door saying, "I'll be right back; gotta get the keys."

Taylor waited for Trey to return with the keys. *He's so cute... I hope his nerves don't get the best of him. This test drive is going to be too much fun.* Taylor envisioned her day ending with her getting a new car and some very much needed, mind-blowing, perm-sweating-out, back-scratching sex.

CHAPTER TWENTY

The roar of the powerful car engine mixed with the loud music blaring from the car's stereo system was no equal to the boisterous squeals Taylor made as she sped along the I-95 highway. With the top down and her hair blowing wildly in the wind, it took all of Trey's "inner married man," to restrain him from jumping into her lap and…

Damn, he thought admiring her breathtaking beauty. *This woman is fine as hell. Here I am riding in a bad BMW with the top down, freezing my butt off, with a woman with Halle's looks and Beyonce's body and all I can do is stare.* Boldly, Trey allowed his eyes to wander down her body, until they rested on his favorite part of her, her thighs. Again the intense desire to rub his hands over her smooth, firm, shapely thighs made his nature rise until the "inner married man," hollered out in his head, "Hey fool, check yourself. You got a wife and two kids at home!" He shook his head and looked around as if Taylor heard the voice as well. He snapped his head forward and concentrated on the blurred white stripes darting by on the road.

"Hey, uh Taylor? I think you should back out off it before we get pulled over."

"Don't you think I could charm my way out of a ticket?" she asked, batting her long lashes. She smirked as she increased the pressure on the pedal bringing the car's speed to nearly 100 mph.

Despite his concerns and against his better judgment, Trey relaxed a little and threw his head back against the headrest. "You crazy girl. However fine as you are, and I'm sure charming as all get down, let's bring those horses into the corral." Then he reminded her, "Besides, I can't let you blow the engine until we sign on the dotted line."

Slowing down to 85 she said, "Oh I see how you roll. Putting on your salesman's hat now?"

"Would Superman leave home without his cape?" he teased. "Of course not." He answered for her. "So I can't leave the hat at home. Gotta keep my eyes on the prize.

"Am I a prize?"

Speechless wasn't a word that normally described Trey at any time, but that question not only closed his mouth; it brought a coloring to his cheeks like a little boy getting kissed in the sandbox.

"Am I?" she pressed.

Playing dumb Trey said with a catch in his voice, "Are you what?"

"A prize."

Taylor's soft teasing laugh tickled his ears. Before he could respond his body slammed back against the leather seats after she punched it and switched lanes like she was the only car on the highway.

"Woooo...this bad boy handles like a dream!"

Trey white knuckled the door handle. "Hey, Speed Racer's sister," he shouted to be heard above the roaring engine and wind. "Slow it down."

"Answer my question." She was pushing 125.

"Yes, yes. You are a prize, a catch, the whole kit and caboodle. Now slow down!"

She obliged him by releasing the pedal and allowing the car's speed to reduce on its own. "So let me see. You find me attractive, charming and a prize. Did I miss anything?"

"Danger Will Robinson, danger Will Robinson," played in his head. Trey was no stranger to flirting; it was something he did himself. But this woman moved him in more ways than he really felt in control of. The prudent thing to do was make her pull over while he took the wheel and as fast as he could fly back to the dealership and turn Taylor over to another sales rep so they could split the commission. Whenever the little bugger dictated to the bigger one, prudence simply became an old-fashioned female name. "Are you trying to seduce me, Mrs. Robinson?"

"Mrs. Robinson," she snorted. "Have we forgotten that you are the ol' married one?"

Trey turned his head away to hide the remorse that came over him. "Umm, take this off-ramp and we'll take it back from here."

"I'm sorry, did I touch a nerve?"

"A nerve? Ah nah, we just need to get back. We've already be gone too long."

"You sure?"

"Yep."

Taylor punched it again while switching lanes and hit the off-ramp exceedingly fast. At the top of the ramp, she hit the brakes stopping on a dime. "Hungry?"

"'More like famished, and very glad to be alive. You do know you drive like a maniac."

"How come when a woman handles the wheel she's a maniac, but when a man drives like I do he's the bomb?" she asked merging smoothly into traffic.

Trey's face lit up. "Oh Lord, not the gender card."

"The gender card?"

"Yep, every woman on the planet has at least a deck full of them."

"Do tell," she said pulling into the parking lot of an Outback Steakhouse. "This I have to hear."

Instead Trey reached for the keys in the ignition and she swatted his hand. He reached again and this time she finger-plucked his forehead. "And violent too," he said rubbing the spot she hit.

"And sometimes I bite," she responded shoving the keys down her cleavage and stepping from the car. "Don't think you're off the hook from explaining that gender card comment either."

Exiting the car Trey rolled his eyes skyward and bowed deep at the waist toward Taylor, "Sure thing. You're Goddess," he wisecracked. Following her into the restaurant his view from the back almost, but not quite, topped the front.

"Take a picture. It lasts longer."

"Uh...what you talking 'bout?" he asked, knowing that she must have caught him checking her out in the reflection from the glass doors. He sheepishly hopped in front of her to open the door to let her pass through ahead of him. Again, he couldn't help it. He looked.

For the next two hours, they talked poked fun at each other and flirted, forgetting that they were supposed to be out on a test drive, not a lunch date. Four times Trey's cell phone rang, almost like a warning; each time he ignored it.

"Are you in a rush to get back?"

"Nah," Trey foolishly answered.

"Lunch is on me…you get the room."

Trey gulped and all of a sudden his eyes began to blink uncontrollability. His cell phone rang as if by divine intervention. His pulse quickened as he looked at the phone, while his "inner married man," begged him to answer. Images of Andrea and the kids flashed before his blinking eyes. With every blink, their faces became clearer and clearer. He and Ian had often spoken about what he would do if presented with the opportunity to sleep with another woman. Would he resist temptation or fall prey to it? Now sitting in front of him was temptation personified in the form of the most beautiful, sexy and desirable female he'd met since the first day he had laid eyes on Andrea over twenty years ago. There was no mistaking what she'd just said. She took the lead, not him. It's not as though he pursed her and… he couldn't finish the thought. Wrong is wrong. Right? But if wrong was wrong, why did the possibility of sleeping with her seem so right? There was a war raging inside of Trey, one that he'd never had to fight in fourteen years of marriage. Looking at other woman and having fantasies was one thing, but actually doing more than that was just male bonding talk. Something the fellows did in the locker room of the gym and around the water cooler at work. Talk. Nothing more. True-blue married men simply did not take it past the talking stage.

The ringing phone penetrated his thoughts and just as he inhaled deeply, ready to rebuke the treat to his vows, Taylor reached across the table, snatched up his phone and turned it off.

"I'll be in the car," she said casually. "You drive. Where we end up is your call."

CHAPTER TWENTY-ONE

"Dammit, Trey," Paula said into the receiver. Hanging up, she quickly picked it back up and dialed his cell for the sixth time. This time it went straight to voice mail. "I knew that high-yellow ho was up to some stuff when she strutted her Queen of Sheba behind up in here." She didn't know whether she was jealous or disappointed. Trey was one of the "good ones." In the four years, they'd worked together, she'd witnessed many woman come on to Trey and watched him give as good as he got. But to the best of her knowledge and since the gossip mill never said otherwise, he normally played along to make a sale. On the other hand most of the other sales reps— married or not— would dry-hump a tree if it had breast.

Noticing the biggest skirt-chaser in the dealership fast approaching her desk she tried to appear busy. Her fake nails flew over the keys of her computer, making a lot of noise, but if anyone were to come around her desk they would discover her secret. The computer wasn't turned on.

"Hey," Tony whispered, "you heard from Trey since he and that fine chick rolled out?"

Paula lifted her head slowly, clearly aggravated with being interrupted in her important task. "Tony, can't you see I'm busy?"

"Yeah, whatever. Just answer the question."

She ducked her head. "Do I look like his keeper?"

Tony's laugh as he walked away annoyed her nearly as much as the fact that she found herself feeling envy toward Taylor, which both surprised and upset her at the same time. Trey represented to her everything she wanted in her own man. And now the thought that he could be so easily led astray by a pretty face and a to-die-for body, lessened his value in her eyes. Hopefully, her woman's intuition radar needed to be recalibrated and Trey could restore her faith in men if he'd just come through the door having sent that little she-devil back to the fiery furnace from whence she came.

****

Meanwhile, if men possessed intuition radar, Trey's would be blinking like crazy. Andrea sat across from Pastor Douglas, having left work early to meet him at the church. When the pastor called her unexpectedly at her office earlier that morning, it caught her totally by surprise. After their last phone conversation, Andrea had been ducking him by not answering her cell phone if she saw either the church's number or his home number on caller ID. She even deleted his attempts to reach her by e-mail. The man was persistent though. Somehow he found out where she worked. In her nervous state, Andrea forgot she had given him her business card when he first arrived at the church.

That's all it took for her. One connected call and his urgent plea to speak with her in person about the women's group and Andrea was leaving work early, citing an unexplained illness, to rush to see him. On the drive over to the church, she questioned the validity of his request. On one hand she wanted to believe that's all it was about and on the other, she regretfully hoped it was more than that. This time the quilt that had tip-toed across her heart now tap-danced, stomped and kicked. There was no good that could come of this. A married woman, happily married woman, at that, should not be feeling the way she felt driving down the road. *And just how do I feel?* Like a young girl waiting for her sweetheart to pick her up for the prom. Surely the love she had for her husband could withstand some fanciful lust. There stood a better chance of her winning the lottery she never played than anything happening between her and the handsome pastor. *If lusting after him is wrong, then I don't want to be right.* As the play on the old soul song played in her mind, she knew it was definitely wrong. The correct thing to do would be for her to turn her car around and either head home or back to work.

Unfortunately, no one went through life doing the right thing one-hundred percent of the time and with that weak thought, Andrea found herself now sitting across from the man who made her knees tremble. As she sat, her foot tapped against the linoleum floor causing a rhythmic sound to pierce the silence.

"Thanks for coming to see me, Sister Edwards." His smooth baritone voice made her look down at her silk blouse to ensure he couldn't see the effect it had on her.

"You said it was urgent," she replied. Silently she prayed for strength. "And I'm willing to do anything to help the church."

"That's what we need more of, folk who understand the needs of the church and its leader." She waited for him to continue after he paused as if in deep thought. "Do you understand the needs of its leader, Sister Edwards?"

"I think I do," she answered feeling a little awkward.

"May I share something with you, Sister Edwards?"

"Yes."

"May I call you, Andrea?"

"Yes."

"I'm lonely. I bet you didn't expect to hear that from me, did you?"

"No I didn't," she admitted. "Being lonely is not good for anyone."

"Thank you, Andrea for not stating the obvious."

"Which is?"

"At least I have Jesus and with Him there is no loneliness."

"Well that is true, isn't it?"

"Yes, in the spirit, but in the flesh it is not." He stood up in front of his desk towering over her. Andrea never felt happier to have an obstacle between her and another person in her life. "You see, Andrea, being a Man of God can be very difficult at times."

"I can only imagine."

"Can you? Have you ever wanted to do something that you knew in your heart was wrong, but you wanted to do it anyway?"

If only you knew, she thought, and then said, "Something like what?"

"May I come and sit beside you?"

"Yes." *Oh please Lord, don't let this man sit beside me.* Andrea moved her chair back from the other chair in front of the desk. Pastor Douglas sat down and scooted his chair closer to her so that their knees were almost touching. *Get ye behind me, Satan.*

"Do I make you nervous, Andrea?"

It was his closeness, his cologne and his sexy green Smokey Robinson eyes that were making her nervous. "No, not at all."

"I asked you here under false pretenses and I apologize for that. I needed to see you, and for some reason you stopped taking my calls. And Sunday is just too far away."

"Just around the corner," she said trying to lighten the mood. All of a sudden, she began to feel uncomfortable. There was something in the way that he was looking at her that made her suddenly feel undressed although she had on a two-piece pant suit. "I really do have to run. Gotta pick up the kids." She lifted herself up out of the chair.

"No," he said excitedly, "I mean not yet, please. I really need to talk to you."

Andrea retook her seat and consciously buttoned her suit jacket. The lust she experienced before flushed from her system. He was still a very attractive man and very sexy, but for some odd reason, he now seemed a tad bit creepy to her. What was it that took her from thinking about him during lovemaking with her own husband to now sitting beside him and feeling the hairs rise on the back of her neck?

Without warning the answer came in the most unforgettable, horrible and tragic way possible. Pastor Raymond Douglas, pillar of the church, spiritual leader to the lost and sinful, committed the unthinkable.

****

Afterward, Andrea staggered from the church lost in a fog of guilt, shame and confusion. The fact that a man she thought could be trusted had done what he'd done in a house of worship caused her to lose the contents of her stomach in the empty parking lot. It took her several attempts at pulling on the door handle of her car to realize that it was locked. She unlocked her car and flopped down on the driver seat losing a shoe in the process. Closing the door, Andrea reclined the driver's seat and forced herself to close her eyes and replay what had just happened.

One minute she was sitting in the chair and Pastor Douglas was sitting next to her saying something she failed to recall. Then he grabbed her by the hand, not roughly, but with force and led her over to the couch. That's where it became surreal to her. He started by touching her face and saying soothing words that she still failed to recall and the next thing she knew, his hands were all over her and he was trying to kiss her. She knew she pushed at him and demanded he let her go, but he was too strong. He didn't get violent; he simply imposed his will on her. He didn't tear at her clothes; he gently and swiftly removed them.

Andrea sprung up and pushed the electric button to put the seat back in its original position. She screamed at the top of her lungs and pounded on the steering wheel until her throat became sore and her fist ached. A thousand thoughts shot through her mind, none of them good. How could she face Trey and the kids? How could she ever again pray to God after what she had done? She had played with fire and had gotten burnt.

A movement in her rearview mirror caught her attention. Sister Allen was fast approaching her car. Andrea grabbed her keys off the passenger seat, started the car and sped off just as she walked up to the driver side door.

"What in the world?" Sister Allen jumped back to prevent getting her foot ran over. She spotted a shoe in the space where Andrea's car had just been. She picked up the shoe and turned around to find Pastor Douglas looking out of his office window.

****

"Wasn't that Sister Edwards pulling out of here like a madwoman?" Sister Allen interrogated the Pastor as she stood in front of his desk holding the shoe in her hand.

"Yes."

"What would make her drive out of here like that and leave her shoe behind?"

"You know I can't divulge my counseling sessions with you, Sister Allen," he smugly answered. "Now if you would excuse me, I must prepare my sermon for Sunday's service."

The dismissive tone to his voice didn't escape Sister Allen as she spun on her flat rubber-soled heels and walked out of his office, very disturbed in her spirit. Something was indeed rotten in Denmark, and Philly was a long way from Europe. Sister Allen moved as quickly as her sixty-three years-old legs could carry her. She almost stepped in the offering Andrea had left in the parking lot. She had to get home and share her suspicions with her husband. Sure he often accused her of being a nosy-body, but this time, she might not have witnessed the act, but that didn't prevent her from reading the play. Sister Edwards and Pastor Douglas were fooling around and had had a lovers' spat.

****

"You got to be kidding me!"

Trey picked up his pants off the hotel's carpeted floor, keeping an eye on Taylor lying spread-eagle on the king-size bed wearing only a black lace bra and a matching lace thong, Trey prayed harder than he'd ever talked to God in his life. He prayed for strength, forgiveness and that his lower region didn't stay in the shape it currently was in. "I'm sorry, Taylor. I just can't go out like this." Even though it was his voice saying the words, he found it hard to believe it was actually him speaking them. "Please," he pleaded, totally unable to stop salivating over her incredible, smooth, luscious, sexy and Lord-have-mercy body. "Get dressed. We've been gone so long they probably put an APB out on us."

He watched Taylor open and close her exposed legs. The mere fact that just minutes ago he was all over her, kissing those soft, supple lips and taking off her clothes caused him pleasure and pain. He couldn't get out of his pants quickly enough. If she hadn't called him "Baby Boo," it would have been on and popping for sure. Immediately when she made that mistake, though, reality slapped him upside the head. That's the pet name that Andrea had starting calling him way back in high school. Once Taylor let those words loose, she unwittingly dispatched the "Protector of the Vows."

The devil that sat on Trey's left shoulder encouraged him to do his thing. It was okay, because he was a man. The voice spoke straight to the area of his body that wanted to hear such words. But the angel on his right shoulder pricked his ears and opened them wide enough to hear her moan his wife-given pet name. After that, the big head took over despite the little rigid one demanding he get back in there and take one for the team.

"You got to be kidding me," she repeated. This time there was no mistaking her displeasure. She wasn't used to being rejected.

"I'm married," he said weakly.

"Hell, I knew that. So did you before we came up in here."

Now fully dressed, Trey found the needed strength to look away from her. "This ain't happening; I'm sorry."

"Sorry, sorry…what type of game are you playing?" she demanded. "You just wanted to see if you *could* hit it?

"You came on to me." He regretted saying the words as soon as they came out. It was beyond weak to blame her for his weakness. Trey bowed his head to hide the tears that arrived unannounced. The tears weren't for him or Taylor; the images of Andrea and his kids danced in his mind's eye.

"Trey," she said softly, "look at me."

He slowly and reluctantly lifted his head and watched as Taylor scooted toward the edge of the bed. Then she tossed her hair back and stood up. With her hands on her hips and her legs spread shoulder width apart, she asked, pacing each word, "Are you sure you want to leave?"

Trey visually gobbled her up, silently pleaded with God to give him a pass on this one and stated briskly, "Hell yeah, I'll be in the car. And with that he grabbed the car keys from off the mirrored dresser and practically ran out of the room, leaving Taylor open-mouthed and thoroughly pissed off.

****

They rode back to the dealership in complete silence, neither of them bothering to turn on the radio to break the quiet storm that loomed inside the car. Taylor cut laser-beam eyes at Trey periodically hoping he would say something so she could cuss his sorry, lame, tired-behind out. Since she was old enough to wear a training bra, no male had ever turned down the chance to get her into a bed, back seat of a car or in the haystack loft at her granddaddy's farm. In truth, she didn't know how to take being rejected. It's not like she had any feelings for Trey— or for any man at all.

It never entered her consciousness that a guy would have her darn near buck-naked and ready to do any and everything and he would stop before anything really kicked off, all because he was married. If that was so important, why start something he wasn't man enough to finish? She had been with dozens of married men and not one of them had allowed that fact to stand in the way of them getting what they wanted. Of course, they only got their desires met after they supplied hers.

So what made this guy so different? Probably if Taylor wasn't so angry, she would have pondered a little longer on that. Instead she looked at Trey as he turned into the dealership and came to the only logical conclusion. He was gay.

CHAPTER TWENTY-TWO

"You still want to buy the car?" Trey asked sheepishly.

"Yes, at least that can perform."

Taylor trailed behind Trey as he quickstepped through the dealership's entrance, without holding the door for her. They marched past a steaming Paula and a snickering Tony. He avoided making eye contact.

"Hello," Taylor said sweetly to Paula. She winked at Tony as she followed Trey.

"There goes Superman followed by his kryptonite," Tony cracked.

"Oh shut up."

Trey couldn't wrap up the deal fast enough. He just wanted to get Taylor out of the dealership. While she signed the paperwork and the service department detailed her new BMW, she appeared oblivious to Trey's discomfort. In fact she barely looked at him.

After the service department informed Trey the car was ready, they walked outside to inspect the car. Satisfied with the new shine on her new purchase Taylor accepted the keys from Trey and slid into the driver's seat. Her exposed legs as she slithered into the car almost made him plead insanity and ask for a second chance. However in an effort to save himself he abruptly closed the car door, almost slamming her foot against it and waved her off. Before he could escape back into the safety of his office, Taylor rolled down the electric windows and said, "If you're on the down-low, you should let your wife know." And with that she sped off leaving Trey standing in the lot with a dumbfounded look on his face.

He jumped forward startled when he felt a slap on his back.

"Chill big man, just wanted to give my props to the big dog."

"Props for what? What you talking 'bout, man. I sell cars everyday," Trey stammered attempting to cover up his nervousness.

"Yeah, all right. You sell cars," Tony said beaming. "You are the man, Trey, for real. You are the man." Tony stepped off clapping his hands and looking back at Trey eyeball him.

Damn, that's all I need is that fool running around here running off at his mouth, he said to himself. Trey traipsed back inside the dealership only to run smack into Paula. Without saying a word she snatched his hand and pulled him along behind her into his office. She pushed him in and shut the door. "Have you lost your mind?"

Composing himself, Trey moved around his desk and smoothed down the front of his slacks before sitting down. "What are you babbling 'bout?"

"You know darn well what I'm talking about," Paula responded, not backing down. "Do you realize how long you were on…that test drive?"

"She bought the car didn't she?"

"Trey, please don't act like it took you that long to sell a car."

"I appreciate your concern, but last I checked I didn't answer to you," he snapped.

"Right, you are absolutely correct," she agreed. "Think about this Trey, just because the candy is offered, doesn't mean you have to accept." Not giving him a chance to respond, she spun around, opened the door and stormed back to her station.

A soft knock on his office door interrupted his racing mind, "Hey what's up, Dex?"

"You okay?" Dexter asked with concern. "You were on that test drive for quite awhile."

"It's cool, took a little longer than I thought it would. She was a tough nut to crack."

"You sure?"

"Yep, just a test drive and a sale."

Nodding his head but in no way convinced, Dexter shook Trey's hand. "Hey brother, I'm not one to judge and Lord knows I've messed up enough before I accepted Christ into my life…but anyway…you're a good man, Trey. Sometimes good men get tests thrown their way to see how great they can become. Know what I mean?"

"Just a test drive," Trey reassured him as he watched Dexter leave his office.

If guilt was a dessert best served cold, Trey's insides were frozen. The picture of Andrea on his desk demanded to be acknowledged, but he couldn't bring himself to look at it. To avoid her accusing eyes in the picture he placed it facedown and picked up the phone.

"Ian, where are you? I need to holler at you as soon as you get this message. Hit me back with the quickness."

Trey replaced the receiver. Just as he pushed back his chair, he noticed a pink slip of paper on his desk. It was a message receipt from Paula. Picking up the piece of paper he read what was written on it. Letting out a loud groan he looked at his watch to check the time. Hoping beyond hope that he wasn't too late, Trey dialed the phone. As the phone rang, he was shocked to find himself mouthing the Lord's Prayer. He hadn't prayed this much since…ever. "Yes…yes, Mr. Davis. This is Trey Edwards. I'm so glad I caught you."

Mr. Davis's deep bass voice was like a lifeboat coming to save a drowning man to Trey; he prayed that the boat didn't have a leak. "Please tell me you have good news for me." He listened intently as the mental boat started taking on water. "After all this time, it still hasn't been approved?" he asked. "Yes sir, I understand. I'll have my accountant send over those tax returns as well. Mr. Davis, I really need you to come through for me. I stand to lose a lot of money and even more if this loan isn't approved."

Trey thanked the loan officer for taking his call and hung up the phone as the boat went completely under.

****

Mr. Davis hung up the phone and looked up to find one of the bank's vice presidents standing in front of his desk. "Hi Paul, what brings you down here to mingle with us little people?"

"Don't forget, I was once a little person myself. Have you spoken with the gentleman who applied for the loan on a car dealership?"

"That was him on the line. Why?"

"Did you tell him that his loan was close to approval?"

"I didn't want to speak too soon. I informed him we needed those other tax returns."

"Good. Word just came down from corporate and all small business loans are being held up until further notice."

"But this one is ready for approval."

"He doesn't know that, so when he calls back tell him you haven't gotten an answer yet."

"But Paul…"

"Orders ,Gary. We might not like them but we have to follow them."

****

The four walls of his office were closing in on him. As Trey sat at his desk staring at Andrea's picture, the contrition and regret that he'd attempted to forced down began to well back up inside of him. All of a sudden his mouth got dry and his shirt collar began to tighten. His was wild with worry that right now Andrea was somewhere receiving some telepathic messages from the picture he held in his sweat- soaked hands. So he allowed the picture to slip from his grasp. The glass picture frame cracked upon impact with the desk from the height he'd dropped it from. He couldn't recall when he had stood up. The walls… weren't they further apart? Unloosening his tie and unbuttoning his shirt at the neck didn't help one bit. Sweat poured down his brow and dripped into his eyes. No longer did the fantasy of Taylor arouse him; instead it made him sick to his stomach. If his wife found out about his slip-up with her and she also found out about him taking the money without telling her, there wasn't enough police protection in the entire city to save him from her wrath. How in the hell do walls move? Perspiration ran down his face and drenched his underarms. The contents of his supper with Taylor threatened to erupt. Andrea's eyes seemed to burn right through him, reading his mind and damning his soul. With purpose he tossed the cracked picture frame into the trash can behind his desk. Even that didn't help; it fell face up in the overflowing receptacle. The eyes never left him as he went back and forth in the narrowing space.

Trey walked dejectedly toward Paula who was letting the last customer out of the door. Touching her arm he said, "It was just a test drive."

"Trey, the devil is always on his j-o-b, that's why we always have to be on ours."

"Dexter got to you too?"

"Rather anyone thinks so or not, I always knew my God. Don't let the breast fool you."

"Good night, Paula."

"Good night, Trey."

****

Trey drove around aimlessly afraid to go home. In his guilt, he was certain that Andrea would read his face like a book and determine what he had come close to doing. He needed a smoke-screen fast. If anyone could tell when he was trying to pull a fast one it was her. She told him that he had a tell-sign whenever he wasn't being completely honest with her and after all this time she hadn't told him what it is. For the life of Trey, he hadn't been able to figure out what he did that gave him away. And for that reason, he almost never told her anything more than "white lies." Shoot, Andrea had detected that he sold the insurance agency simply by the tone of his voice over the phone. She could put a bloodhound out of business. So under the high-beam of interrogation, he knew he would crack.

As he found himself turning back onto the same street for the fourth time, he recalled his father's warning on the morning of his wedding: "Son, never do anything to that woman that you couldn't live with if she did the same thing to you. If you haven't gotten enough pleasure from other women in your life, it's too late now. Besides, a woman knows her man's scent. So if you come home smelling like Dove and all you guys use is Zest, well you know the rest."

Trey self-consciously sniffed the air, praying that it was just his imagination alone that picked up the smell of Taylor's perfume. Picking up his cell phone, he speed-dialed Ian's cell. "Hey man, hit me back." He needed to confess his sins.

While her husband drove around the city, Andrea was at home driving herself crazy. She was walking a marathon around their bedroom. The images of what happened between her and the Pastor flashed across her mind. With every scene, it took all of her willpower not to scream or pound her fist into anything in front of her. Every time guilt entered her heart, anger jumped in as well. Her emotions were running wild and out of control. Andrea looked down at her hands to find that unknowingly she'd pulled some hair from her head. Hot tears poured from her bloodshot eyes.

It was her fault, she scolded herself. If she hadn't given off the wrong signals… No! It wasn't her damn fault; that man had no right to do what he did and in the house of God no less. She didn't invite him or entice him in any way. Her mind had screamed for her to get out of there and she hadn't listened. Sure there was an obvious attraction and maybe a little flirting over the phone, but that was not enough for him to think that she was open to being taken on a couch. Just as her anger started to pick up momentum, shame held up a stop sign.

It was her fault. Trey would know what she had done as soon as he saw her face. Andrea looked at herself in the bathroom mirror, fully expecting to find a scarlet letter plastered on her forehead.

Andrea replayed her mother's words to her on her wedding day, "Don't do anything to a man that you don't want done to you. Men don't have the market cornered on cheating."

"Hey girl," she said into her cell phone, "Call me back when you get in." Andrea needed to confess her sins.

CHAPTER TWENTY-THREE

"Is Mommy ever coming downstairs?" Brittany asked her big brother as they slouched on the comfortable suede sofa in the basement family-room. "And when is Daddy coming home?"

Brett pleaded with his little sister to save her questions until the commercials came on. Brittany complied with his request. Once Bart Simpson faded from the screen, she hit him with a barrage of questions. To his credit, Brett answered every one until Homer bounced back on the screen. "Go get some ice cream," he suggested.

Brittany gleefully followed that suggestion and if she got caught eating more ice cream, she could always say that Brett told her it was okay.

Trey found his daughter hand-deep inside of the ice cream carton with strawberry ice cream dripping from her mouth. The sight of Brittany sitting at the island in the middle of the kitchen devouring the ice cream sent chills down his spine. "Daddy, Brett told me I could get some," she shouted as she spotted him blocking the kitchen door well.

"Is it good?" he asked, kissing her ice cream-smeared lips.

"Delicious," she said smiling up at him. "You have ice cream on your mouth." She giggled.

He licked his lips and asked about the whereabouts of Andrea and Brett. He left her alone to enjoy her favorite dessert. "Don't forget to clean up after yourself."

"I won't."

He mentally jotted down a note. Give Brittany some Pepto-Bismol before she goes to bed.

Dreading the thought of facing Andrea, he decided to check on Brett. He found his son flipping through the channels like a remote-control veteran. "Hey Dad, when you get home?" He raised his hand so Trey could give him a high-five. Instead Trey reached in for a bear-hug. He held on until Brett complained about not being able to breathe.

"What you watching?"

"Nothing. Just flipping."

"No wrestling?"
"Nope."
"No game on?"
"Nope."
"No good action movies?"
"Nope."
"Nothing on where people answer questions with more than one word?"

Before Brett could respond, Trey grabbed his arm and lifted it up to tickle him. He felt someone jump on his back. He turned around to find that Brittany had come downstairs to her big brother's defense. "You gonna make him wet himself, Daddy," she shouted.

"Tickle him, Brittany," Brett squealed.

Pretending to weaken, Trey rolled off Brett and allowed his two hearts to overwhelm him. Their shared squeals and laughter worked their way up the steps, through the living room and up to the top of the stairs where Andrea stood. She had heard Trey come in the house when he first got home and instinctively almost ran down the steps to greet him. But fear paralyzed her and twenty minutes later, she still stood in the exact same spot, not having moved a muscle.

****

The light on the answering machine was blinking as Tina followed her three daughters into the house. "Did you like the service, Mom?" Rochelle nervously asked.

"It was…interesting." She replied. "What was wrong with that woman who sat in front of us?"

"Huh?"

"The one who started flopping all over the place like she was having a seizure."

"She caught the Holy Ghost."

"The what?"

"The Holy Ghost. You know that's when the spirit of the Lord enters into someone."

"Well it looked like the spirit of a drug withdrawal to me." Tina flopped down on the weathered couch and kicked off her too-tight shoes.

"I'm glad you went to Bible study with us."

"Me too," she had to admit. "I'm trying, baby."

"I know Mom." Rochelle left her mother alone with her thoughts.

The blinking light attracted her attention, but Tina didn't feel like hearing another bill collector make threats. She pushed the delete button without listening to the message.

If everything went right tomorrow, she would have the money to pay her bills on time. Until then it wouldn't hurt to smoke a little weed just to calm her frayed nerves. Tina reached under the cushion and pulled out her hidden stash.

The strong pungent odor hit Rochelle's nostrils as soon as she hit the bottom of the stairs. She walked into the living room to find Tina kicked back on the couch with her eyes closed, smoking a joint and humming a gospel song.

****

Ian rolled over and attempted to catch his breath. "You want something to drink?" he asked his bedmate.

"What you got?"

"Wine, juice or water."

"Red wine?"

"Yep, straight from Italy."

"How chic."

"Not really. It came with the box." They laughed as Ian hopped out of bed and went into the kitchen to retrieve the wine. Spotting his cell phone on top of the plug-in electric fireplace, he looked at the screen to see how many calls he'd missed. He walked back into the bedroom with two glasses of wine and the cell phone wedged between his ear and shoulder. He handed over one of the glasses. "Man, Trey has been blowing up my cell. I wonder what he wants."

"Put the phone down. Whatever it is can wait."

Ian took one look at Taylor's nude body and quickly forgot all about his best friend.

****

Like it was Sunday morning, Trey quietly rolled out of bed hoping to get dressed and out of the house without waking his wife or the kids only to find out that Andrea was already in the shower. If he didn't know better, he would swear she had placed her pillows in a way to make it seem like she was still under the covers.

Little did either one know, but as Andrea let the shower water wash her tears away and Trey jumped into the hallway bathroom shower, they were experiencing the same emotions: shame at what they had done and fear of the other finding out.

CHAPTER TWENTY-FOUR

The tension in the board room was so thick it would take a chain saw to cut through it. Pastor Douglas sat at the head of the long highly polished oak table and made direct eye contact with everyone sitting at the table. Only Sister Allen gave as good as she got, while the male members of the Deacon board either dropped their eyes or pretended to shuffle paper.

"I suggest we bring this meeting to order," Deacon Allen said in taking up his role as head deacon. "Pastor, we appreciate you taking time out of your busy schedule to meet with us this morning."

"Brother Allen, I serve this church at the Lord's will and the church board's discretion." Pastor Douglas said.

"You got that right," Sister Allen smartly muttered loudly enough for the eight- member board to hear.

"Please dear. Let's remember we are in the house of God," he reminded his wife.

"With all due respect, Deacon Allen, may I ask why Sister Allen is present?" Pastor Douglas shifted in his chair and smiled sweetly at Sister Allen.

"Well, Pastor, Sister Allen," he started off saying, "my wife is here because she has leveled some serious charges against you."

"Such as?"

Clearing his throat, Deacon Allen looked around the table for moral support from the other deacons, but not one of them returned his glance. "Pastor, I'm a direct man. So I'll just come right out with it. My wife, Sister Allen has reported to this board of deacons that she believes that based on what she observed the other day between you and Sister Edwards…"

"And just what did she observe?" Pastor Douglas asked, interrupting the deacon.

"I saw…"

"You saw what?" he cut Sister Allen off. Pastor Douglas lifted himself up from the chair and walked around to place a hand on her shoulder. "Just what did you observe, Sister Allen?"

Deacon Allen noticed his wife cringe before she shrugged his hand off. "While I didn't see anything concrete, I did notice her weird behavior, pulling out of here like a bat out of…"

"Honey!"

"Hell, there I said it." She stubbornly plowed forth. "The woman left her shoe in the driveway and some vomit as well."

The other deacons stirred uncomfortably in their chairs still pretending to shuffle paper.

Pastor Douglas took his time walking back to the head of the table. With his back to the room no one could see the contempt on his handsome face. Before he turned around he put on his best poker face. "Brothers and Sister, I do agree that the impression of impurity may be apparent." His voice was soothing. "Especially to those who may seek to find it. However my encounter with Sister Edwards was as pure as any other encounter that I have had with any member of this congregation."

"I know what I…"

"Let him finish, dear," Deacon Allen said.

"Now I say to you, "he said warming up, "I say the devil is a liar. And anytime he can slither his way into God's house, believe you me, he will. Only the devil or believers of his evil ways, mistake a counseling session as anything other than that."

"Did this fool just call me a devil worshipper?"

"Enough, Helen! There will be no name calling. This man is still our Pastor," Deacon Allen scolded his wife. "Besides, Pastor Douglas wasn't calling you anything of the sort. Right?"

Now in control of the room, Pastor Douglas smiled kindly at Sister Allen. "No way did I mean to insinuate that a woman of God such as Sister Allen lived for anything other than our God. This goes against everything I believe in and I ask that this information doesn't leave this room. Agreed?" He waited for agreement from everyone, including Sister Allen who was fuming. He breathed in deeply. "Very well, for the sake of cohesiveness and the ability to do what I have been sent here to do, I will share this with you. As I'm certain you all may have noticed, Sister Edwards and her children have been attending church without her husband. She came to me seeking guidance and advice on how to bring her husband back into the fold. Also she shared with me some issues they were dealing with in their marriage and need I say I really can't say anything more than that. During the course of our session she became very upset and ran out of here before I could stop her and offer prayer." He figured adding the "prayer" part would be received well.

"So what my wife, witnessed was the aftermath of a counseling session between you and Sister Edwards?"

"Nothing more."

"This meeting is adjourned," Deacon Allen stated flatly.

The other members of the board couldn't get out of the room quickly enough. In the parking lot Sister Allen glared angrily at her husband. "You fell for that crap?"

"The man was lying through his capped teeth," her husband replied. "Now get in the damn car."

****

Trey drove into the parking lot of Fortune Motors. Completely absorbed he parked in what was no longer his privileged parking slot. The blaring of a car horn startled him. Tony was behind him, impatiently riding his horn while flagging Trey to move his car. "It's still mine," he hollered out of the car window.

Dejectedly Trey found another spot to park. Stepping out of his Benz, Trey reached into the back seat and removed his black leather Gucci briefcase and a tan cashmere overcoat. He spotted Tony coming his way so he steeled his emotions to ignore him if he started talking any foolishness.

"Good morning, Trey," Tony said. "Another bad suit."

"Thanks," Trey replied sliding his arms into the coat.

"I'm looking forward to going head to head with you this month."

"Me too. I'm getting tired of parking over here on the back forty."

Tony laughed and stepped back so Trey could pass by. "Hey Trey, got a question for you?"

He stopped and slowly turned around to face Tony. "I'm listening."

"Do you think I'm as good as you are?"

"You for real?"

"Yeah."

"Why you asking me that?"

"Because I got much respect for you."

"Tony," he said slightly taken aback, "you have the potential to be one of the best to have ever walked through those doors. Always treat the customer with respect and never count your pockets until the deal is done."

"Am I as good as you?"

"Yes." Trey walked away while Tony stood frozen, grinning like a child earning his first gold star.

Trey noticed the new car display as soon as he walked through the doors of the dealership. Two glass-polished Aston Martins set side by side on the showroom floor. One was pearl white with white leather interior and the other was black on black. "Paula, when did these come in?"

"They were here when I got in," she responded. "I got dibs on the black one."

"I heard that," he said admiring the cars from bumper to bumper. "Dex pulled it off. Is he in?"

"Yep, he was asking for you."

Like always Trey felt the rush of power he experienced every time he entered Dexter's office. "Dex, the Aston Martins are off the hook," he exclaimed with excitement.

"It took a while, but we finally are an official Aston Martin distributor."

"So I guess retirement is being pushed back?" he asked, taking a seat in front of Dexter's desk.

"Not really," he said. "Just putting another bullet in the gun."

"I'm feeling that."

"I knew you would." Dexter said. "Too bad you'll be leaving us soon. Have you heard from the bank?"

"Man you would think I was asking for the entire bank."

"Still not approved?"

"Nah."

"Keep the faith, brother, every thing in God's time."

"He need to get a new watch," he instantly regretted his slip of the tongue and the look on Dexter's face made him feel stupid for doing so. "I'm sorry, just getting a little nervous. I stand to lose a lot of money in the next few weeks if they keep dragging their feet on this thing."

"Faith the size of a mustard seed can move mountains. Have you prayed about it?"

"I've darn near begged God for the loan approval."

"Praying isn't begging, Trey. Praying is about talking to God and asking Him about His will and purpose, even if it doesn't line up with our desires."

Not wanting to hear another sermon, Trey attempted to excuse himself. However, once Dexter got on the subject of God he was not to be deterred. He began to lecture Trey on having faith, belief and trusting in God in all areas of his life and not just what Trey wanted to obtain.

Out of respect Trey sat still and listened although he wanted Dexter to shut up. "I hear you, Dexter. But man, I'm just not into God like you are. I mean don't get me wrong. I believe in a higher power. I simply don't feel the need to go around preaching to everybody."

"What you consider preaching, I consider witnessing to you about the goodness of the Lord," Dexter calmly explained. "People talk about war, politics, sports and anything else that pops into their minds. But when it comes to talking about God all of a sudden, no one feels comfortable talking about Him."

"It's not always appropriate." Trey stated firmly.

"Do we talk about business?"

"Yes, we are in a business setting," Trey answered.

"Well, this is a Christian owned and run business, so with that being the case do you think it's wrong to speak about the head of this business?"
"You are the head of this business."

"No I'm not. Once I turned my life over to Christ, He became the head of my life, in business and out."

Rubbing his eyes, Trey's neck began to stiffen. He cracked his neck making a loud noise.

"You going to break your neck one of these days doing that," Dexter warned him.
"My man Ian says that all the time."

"Trey, I'm not trying to convert you to my way of way of thinking. I'm simply sharing with you."

"I know."

"Actually I feel a need in my spirit to talk to you."

"That's what you've been doing," this time Trey didn't try to hide his annoyance.

"Did you know I was married before?"

"We never talked about it," Trey said. "But that night we went out the chick at the door told me she was your ex."

"Woman," he corrected. "The woman at the door. Yes that was my ex-wife. And you know why she's my ex?"

"Didn't even know you were married in the first place."

"Infidelity. I committed adultery."

"You got caught?"

"We all do," he responded, "even those who do things in the dark. Sometimes we forget that nothing stays hidden from the light."

"What light?"

"The light of truth."

"You trying to say something to me, Dexter?"

"Do you know why Adam and Eve disobeyed God and ate from the tree He warned them to stay away from?"

"Not really," Trey admitted truthfully. "Never gave it much thought."

"Because they allowed themselves to be deceived by sweet nothings being spoken into their ears. Think about it Trey, at the first sign of temptation, they gave into it. And if two people who walked with God and spoke directly to Him could give into it. Doesn't that tell us that temptation is a powerful weapon that is used to disconnect us from God's will and purpose for our lives?"

“What does that have to do with me?”

“Temptation confronts us all in many ways, be it a woman, drugs, love of money or something else.”

“Why don’t you come straight out and ask me what you want to know,” Trey blasted. His desire to unload was strong but his fear of being judged unfavorably by Dexter was even stronger. If he felt this bad over what hadn’t happened, then he surely didn’t what to imagine how terrible he would be feeling if he had given into his lustful desires.

“Only if you want me to know,” Dexter replied. Trey recognized his concerned tone, one that he’d been hearing a lot lately.

That was just it, Trey didn’t really want anyone to know, but then again, if he didn’t unload on someone, the guilt would surely eat him up. “Dex, I messed up, well not really but I almost did big-time.”

“The test drive?”

“Yeah.”

“Did you?”

“No, but I wanted to.”

“You stopped or did she?”

“Me.”

“It takes a strong man to overcome himself.”

“And a weak one to do what I almost did.”

“Trey, many men in the Bible faced…”

“No offense man, but talking about some cats from over a thousand years ago…”

Dexter cut Trey off. "Trey the stories in the Bible are as relevant today as they were thousands of years ago. Those stories have laid the foundation of life as we know it."

"I almost cheated on my wife," Trey said his voice clearly expressing the pain he felt in his admittance of guilt.

"And you were wrong to do so. However you didn't go all the way. And believe it or not that really says something about the character of man you are," Dexter assured him. "Trey I tell you again, God has a plan for your life if you just open yourself up to Him."

"Organized religion is not my thing," Trey said.

"I'm not talking about organized anything; I'm speaking about you having an intimate, personal relationship with the Lord and Savior Jesus Christ."

"If I started that now, wouldn't it come off like I'm only doing it because I almost screwed around on my wife and I really need this loan to come through?" Trey asked. "Wouldn't it seem like I was trying to pimp the Lord?"

"Trey, most people turn to God when all else have failed. In my humble opinion it doesn't matter when one comes to Him as long as they do."

"I hear you."

"Brother to brother, Trey may I ask you to do something with me?"

"Pray?"

"Yes."

"Here in the office?"

"Yes."

"Now?"

"Yes."

Trey's discomfort showed all over his face as well as his body language. All he could think about was the others in the office hearing him and Dexter praying. As if he didn't have enough to worry about. He looked at Dexter with desperation in his eyes. If only he could melt into any kind of liquid then he could slide out of the chair and under the door. Now was the time for long-forgotten childhood super powers to kick in. "I can't." He finally spoke.

"You can't lean on the Lord?"

"I can't ask Him to forgive me when I can't forgive myself."

CHAPTER TWENTY-FIVE

While Andrea sat in her office and Trey slumped in his, both dealing with their demons, Tina was nervously waiting to exorcise her own. Trying not to lose her sanity and pull out all of her hair, she sat quietly as the social worker flipped through some papers on her cluttered desk. The woman hadn't spoken a single word to Tina since she'd called her into her cramped windowless office.

"Miss Jenkins," the social worker began speaking in a tone that made Tina's skin tingle. "As you well know the mayor has taken it upon himself to reduce the welfare roll."

Tina loathed the superior attitude. However, self-preservation warned her to mind her manners; for now. "Right, that's why I'm here."

"You are here, Miss Jenkins because you received the letter that came with your check.

If you hadn't kept this appointment it's very likely your forthcoming checks may or may not have reached you."

Some heated words warmed her tongue dying to get out. But instead Tina checked herself and responded in a cool restrained tone. "Miss Connor, I'm very much aware of the program and about losing my check. I came here today, Miss, to get into this thing and turn my life and my girl's lives around."

For the first time since Tina entered the office, Miss Connor really looked at her having felt the sincerity in her voice. "Please accept my apologies, Miss Jenkins." Then she added, "No excuse, but it's been a horrible morning. Most of the people I've seen so far have either come in here whooping and hollering about losing their check, or failed the written or urine test, if not both."

"The test was hard and it's not like yaw gave anybody time to study for either one," Tina joked to lighten the mood and still her nerves. *Dang, a drug test too*, she thought.

She chuckled at Tina's humor and picked up the folder that contained the scores from the test Tina took earlier in the morning. "You know this program really can change your life."

Tina nodded and thanked God that she hadn't thrown the letter away as she'd started to after the mailman delivered it a couple of days ago. After talking with Rochelle and Andrea for support, she decided to take a leap of faith and believe that the Lord really did look out for babies and fools— even fools that had babies too young to know better.

"First off let me tell you, Miss Jenkins," Tina noticed a change in her. "I must say how proud I am of you and how proud you can be of yourself." She paused. "No one has scored well in every area of this test since we started." The test consisted of math, reading comprehension and a social adaptability portion. "You have scored…" She paused again, "You have scored 35 percent higher than you needed to pass." She placed the folder down and sat forward in her chair. "Miss Jenkins, you are a perfect candidate for this program and I would like to offer you the opportunity to get off welfare once and for all and enter the work force."

"Oh my God!" Tina shouted as her hands flew up to cover her face. "Oh my God…are you saying I pass the test?"

"Yes dear, you most certainly did pass the test."

"Oh my God," was all Tina could think to say. She didn't know whether to cry, shout louder, call home or hug Miss Connor. Over and over again all she could say was, "Oh my God."

"Now Tina all you have to do is go down the hall and ask for Miss Craven. She will administer the drug test and then we are in business."

"Umm…bout that drug test."

****

Taylor waited for the ring tone song to end before leaving her message. "D-Jay, it's me again. Call me when you get this message." Without giving him another thought, she leaned back in the chair and turned her full attention to the owner of the Blue Way. "Now where were we?"

"You done making calls," he asked.

Taylor smiled her sexiest smile, batted her long lashes and proceeded to charm the club owner into spending more money on renovating the club for

Ian's Friday night showcase. "There will be press and I'm talking lights, camera and action. Now do you really want your club to get that type of exposure and it not be up to par? We want folks talking about the Blue Way like it was 1965 all over again."

"Pretty lady, you could charm the clouds from the sky," he replied. "Okay I'll redo the stage."

"And the sound system."

"And the sound system," he agreed. "But pretty or not if this place ain't packed on Friday and I don't make my money back, I do expect some other form of compensation from you."

Since this wasn't Taylor's first rodeo. She knew exactly what "compensation" meant. The man couldn't care less that she was young enough to be his grandchild. He'd been quite up front about his lustful desires. And she had used that obvious attraction to her advantage, talking him into spending money on new tables and chair, as well as putting down new flooring throughout the club. Gone was the old stained tile flooring that had lumps and bumps throughout. Now the floors were covered in a rich, dark hardwood laminate and the dance area was covered in a marble-like material that made the club go from looking like a hole-in-the-wall to high-end. Taylor still felt the need to remind him that since Ian started performing nightly at the club, his business was booming with new cliental and older ones returning that had simply taken their entertainment dollars elsewhere.

"So it's not like the money you're spending is money you already had," she shrewdly reasoned for him. "Just think after Friday night, all of Philly will be talking about your club again. It will become the new hip place."

"Girl, if you can really pull that off, I can die a happy man. You know now, back in the day, this joint was the hip place let me tell you." And he did. Taylor sat and listened to the older man reminisces about yesteryear for over an hour until Ian and the band showed up for rehearsal. As Taylor stood up to go greet the boys the older man grabbed her hand and said, "I'm sorry for coming on to you. You young enough to be my grandchild. Hell I got three grands your age. Your beauty is no excuse and I do know better. Again child, I'm sorry. God has blessed me with you and that boy of yours." He wiped his leaking eyes. "Sorry."

Taylor watched him walk off and she thought she noticed a little bounce in the old man's step. In all of her dealings with the opposite sex, not one had ever past on the chance to sleep with her like Trey and now another first, a man had apologized for making an advance at her. Was she losing her sex appeal or were the men in Philly just crazy? The looks from the guys in the band answered her question for her. She glanced down to find that her skirt was hiked up on her firm thighs and every guy in the club including Ian was shamelessly admiring her legs. Their lustful stares confirmed it— she hadn't lost a thing, they were simply crazy. "Take picture boys," she called out using one of her favorite lines. "It'll last longer."

"Let's get to work, fellows," she heard Ian say as she spun on her high heels and grabbed her purse off the table and strutted out the door, blowing the band air-kisses.

****

"Yes! That's the groove there, fellows!" Ian shouted placing the microphone in the stand. The guys in the band gave each other high-fives. They were rehearsed and ready for the big showcase on Friday night. Ian insisted on two practices a day and had even fined a couple of guys for showing up to the club late. Now days before performing in front of record industry executives, the band had come together on one accord. To a man, each knew that this night could change lives. A musician could perform in front of three drunks with hearing aids in a one-barstool-joint, his entire life and never get heard by anyone with some clout in the industry. Music wasn't just about raw talent, it really had a lot to do with who knew you, how you look, are you marketable and more importantly— can they make money off you.

Ian knew that from experience and too many disappointments to count how tough it was to catch a break. He'd been at this since graduating high school and full-time as a "j...o...b" for close to twenty years .Being known around the city as a top-notch vocalist and having his small degree of notoriety wasn't enough for him anymore. Taylor had rekindled a dream that he'd long since allowed to stay sleep. So now for him, singing was his long-time lover that returned home to daddy. "Okay listen up," Ian shouted to get the bands attention. "First off, I want to thank each and every one of you for the great job you're doing." They applauded and patted each other's back. Ian held up his hand to settle them down. "Look I know I bugged out a couple of times."

"Na not you," the drummer teased.

"Yeah me. I wanted to say I'm sorry and everybody that I fined will get their money back."

"How 'bout more dough for the gig?" One of the guys hollered out. Soon the others joined in with their opinion of how much that should be.

Ian waited for them to get it out of their systems. Once they noticed he wasn't responding, they quieted down. "Taylor and I spoke about that the other day," he said, "and I decided to split the money equally."

That really set the guys over the edge with excitement. For many of them playing music barely covered the cost of getting to a gig, they played for the love of music and hoped that someday their passion would equate to better paying jobs. Most of the fellows worked full-time jobs and supplemented their income with what they made gigging around town.

"Hey Ian, we were thinking…" The drummer stepped out from the crowd. "Since you're in a generous mood, how about the band get some props as well."

"Like what?" Ian asked.

"We should have a name." Immediately all at once the guys shouted out different names until one name received a unanimous vote. They settled on a name for the previously unnamed band. No one knew what it meant or if it was even a real word. It simply rolled off the tongue and sounded unlike any other band name any of them had ever heard.

"Hold up," Ian said trying to pronounce it. "Kwa…zeke?"

"Na man…a 'q' like in quasar. It's 'quazeke," the drummer explained.
"That ain't no darn word," Ian said incredulously.

"It is now," they all agreed. So the bands official name became "Quazeke.'

CHAPTER TWENTY-SIX

Sometimes problems are solved by corporate agreement and then there are problems that loom as large as Mt. Fuji. As Trey drove into Center City, he felt like his problems were mountainous and if there wasn't an intervention of a divine nature or otherwise, he would be buried underneath the avalanche.

Before he'd left Jerry standing in the parking lot all pissed off because he needed the rest of the day off, Trey had once again called the bank to find out whether his loan request was approved. The loan officer's answer almost floored him. He could still hear the man's apologetic tone as he told Trey, "I'm sorry, Mr. Edwards but at this time I don't have good news for you. I think it would probably be in your best interest to place your request elsewhere. Again, I'm sorry."

Trey remembered putting the phone to his head like a gun and pulling the trigger. Never in his life did he think that he would lose one-hundred thousand dollars in just twenty seconds. But that's exactly what the phone call to the bank meant, the loss of his non-refundable deposit on the car dealership. *Maybe the old dude will give me back my money if I explain everything.* Even as the thought popped into his mind, reality scolded. *Yeah right, sucker.*

Trey caught a glimpse of his lips in the car's rearview mirror. They were moving. He was speaking. But although his mouth was moving no clear sounds were reaching his ears. Trey momentarily took his eyes off the road to look at his full impression in the mirror and in doing so his left hand holding the steering wheel started turning the car across the lane he was driving in. A loud, blaring noise jolted him into paying attention to his task at hand: driving a car. He stomped on his brakes and snatched the wheel back narrowly missing a multi-colored older beat-up car that had stalled out at the light. The woman seating in the car continued to pound on the car horn looking wide-eyed like a deer in headlights before impact.

Trey nodded his head at the woman as a way of apologizing and made it through the stoplight on yellow. He stole another look at his reflection and to his total surprise his mouth was still moving. *Maybe I'm having a stroke.*

Just in case he decided to pull over and conduct a full-body check. Trey maneuvered his car into the nearest parking lot. Cutting the engine off, he slowly stepped out of the car with sweat starting to bubble on his forehead despite the cold November winds. Trey ran his hands down the entire length of his body, shook his head and bent over to touch his toes. Then he shook his left arm and paused for a moment to see if he felt any tingling on the left side of his body. He bent down to look in the side mirror. He looked normal. Then like a great idea that comes after hours of searching it hit him. He had been praying. Praying wasn't a daily doing in Trey's life but on occasion he sent some words up. So why was this time so different? Why did he feel so strange?

As if the answers came from heaven, Trey looked around the parking lot he had driven into. It was the parking lot of a church. And not just any church. It was their church— well Andrea's, since he hardly stepped foot inside anymore. Trey started walking toward the church before he could stop himself from doing so.

The big oak doors opened with a small squeak as if not to cause a disturbance. Trey shyly walked into the sanctuary half-expecting to find a full-blown revival service underway. It was empty. Standing at the back of the sanctuary looking up at the alter took him back fifteen years to the day he and Andrea stood in front of a packed church and exchanged their vows to love, honor and cherish each other till death do they part. *Till death*. When Andrea found out about his run-in with Taylor and his losing the money, death would be the least of his worries. It might even be an escape.

"May I help you?" A male voice interrupted his reverie.

Trey's eyes followed the voice. Standing behind the podium he was startled to see a tall, well-dressed man standing behind it. In Trey's clouded frame of mind, he hadn't noticed him when he entered the sanctuary. "Pardon me?" he stammered totally taken aback.

"Are you allright, brother?"

"Yeah, umm…yeah. I'm cool."

"Well then, how may I assist you?"

Trey slowly approached the front of the church without answering. Once he located the regular area of the pew where he knew Andrea normally liked to sit he sat down. He hadn't been inside the church in months. If memory served him, the last time was actually six months ago, the last Sunday that the old pastor preached his last sermon. Looking up at the man staring at him strangely, Trey wondered if this cat in the gray pinstriped suit was the guy that took his place. "Who are you?" Trey asked.

"I'm Pastor Douglas."

"So you the dude that took over." He quickly corrected himself. "I mean the new pastor."

"That's okay. I am a dude and yes I'm the new pastor." His warm smile and laugh put Trey at ease.

"My bad, Pastor. No disrespect intended," Trey apologized.

"None taken," he assured Trey. "Would you like to be left alone?"

"I don't know," Trey admitted, "I don't even know why I'm here."

"I'm sure many people feel that way," he said. "If I can be blunt with you," he paused.

"Go head."

"Walking into the House of God in the middle of the day and looking like you're carrying the weight of the world on your shoulders is a strong indication to me that just maybe you needed a place to release that burden. And from my experience you've have picked the right place."

"Really?"

"Really. I'll leave you alone. If you want to talk I'll be in my office, its right through these doors, down the hall on the left." He walked through the door he had indicated leaving Trey to ponder his next move.

The quietness of the empty church quickly became unsettling to Trey. It was as if Pastor Douglas took all sound with him. Trey sprung to his feet for no reason other than to make some noise. Then the internal battle started. One half of him wanted to sprint out of the door and the other half wanted to go talk to the pastor. Trey estimated that the pastor was around his age and seemed to be a nice enough guy. At least he didn't get all preachy on him like Dexter. What harm would it be to speak with someone who didn't have a dog in the fight? It wasn't as if he needed counseling or anything like that. Beside with the guy being so young, Trey decided he might be a little more understanding about his plight. As he took his time going to find the pastor, he wondered why Andrea hadn't mentioned that the new preacher was young, attractive and a sharp-dresser. He had assumed that the guy who took over for the old one who married them would be more like Billy Graham than Creflo Dollar.

****

Pastor Douglas rubbed his sleep deprived eyes. All he wanted to do was go home to his two-bedroom condo and totally shut down. The lease on his unit was more than the church budget allowed, but what they didn't know wouldn't hurt him. Besides, playing Shepard to a bunch of stuck-in-the-past sheep was becoming more than he'd bargained for when he accepted the position. Not that he had any say in coming to the church, not with what happened at his last assignment. *Boy you blew that one.*

He reflected on his last church. In five short years he went from preaching in the basement of a hardware store to ten-twenty worshippers to having one of the biggest churches in five counties down in Georgia. To go from preaching in front of three thousand folks on any given Sunday and answering to no one, to now standing in front of three-four hundred tops depending on the weather was truly a let-down. Not to mention that darn noisy-behind Sister Allen. For some reason he couldn't put his finger on, that woman had never taken to him. Although it was never spoken, he knew that the one lone vote against him becoming full-time pastor belonged to her. What a bunch of crap, having the entire church vote. Inwardly he smiled because he had shown them though. He preached his butt off that Sunday and was overwhelmingly voted into his post. At first the congregation consisted of a few die-hards and some stranglers that popped in and out. But now he preached to a packed house full of woman. He had no doubt that they came faithfully because he was single and everyone assumed that pasturing a church meant getting paid the big dollars. Not at this church it didn't. The deacon board ran this church and controlled the money like the Apostle Paul himself was the treasurer. Something had to give however, whether they wanted to or not. It was time for this church to get bigger. And to get that way it meant, they would have to build a new one not just keep repairing this old building. There was more than enough in the "building fund" to purchase some land. And come hell or high water, no matter what he was going to lead this flock out of the wilderness and into a new state of the art mega-church that could seat five thousand.

Pastor Douglas felt a new surge of energy like always when he thought about his dream. Yeah, he messed up before, but not this time. He would have to control his urges and stay rooted in the Word. No more would he allow the devil to use his weaknesses against him. It cost him once back in Georgia and almost cost him again by allowing Andrea Edwards to work her voodoo on him. It was always a woman who got him into some mess. Thank God the board believed his version and Deacon Allen had reined in his noisy wife. There was no way he would have another scandal on his hands. Na, no way would he do a "Jimmy Swaggart." What folks don't know won't hurt him.

Surely God would forgive him for his slip-up. Men weren't designed to be perfect just perfected through Christ.

The knock on the open door and the darken door well brought him back to the present.

"You got a minute, Pastor?"

"Sure, sure come in," he responded not surprised to see the guy from the sanctuary.

"I'm not bothering you am I?"

"Stalling?" He playfully asked.

"Something like that."

"Take a seat, no cover charge like on Sundays."

"They really do that now?"

"I was joking."

"Gotcha."

The two men shared a laugh. "I'm sorry; I didn't tell you my name."

"I figured you would in your own time."

"Trey Edwards," he said. "You might know my wife, Andrea."

Lawdhavmercy! The bullet that narrowly missed its mark in Macon had somehow made it up 95 North and was about to hit him square in the forehead. He closed his eyes so tight his chin met his cheeks. All sense of rational thought left him and the power of speech escaped as well. In just moments all of his dreams would be permanently put to sleep forever. The hot slicing lead would enter his frontal lobe like a hot knife through butter. If God was merciful he would die feeling no pain. *Please be merciful Oh Lord!*

"Hey Pastor, Pastor you okay?"

Pastor Douglas slowly opened one eye and then the other to find Trey standing beside his chair, and without a gun in sight. Relief replaced panic. But before he got too excited about still being alive he pushed away from the desk and stood up to demonstrate his height advantage to the possible assailant. "Yeah, yeah I'm fine." He threw some bass in his voice for effect.

"What you get caught up in the spirit or something?" Trey asked.

"One never knows when it will hit you," he responded throwing back a glass of water like it contained something stronger. "Ah, Andrea you said."

"Yeah my wife normally sits where I was sitting in the pews."

"Oh yes, lovely woman, a true asset to the church." He quickly added, "Don't know her that well though." He remained standing and refused to give in to his quavering knees. As long as Trey stood so would he. If this jealous husband came looking to throw-down, he would be prepared for the assault.

"Look here, Pastor. I've taken up enough of your time," Trey said. "I'm gonna take off. Thanks for…you know."

"No problem, brother," he said much too excitedly. "Anytime, the church's doors are always open."

The two men shook hands. One walked away wondering why the other's hand was so sweaty and one dropped to his knees and ran his sweaty hands over his face filled with regret, fear, joy and thanksgiving that the bullet hadn't made the trip.

Just when he thought it was safe to take his feet the sight of a lone woman standing in the door kept him on his knees.

"Hello, Raymond. I bet you didn't think you would see me again. Did you?"

CHAPTER TWENTY-SEVEN

Since the invention of the automobile, it has been widely accepted that next to a dog, a man loved nothing more than his car. Some men have even described their cars in explicit terms normally reserved for locker room lies about their sexual prowess. Other than the wonders of the movies, though, no human being, male or female, could say that their car got them home without any assistance from the driver. Well, that was until Trey ran out of the church, nearly running into a woman entering the building. He hopped into his Benz and forty minutes later he sat in the alley driveway of his home. He remembered getting in the car and even putting the key in the ignition, but after that, he was operating on auto-pilot. His mind wandered from one subject to another without a single thought standing still long enough to identify. All he knew was that the floods were coming and not knowing how to swim was definitely not going to help.

Trey moved the rearview mirror so he could get a full view of himself. The expression of guilt was written on his forehead in bright, bold ink. To the naked eye of other folks they wouldn't be able to read it, but to the trained, keen, look-into-your-soul-and-read-you-like-a-book eyes of his wife, his face read, "I done wrong." *Damn, it's rough going through life sober.* Trey wished he had acquired the taste for alcohol early in life. If he planned this correctly, he could go in the house, feign an illness like impeding stroke or a mild cardiac infarction, get in the bed and sleep until Taylor and the owner of the dealership either died or were picked up by aliens. "I could kill them," he said out loud. Immediately the sounds of bars being slammed together and the shortness of breath that came with being in an enclosed space overwhelmed his senses. *Somebody is gonna die.* "Please Jesus be the merciful, forgiving God that everyone claims you to be."

A banging sound startled him. Trey peered through the front windshield to investigate the source. Brittany was knocking her little knuckles against the window in Brett's bedroom. Trey reluctantly stepped out of his car and plastered on a fake grin as he waved to his precious daughter. In a flash she disappeared from view and within seconds Brittany bounded out of the garage door and jumped into his unexpected arms.

"Daddy, Daddy you home," she shouted in his ears raining kisses all over his face.

In spite of how he felt just holding his little girl started to melt away the cold icy grip of despair. Holding Brittany tight enough to crack a rib, Trey accepted the kisses and returned some of his own. Loosening his bear-hug he looked deeply into her soft greenish brown eyes seeing the gift of life and unconditional love gleaming behind her long lashes.

"You okay, Daddy?"

"Of course, why you ask me that?"

"Cause."

"Cause what?"

"You have tears in your eyes."

Trey blinked his eyelids repeatedly and faked a wide-mouthed yawn. "No tears, baby girl. Your Daddy is just tired." Figuring it was never too late to set things up he added, "Also I'm not feeling my best. I think I'll go to bed early tonight."

"You can't," Brittany stated flatly.

"Why not?"

"We have company."

"Who?"

"Uncle Ian and his new girlfriend."

"Your Uncle Ian doesn't have a girlfriend," he said putting Brittany down.

"Uh huh," she said grabbing his hand to lead him into the garage. "Come on I'll show you." Then she stopped in her tracks and turned around. "Now

Daddy," she said in a whisper, "she is very pretty so don't stare at her and make Mommy jealous." Having said her peace, Brittany resumed pulling her father through the garage and up the stairs into the house.

Entering the house Trey made out Andrea's voice, then Ian's cackling laugh. And then he heard a sound that practically sent him into major cardiac infarction. Not wanting to believe his ears Trey pulled his hand away from Brittany.

"Come on Daddy."

"I'll be right there. I need some water." Before he could tell her to hush up, Brittany ran into the living room hollering, "I told you Daddy was home, Mommy."

"Where is he?" he heard Andrea ask.

"In the kitchen," Brittany answered.

"Trey," Andrea called out, "Come here there's someone here with a surprise for you."

"I'll be right there," Trey said. *Where was an earthquake when you needed one?*

Trey sprinted into the kitchen and snatched opened the door on the "hated fridge," and gulped down half of the orange juice straight from the bottle. More liquid wound up running down his chin than in his mouth. *Okay keep your cool*, he told himself. He needed the pep talk. *You can handle this. You've been in tighter spots then this.* He proceeded to pace the kitchen. He simply needed more time to sort things out. Going to the church hadn't helped and prayer took too long to go into effect. The saying that old folks often said played in his head. "God might not come when you call him, but He's never late." According to Trey's watch, now was as good a time as any. Thinking fast he poured the remainder of the juice into the sink. "Hey baby," he shouted, "we're out of juice. I'm gonna run to the store. I'll be right back."

"Man you trying to avoid me?"

For an instant Trey lost his ability to stand up straight. His knees buckled slightly and he dropped the bottle into the sink breaking it on contact with the stainless steel. Ian rushed over to Trey's side and wrapped his arms around him to give him some support.

"Whoa big boy," Ian said, "you been out drinking?"

Trey regained his balance and pulled away from Ian. Without responding he bent over the sink picking up some of the bigger pieces of glass.

"Trey, are you okay?"

"Yeah man, you sneaking up on a man, made me break this damn bottle."

"I made you…" Ian snapped back. "You the one dropped the thing, up in here looking like you 'bout to fall on your butt."

"My bad. Messed up day at the dealership," Trey told him.

"I heard that."

Turning around to face Ian, he extended his hand, but Ian moved in for a hug. "Good to see you."

"Yeah man, it's been a while," said Ian. "Wanted to stop by and share some news with my best friend and his wife."

Trey finished removing the broken glass from the sink and after throwing the pieces into the garbage can under the sink he beckoned for Ian to sit down at the kitchen table. "So what's up?" he asked.

"Sorry I didn't get back with you the other night when you called," Ian said. "I was kind of busy, if you know what I mean."

Trey didn't, but he decided to stay quiet in case Ian wanted to enlighten him further. Once he determined that Ian wasn't going to by the silence that filled the air he admitted he didn't have a clue. After Ian explained in vivid details about he and Taylor's bed romps, he wished that he had been kept in the dark. "So you and Taylor are…what…seeing each other."

“Were you listening?”

“Yeah.”

“We are seeing, touching…”

“I get the point,” Trey didn’t want to hear anymore. “I thought you weren’t really that much into…you know.”

“Bro, I can take some and leave the others, but she’s different, man.”

This wasn’t happening. This was all he needed Taylor running off at the mouth and tells Ian that they had almost gotten busy. Oh hell, now he stood to hurt his wife and his boy and for what, nothing happened. What was next, his mother would call and tell him that the milk man was his real daddy? Trey needed a drink.

“Hey man, did you hear me?” Ian asked loudly forcing Trey to snap back.

“Huh?” Trey babbled, “What you say?”

“I said she’s in the living room and we wanted to announce to you guys that we are a couple.”

“Has she said anything about me?”

“What? Why would Taylor talk about you?”

“No reason.”

“Oh you mean about the car?”

“Yeah, yeah. I sold her a car.”

“Yeah, man. She said you hooked up her.”

“That’s it?”

"Yep. Why?"

"No reason."

"Can we go into the living room now or do you have to break some more stuff."

"Ha ha funny man. You go head. I'm right behind you. I have to make a call."

"You know you acting kind of strange."

"Na, I'm cool. Just got a lot on my mind." Trey flagged him off. "Hey I'm happy for you though."

"Yeah I can tell. See you in the living room."

Trey could tell he had offended Ian, but that was the least of his concerns at this time. Once he figured a way out of this predicament, he'd make it up to everybody. The only thing missing was the way out. For the second time today Trey felt an overwhelming urge to pray. At least this time his mouth hadn't taken over, but none- the -less, he was still consumed with a tremendous urge to seek guidance and counsel from above. Instead of feeling peace, the sensation unnerved him. He couldn't figure out where it was coming from. In forty years of living, Trey had never really given much thought to prayer or any effect if any it had on his life. Sure Andrea prayed like she and the Lord were in the same room. And sometimes he would indulge her by praying with her and the kids, but all he did was repeat what he'd heard her say or other people say in church. Even as a child growing up in his parent's household, prayer wasn't a big thing. They said grace at meals and went to church like everybody else, on Easter and Christmas. Andrea, on the other hand believed every word of the Bible and simply believed in God more than he did. But none of that made any difference to Trey as he stood alone in the kitchen fighting the pull inside of him to drop down on his knees and pray.

His dilemma was solved for him. Andrea burst into the kitchen and quickly pecked him on the cheek, grabbed him by the hand and dragged Trey behind her into the living room before he could say a word of protest.

Trey dutifully followed resigned to his impending fate. It was a good life he thought, he had lived, loved and could probably say, was loved in return. Now to have it all come to an end, well if all went right he would get to spend some time with Tupac and Elvis.

"Baby, you remember Taylor," Andrea gushed. "She's Ian— no I'll let him tell you."

Trey lifted his head and looked defiantly into the eyes of one of the storm. "Yes, we met at the club and I sold her a car. Hi Taylor, nice to see you again. I mean not that I've seen you any other time." He couldn't stop the rambling words from pouring forth.

He noticed the weird expressions on their collective faces, but no one said anything until Taylor returned his greetings and commented how lovely their home looked.

"Thanks," was all he said.

"Like I told you in the kitchen," Ian said, "Taylor and I have decided to see each other exclusively."

"Isn't that fantastic, Trey?" Andrea asked.

"Yeah, yeah, wonderful news. Now we can stop wondering if the boy was going to grow old and become Catman." Trey nervously joked.

"Yeah right," Ian shot back. "Not everybody can find the woman of their dreams in high school."

"That's true, sometimes it takes a while," Andrea agreed.

Trey averted direct eye contact with Taylor and stepped toward Ian to embrace him. Andrea quickly scolded him for not congratulating Taylor as well. Awkwardly Trey walked over to Taylor and said, "I'm happy for you too." Then he stepped in to give her the old butt-out-no-contact-hug. Taylor moved into his body and hissed so only he could hear, "Get it together, fool."

Trey moved away from her so fast he tripped on his own feet and landed head first into the couch and was back on his feet in almost one motion. "Wooooo, gots to be more careful," he said trying to hide his embarrassment with humor.

"Trey, have you been drinking?"

"I asked him the same thing, Andrea," Ian said.

"Go on girl. You know I don't drink."
"You sure are acting a little off." Andrea said.

"Must be light-headed selling all those cars," Taylor piped in.

"Yeah yeah, na na. I'm just not feeling too good."

Andrea approached him and felt his forehead. "You do feel warm."

"Hey, I hate to be a poor host, but if you guys don't mind I think I'll turn in."

"No problem. We out anyway," Ian stated. "Our traveling good news show is going on the road."

"What you mean?" asked Andrea.

"We're going to see his Mother," Taylor answered.

"Oh yeah, almost forgot," said Ian. "I also wanted to give you guys' two tickets for the big showcase this Friday that my baby set up at the Blue Way."

Andrea insisted they pop open a bottle of wine to celebrate. Trey begged off and just to show how ill he really felt, he coughed and began breathing heavily.

"That's cool, man. Go get in bed. You look like crap," Ian said.

He excused himself after offering his apologies and sick-walked up the stairs just in case they were watching. Trey stopped in Brett's bedroom and found both kids fast asleep on the floor in front of the TV. He decided to leave them for Andrea to deal with. Trey entered the master bedroom, closed the door and went over to kneel down beside the bed. He recalled one sermon long ago when a preacher had said that at some time in a person's life they would fall to their knees and call on the name of Jesus. Never in a million years had he thought he'd be that person.

Hypocrite! That one word exploded into his thoughts. Trey stood up. *Hypocrite!* He looked around the room almost expecting to find someone standing in the shadows calling the word out to him. *Lean not onto your own understanding.* Trey immediately ran over to the nightstand to turn on the lamp that sat on top. He planted his feet in a boxer's stance. *Repent in the name of Jesus for the remission of your sins.* Trey grabbed his head with both hands and squeezed his fingers against his head. He was hearing voices inside his own head.

Oh Lord, the stress of the deal and what almost happened with Taylor was driving him insane. He'd heard about this. Severe guilt could make a person go nuts. They struggled and wrestled with it until they couldn't take it anymore and their minds snapped. Then they spent the rest of their lives drooling and thinking it was 1945 over and over again. He was too young to dwell on 1945.

Hypocrite, he thought. But did not going to church on the regular mean he wasn't entitled to ask God for help? Or did it mean he only wanted to pray because his butt was in the fire and he didn't want to get burnt? He could ask Andrea. She would know. No he couldn't do that. She would want to know why he asked. Asking her would be like walking up to the gunmen, putting the gun to his own head and pulling the trigger for the guy. No he was smarter than that. It was better to wait for the bullet to come out and find a way to duck quickly enough to avoid getting hit. *If you were that smart you wouldn't be in this mess.* Trey's head snapped around. He had to get a grip. It wasn't that bad. Besides more than half the money in the account was his anyway and as for Taylor, it's not like he got to enjoy her.

The cloud of gloom and doom that was over his head started to dissipate. He was making this much bigger than it was and giving this junk way too much power over him. *See that's why people do all that praying. They can't figure things out for themselves.* Feeling like he was back in charge, he stripped down to take a shower. *No man will leave this life and not confess that Jesus is Lord.* "Oh no not again," he sighed. Why was he recalling stuff he heard in church when he didn't even go that much? Stress. That's all it was. It will pass.

Attempting to practice the power of positive thinking techniques he often read about Trey entered the shower and tried to relax under the hot water cascading down on his head. It didn't work.

****

A single glass of wine to toast Ian and Taylor turned into an impromptu party. Somewhere between the cracking of the first bottle of wine and the second one being opened Ian had cranked up the stereo and began to sing along with a Luther song that blared from the speakers.

"You are so good for him," Andrea told Taylor as they watched Ian sing into the ice cream scooper that he was using as a microphone. The ladies were seated side by side on the tan leather couch in the living room as Ian entertained them in the center of the large open room.

Taylor waited a beat to respond. Being in Trey's house, chit-chatting with his wife was a tad bit surreal to her. She felt like she was in an episode of a nighttime soap. She truly believed that if Andrea had even the slightest clue that just a couple of days ago she was in a hotel room with her husband, the wine bottle she was now pouring red wine from would be used as a upside-her-head weapon. "Yeah, he's kind of good for me too," she finally said. What Taylor really meant was he was good for her pockets and if playing "girlfriend," kept Ian happy and content. She would fulfill that role to its fullest, or until it no longer served her best interest. The feedback she'd gotten from a past bedmate of hers after he heard the demo tape of Ian performing two cover-tunes and a song he wrote had her over the moon. Come Friday night's showcase in front of the music executives, there would be no stopping her. Ian was just the first artist in her stable. And Taylor Daniels was going to ride him all the way to the bank in her brand-new BMW that he'd paid for although he didn't need to know that. No matter what it took on her part, Ian was getting signed to a major label. So if he wanted to parade her around town as his woman, C'est la vie.

Andrea lifted her glass toward Taylor. "Again, here's to you and Ian and all the very best as you guys embark on this journey in life."

"Thanks," Taylor felt a twinge of guilt that she quickly rebuked. "Hey little Luther, don't you thinks its getting late?"

Ian spun around on his heels and gracefully danced over to the couch making the women giggle. "Yeah," he said looking at his watch, "we do need to get moving, Mama goes to bed early on weeknights."

Taylor thanked Andrea for a lovely evening as she accepted her leather trench coat from her. The two women air-kissed each other's cheek and then unexpectedly Andrea wrapped Taylor into a tight embrace. The move startled Taylor momentarily, but she maintained her composure and returned the embrace adding a squeeze at the end.

"Well don't be a stranger," she heard Andrea call out as her and Ian walked down the front steps of the house. "Ian you take good care of her."

"I will," he assured her. "Tell Trey I'll holler at him tomorrow."

"Hurry up honey, "Taylor sweetly said through clenched teeth. "Don't want to keep your mother waiting." Even if was just her imagination running away with her, she could smell Trey's cologne on her body, and if she could smell it, then it was just a matter of a sniff before his wife would pick up her man's scent too.

Speeding away from the curb Taylor hit sixty before they reached the end of the block.

****

Closing the front door, Andrea quickly felt the void of being alone. Not to mention the panic of going upstairs and finding Trey awake and wanting to talk or worst— make love. Just the thought of being touched sent a ripple down her spine that raced around and threatened to drown her heart. The burden of guilt that she carried was beginning to become too much for her. She couldn't recall the last time she'd said a prayer or read the Bible.

All of her teachings since she was a child told her to take her troubles to the Lord in prayer, but the dirtiness she felt simply wouldn't allow her to come clean. Although Andrea could cite chapter and verse for almost every scripture that dealt with forgiveness, she simply couldn't forgive herself. And if she couldn't do that then neither Trey nor God Almighty would be able to it for her.

Needing something to do to give her running brain a rest, Andrea quietly gathered up the two empty wine bottles and the glasses. Downing the remainder of liquid from a glass she believed belonged to her, she tip-toed into the kitchen. Despite her best efforts in drinking so much wine, instead of becoming high and having all cares forgotten, it was quite the contrary; Andrea was stone-cold sober and forgetting was the hardest thing to do.

CHAPTER TWENTY-EIGHT

The old grandfather clock in the corner of the office chimed letting all within earshot know that the twenty-first hour of the day had arrived. For Pastor Douglas time had taken him back to another place and time the moment the woman sitting on the couch had stepped through his office door.

"How many times must I tell you how sorry I am?" he asked. "That was the past and God has forgiven me, surely you can do the same."

"Has He or do you tell yourself that so you can sleep at night?" she fired back. They had been going back and forth for over two hours with neither side giving an inch. The ice in her tone sent another cold dagger into his heart. "You were a man of God and you abused your position to satisfy your lust and greed. You destroyed people's lives and then you simply left town without so much as a backward glance."

"That's not entirely true," he responded without any conviction.

"It is true," she shouted. "You seduced women with your looks and charm and you stole money from the church; now tell me how that is not true."
"I have repented of all my previous sins," he stated full of indignation.

"Oh really? So you mean to tell me that you're not up to your old tricks?"

Choosing his words carefully Pastor Douglas cleared his throat and said, "My past is behind me, my present is today and my future is yet unto the Lord that I serve."

"Oh please, save that for the gullible ones that don't know you. Whether you know it or not, I saw you with that attractive woman in the parking lot."

"A faithful member of the church," he blushed knowing she was referring to Andrea. He waited for the other shoe to drop.

"She married?"

"Why?"

"That's your specialty, frustrated lonely married women who eat up your fancy words and attention."

"I don't do that…"

"Oh were you going to say, you don't do that anymore? When you stop? After my sister shot herself over you?

There it was after two hours of going back and forth, the horrible truth behind her sudden re-emergence into his life. Stacey Vincent, her baby sister and the reason he'd lost everything back in Macon. He remembered Stacey lying in a pool of her own blood as he stared into the dark, hate filled eyes of her sister. So many nights he'd lain awake because her image refused to stop laying claim to his dreams. He thought of her every day and begged, pleaded and made offers to God for forgiveness. And up until Andrea Edwards, he had kept his promises to the Lord. The pull of the flesh was so strong! And for Pastor Raymond Douglas the pull on his flesh had always been a pretty face attached to a married woman. It was easier that way— he could remain unattached.

"You just left her lying on the floor bleeding like an animal," she sobbed through tears.

"I called for help."

"From your cell phone."

"I panicked," he told her by way of explanation. "I didn't think she would shoot herself."

"She had lost everything, her husband her kids. All because she thought you really loved her and that God had sent you to be her savior."

"I never…"

She shouted for him to shut up. "You knew she was having problems at home and you took advantage of that."

"Why are you here?"

The next words she spoke chilled him to the bone. "I came to kill you." And with that she pulled out a gun from her handbag that she had sitting on her lap the entire time they were talking.

"Please don't," he pleaded immediately upon seeing the gun pointed at his chest. "I'm a new creature in Christ."

"Doing the same old thing. Answer me honestly. If you can. Did you have sex with that woman I saw you with?"

The truth shall set you free or get you killed depending on who held the gun. He figured the truth would probably save his life. "Yes," was all he said.

"Why?"
"I'm weak."

"Is she married?"

"Yes."
"Having problems with her husband?"

"I think so."

"You took advantage of her?"

"Yes."

"Do you regret doing so?"

"Yes."

"Why? Is it because you're looking at the end of a gun?"

"Yes."

"You are a wolf in sheep clothing and truly a false prophet."

"No I'm not. Even if you shot me dead tonight, I will die believing in my heart of hearts that I was called of God to preach His word and I messed up."

"The Word says many are called but few are chosen. You may have been called, but you were not chosen."

"That's for the Lord to decide. Answering the call of God is a tough decision for anyone to make and choosing to live a life directed by Him is even harder. No man is perfect and I will not sit here and pretend to be anything other than what I am."

"And that is?"

"A man who fell short of the mark, but I re-commit my life to Christ this evening as I ask for His forgiveness and yours."

"What about my sister?"

"Every day and every day for the rest of my life that I assure you." He waited a beat. "Are you really going to shoot me?"

"No," she whispered, "Lord knows I want to and I came here with every intention of doing so."

"And now?"

"The Lord is pulling on me to take the high road of forgiveness."

"Please listen to Him."

"My sister has forgiven you."

Shock registered on his stressed-out face. "She has?"

"Yeah, she has. She sits in a wheelchair without the use of her limbs yet she still has full function of the biggest heart of any person I've ever known."

Hallelujah! Tears that needed to be set free made their escape. Pastor Douglas wept like Mary weeping and moaning. He cried for the woman with the gun, he cried for the woman in the wheelchair, he cried for Andrea Edwards and every other woman that he'd wronged in his entire life and lastly he cried for himself.

With tears streaming down his face, Pastor Raymond Douglas got up from his chair and dropped down to his knees and with out-stretched hands and bowed head prayed the prayer of repentance asking God to forgive him of his sins.

The woman watched him for a moment, then put the gun back into her handbag and walked out of the church full of forgiveness that only a Higher Power can deliver.

****

Tina woke up with a start. The early morning sun came through her slightly opened blinds with a vengeance. The light of a new day blinded her, but her vision was clear for the first time in her life. She still couldn't believe her luck. Who would have thought that some white women sitting in authority over her would give her a second chance? Was it luck or was it an angel looking over her shoulder? Whatever it was, she felt like that old boxer she'd watched in some old movie who said, "Somebody up there likes me." And at this moment, Tina believed that maybe that same "Somebody" liked her too.

After telling the social worker that she had smoked some weed, she was certain her shot at a new life had gone up in smoke. But the kind lady blew her mind when she told Tina that she believed in her and would stall the drug test for one month to give her a chance to get that poison out of her system. And to add sweetness to the sugar, she told her to report for orientation today for her new job. As of today, Tina Jenkins was no longer an unemployed, unwed mother, today she became a working woman. If life was made up of second chances, then she was going to take hers and do something with it. She owed hers daughters that.

Tina kicked off the covers and jumped from the bed. After showering and putting on her best dress (her only dress) she fixed her hair and put on a little make-up. Looking in the mirror she had to admit that if she lost a little weight, she wasn't a bad looking chick. Oh well, one thing at a time.

Upon entering the kitchen she was surprised to find the place spotlessly clean. A note set on the table. She picked it up to read it. "Hey Mom, good luck on your first day of work. We love you and we are so proud of you." It was signed by all three of her girls. It took her twenty minutes to stop the flow of tears and re-do her face in time to catch the bus that would transport her downtown to her new beginning.

****

"Drea we need to talk."

"I'm running late for work," she responded moving frantically around the bedroom. Andrea made every effort to avoid making direct eye contact with Trey.

"How 'bout we do lunch today?"

"Lunch…today…umm…I'm really swamped today. Today wouldn't be good."

"How 'bout I drive you to work?"

"Drive me to work? Ah…that's okay, thanks anyway."

Trey reached out to grab her arm as she quickly snatched her purse from the bed and headed for the door. It didn't escape his attention how she recoiled from his touch. It seemed like she was doing that a lot lately, although he wanted to believe it was simply his guilt-ridden imagination. "Drea, slow down a sec."

"I'm running late if I'm late again it won't look good since I just started," she caught herself.

"Just started what? Are you working on a big case?"

"Yeah, that's it. A new case." She brushed her lips against his and sprinted out of the door before he could ask anymore questions. Running down the steps, Andrea chastised herself again for keeping her promotion a secret and for the life of her she couldn't figure out what made her do that in the first place. Then an idea hit her. At the bottom of the steps she turned around and called out for Trey. When he appeared at the top, she said, "Guess what?" She hesitated. "I got a promotion at work. Sorry I didn't tell you sooner, but it wasn't definite until recent and I didn't want to jinx it."

"That's great. Congrats," he said deeply hurt that she had kept something from him. Then he remembered that he was doing the same thing. "I thought you didn't believe in keeping secrets?

"I know I was being silly. See you later." As an afterthought she abruptly said, "I love you."

It had been awhile since either of them had uttered those words. Hearing her say them only made him feel worst. Trey choked up and started to cough. Once he got it together enough to speak, Andrea had already left the house. So he expressed his love to the quietness of what was once and he hoped would become again— a happy home.

****

Dexter slowly picked himself up off the floor, where he had laid prone after being "slain in the spirit" while praying. Ever since he'd accepted Jesus Christ into his life he'd started every day off with intense communication with The Holy One. His prayers were a two-way conversation. Not for him was simply praying and saying amen. Failure to listen to what the Lord has to say, would have made prayer meaningless to Dexter. He truly believed that prayer was more than asking God for the "want" of the day. Talking to Him filled Dexter with a fire that burned so deep inside of his being that he thought surely one day his insides would explode. After his morning ritual of Bible reading and prayer Dexter was ready to take on any Goliath the world might send his way.

This morning in particular he'd worked up a pouring-down-his-face sweat. For the past half-hour he had stood as an intercessor for Trey. He asked that the Father forgive Trey of his sins of omission and commission, especially his recent near-miss act of adultery. Furthermore he asked God to place a hedge of protection over and around Trey's marriage. The last thing he prayed was for the bank approval so that Trey's dream of ownership could come to pass.

From what he had gleaned from Trey he knew that his wife was a church-going woman and prayed enough for the both of them. So as far as Dexter saw it, if that woman kept praying, it was just a matter of time before her husband's life would be turned over to Christ.

As he got dressed for work he song an out-of-tune version of "Precious Lord." Walking to his car parked out front of his Main Line mansion, he suddenly felt a searing hot poker stab him in left side of the chest. Dropping his briefcase, he clutched his chest with both hands as he dropped to his knees. "Thank you Jesus," he mumbled just before passing out.

CHAPTER TWENTY-NINE

Pulling into the parking lot Trey grabbed the first available space reserved for the sales staff since Tony still occupied his old spot. It would take a pack of wild dogs nipping at his heels to admit it. He was actually proud of Tony and his accomplishments. Beating him once was a big deal and Tony was doing it again thus far. Trey was determined to reclaim his throne this month and go out with a bang before leaving to run his own show.

Driving in one of his favorite songs of all times came on the radio; "My Way" sang by the Master, Frank Sinatra. Simply listening to the words of the song and its central theme gave him a renewed desire to maintain a positive out-look on his current dilemma. He was going to call the bank one last time and if the loan wasn't approved he would take his business elsewhere. No more sitting around being passive, it was time to get aggressive. There was no way in hell he was going to lose one hundred thousand of his and Andrea's hard earn money. More importantly, Trey wasn't willing to see his dream crushed under the boots of some number cruncher holding onto a dollar tight enough to make ole George squeal without doing whatever it took to make it happen.

The solemn air inside the dealership met Trey at the door. He looked around for Paula, but she was no where in sight. Two of his co-workers were huddled by the coffee machine in what appeared to be a deep conversation. Gingerly he walked up to them.

"Good morning fellows."

The taller of the two gave Trey a weak wave while the shorter one gave him a head nod before walking off. "Hey Trey," the tall one said.

"What's up?" Trey asked. "What's up with him?"

"You haven't heard?"

"Heard what?"

"About the boss man."

"Jerry?"

"Na, Mr. Fortune."

A feeling of dread came over him. "What about Dexter?"

"Dang, man I hate to be the one to tell you I know how tight you are."

He felt himself start to panic as Trey pleaded for him to spit it out.

"A neighbor found him lying face down in his driveway."

Before the last word was past his tongue, Trey had spun on his heels and at top speed ran out to his car.

"Trey…Trey…hold up, man."

"Not now Tony," he barked.

"If you're going to the hospital, I want to come with you."
"Get in."

Tony slid in beside Trey and almost lost a leg as the car door slammed against it as Trey sped off before he could get fully situated in the passenger sit. "Whoa bro, watch that truck!"

Trey appeared to be oblivious to the other drivers on the road as he hit the accelerator and raced through the red light narrowly missing the truck.

"Hey man lets get to the hospital in one piece."

"Shut up!"

"Do you know what hospital he's in?"

That question only seemed to fuel Trey's desire to fly. "No," he stated through clenched teeth. "Do you?"

"I heard Jerry say they took him to Brynn Mawr."

"Do you know what happened?"

"Nope. I think Paula does."

"Where was she?" he demanded weaving in and out of traffic.

"In the bathroom bawling her eyes out," Tony explained holding onto the car handle for dear life. "She was the one took the call."

"Any body know what actually happened?"

"Jerry said something about a possible heart attack."
"Where was Jerry?"

"I don't want to tell you."

"Tell me!" The sharpness of his words left no room for doubt that he wanted to know.

"In Dexter's office."

"That son of a…," Trey pounded the steering wheel imagining it was Jerry's puffy face.

While Trey was punching his face in effigy, Jerry was sitting behind the big desk envisioning the day he officially took over the dealership. First order of business; get rid of Trey Edwards.

****

Slamming his car into park, Trey jumped out of the driver's seat with the engine still running. After Tony performed the motion of the cross over his chest, he turned the car off, set the alarm and ran after the fleet-footed Trey.

"Hey man, slow down I'm not trying to be up in here visiting both of you," he hollered out. His words having more meaning after Trey almost ran smack-dab into an ambulance pulling into the driveway.

Tony met up with him at the hospital's sliding glass door. Huffing and puffing he asked, "Since we're not family do you think they'll give us any information?"

"I'll say I'm his brother," Trey said standing in front of the automatic doors. Being directly in front of the doors set off the motion sensor and the doors repeatedly opened and closed.

"We going in?"

"Yeah…umm…just getting my head together?" Trey responded. Hospitals always unnerved him. Other than the birth of his children, hospitals were harbingers of death. The last time he'd seen each of his mother's parents they were in hospital rooms hooked up to more wire than a stereo system. And the smell of the place, a mixture of bleach and blood stayed locked in his nostrils for days.

They backed away from the doors to allow a nurse to wheel a patient out. Trey looked at Tony for the first time since they had jumped into his flying saucer. "Dang," he nervously snickered, "I guess I was driving kind of fast over here, huh?"

"Kind of? Nah Speed Racer, not at all."

"How's your leg?" he asked, acknowledging he had taken off before Tony was fully in the car.

"Still attached to my hip."

"Sorry 'bout that."

"No biggie."

"You think he's allright?"

"I hope so, but the only way we gonna find out is to go inside."

"I'm scared, man. I didn't realize until now how much the brotha means to me."

"Yeah, it's obvious to everyone at the dealership how tight you guys are."

"Really?"

"Yeah."

"You know we never get together outside of work that much, hardly ever."

"Well I guess your relationship transcends the workplace whether you hang or not."

"He's always preaching to me about God and stuff," Trey said swallowing back tears.

"Yeah, he is a walking advertisement for the Lord."

"He ever witness to you."

"Not really, he would just say stuff that kind of let you know he was religious and all."

"For the past few months he's been trying to get me saved."

"From what?"

"Hell if I know." Trey pondered that question a little longer. Then he looked Tony straight in the eye and said, "I guess from myself. Let's go check on Dexter."

****

"Time of death, eleven forty-eight am," the white-haired doctor recited to the nurse. "So young and he looks to be in good shape."

"I'm certain his family will probably want an autopsy done," the nurse said.

"I would recommend it." He shook his head sadly as he backed away from the stretcher. No matter how long he'd practiced medicine, nothing took more out of him than announcing the time that a human being went from having tomorrows to having none.

"Have someone notify the deceased's next of kin."

****

It felt so good to get out of the office and spend some face-time with her best girlfriend, especially since it had been awhile since they'd had a chance to catch up on the soap opera called life.

Tina sat across the table from Andrea, beaming sunshine from her face. "Girl, can you believe it? I actually gotta a job."

"I'm so proud of you. I knew you would get it together once you gave yourself a chance," Andrea said truly happy for her.

"I must admit though, it wasn't just me. Having my girls believe in me and that nice social worker really helped me a lot too."

"Of course."

"And although you might fall off your chair," Tina gushed, "going to church has kind of made a difference as well."

The mention of church suddenly made Andrea feel slightly uncomfortable. Tina caught a quick glimpse of the sudden mood swing and dismissed it. "That's good," was Andrea's comeback.

"That's good. All this time you been ragging on me about going to church and now I tell you I'm going and all you say is, that's good."

Momentarily the placement of her eating utensils became very important. Andrea rearranged her knife and forks as well as the water glasses on the table. The hum of the lunchtime crowd at the busy downtown eatery got a little louder to her; despite her best efforts the image of her and the Pastor on the couch bum-rushed her mental DVD player. Then all of the guilt and shame that had become her constant companion since that horrible day joined them at the table. Andrea's eyes took on an out-of-state glare and her hands began to shake uncontrollably.

"Girl you are beginning to scare me," Tina said "Talk to me."

Andrea neatly placed the napkin onto her lap and breathed in deeply. Composing herself she looked at Tina and smiled weakly. "I had sex with another man."

Tina's expression went from fear to shock to total disbelief and finally landed on absolute bewilderment. "Come again."

"It just happened."

"Come again."

"You heard me."

"Girl, does Trey know."

"Of course not."

"Keep your mouth shut. I know you believe in cleansing the soul and all. But girl there are some things you take to the grave."

"How can I walk around with all this guilt inside and not tell him?"

"Easy…keep your mouth shut and put it out of your mind." Tina reached across the table and took Andrea's trembling hand in hers. "It was just a fling, right?"

"Not even that."

Time took a break as the two women talked. For the first time in their relationship, Tina took on the role of care-giver. She patiently listened as Andrea erupted like a volcano, releasing the hot lava of pent up emotion she'd kept bottled up since that fateful day.

Hearing Andrea's story and the hell she had been going through tore at her heart-strings and brought tears to her own eyes. She wanted to drive over to the church and cut his genitals off with a dull butter knife. It was apparent that her friend was taking the full blunt of the blame all on herself. In Tina's experience with men, she knew that it wasn't hard to be swayed by a man showing attention and making a woman feel like she was the sexist, hottest lady on the planet, especially if a woman wasn't getting it from her own man. Even though she believed that Andrea had the life of her dreams, listening to her now convinced Tina more than ever that although the grass may be greener on the other side it still needed to be mowed.

"Sweetheart, you have to forgive yourself," she told Andrea. "Everyone makes mistakes, hell I know that better than anybody. You're a great person, a wonderful wife and a fantastic mother. Don't let this make you feel any different about who you are."

"Don't forget adulterer, sinner and a big helping of slut for dessert."

"Don't even go there. You are the straightest arrow I know and one mistake doesn't change that."

"Then why do I feel so dirty?"

"If you didn't, you wouldn't be you."

"This could ruin my marriage."

"You know why I don't think it's a good idea to tell Trey?"

"I'm listening."

"From what you've described to me, it sounds a lot like date rape."

"Date rape?"

"Yep, that's when a female may give a certain signal to a guy that she wants to, but before it gets out of hand she says no or stop and he doesn't."

"He didn't do that."

"Stop making excuses for his sorry ass. He had no business as a preacher coming onto you in the first place and taking advantage of you in the church of all places. He needs his ass kicked!"

Andrea sighed deeply and catching a glimpse of her watch she noticed how much time had passed. "Girl, I don't want you getting fired because of me. With all that's going on with me I couldn't take that."

"This is about you. I'll call in sick if you need to talk some more."

"No, I'll be allright. We'll talk later."

Walking outside after paying for their uneaten meals, Tina made Andrea promise that she would think twice-three times if necessary before confessing her infidelity to her husband. "Girl, there's no telling what he would do," she told her. "And I know you don't want to find out."

The sharp shrill coming from Andrea's purse startled both of them. Pulling her cell phone from her bag, the name and number displayed on the caller ID pierced her already pained heart. "It's Trey," she said.

"Stay calm. It's not like you guys haven't been seeing and speaking to each other."

"Hello." Her voice shook. "Oh my God, Trey. I'm so sorry. I'll be right there."

"What's wrong?" Tina frantically asked. "Everything okay?"

"No. Trey's boss just died. Girl I gotta go. I'll talk to you later."

They quickly embraced and give each other cheek pecks. Andrea ran to the underground garage to retrieve her car as Tina did her best Marion Jones impersonation as she high-tailed it back to her file clerk job at City Hall.

CHAPTER THIRTY

The reminder of the month crawled along like a snail on life support. The unexpected death of Dexter Fortune rocked everyone who knew him, from business associates to his employees and family members. Since death always came in threes, some of the salespeople at the dealership silently wondered who would go next. As the days went by and none other fulfilled the urban myth, things at the dealership started to take on the natural order of business-must-go-on. That was the case for everyone except Trey.

Since the very well attended funeral several weeks before, no one had seen or heard from Trey in weeks. He hadn't returned either Paula's or Tony's voicemails. Even Dexter's brother Ryan tried reaching out to him. Ryan had moved up from Atlanta to take over his big brother's business interest and await the reading of Dexter's will. Reluctantly Ryan left Jerry in charge of the dealership as he dealt with both his own business and Dexter's huge and profitable empire. He assumed that his big brother had left his dealerships to him, since Dexter was divorced and didn't have any kids. There were no other siblings and prior to moving to Atlanta four years ago to start his own real estate firm, Ryan had been a partner in the Philadelphia dealership as well as its sales manager. So he knew the car business as well as his big brother. And like his father said the other night on the phone, "I'm sure Dex left you his businesses because he would want them to stay in the family." But to find out for certain, he had to wait for the attorneys to schedule the reading of the will next week. Until then he would carry on and try not to run himself ragged. If he had learned anything from Dexter it was delegation, so for now he would continue to use the people in place to help the transition go smoothly. Whether Trey came around or not, he had no intention of sticking with Jerry as the general manager of the Philly dealership. Prior to Dexter's untimely death he'd practically begged Ryan to come back and run the shop. He couldn't figure out why Trey would turn down such a tremendous opportunity. But he intended to get to the bottom of that situation sometime in the upcoming weeks.

Oh well no sense putting this off any longer, he mused. Tapping the intercom he spoke directly into the microphone. "Paula, could you please ask Jerry to come see me as soon as he gets a chance?"

****

In past years Thanksgiving was the favorite holiday for the Edwards clan. Every year family members from both sides gathered at the home of the designated one for the annual gathering. This year it was Trey and Andrea's turn at hosting the major family event of the holiday season. They were expecting at least twenty to show up.

Andrea's greatest concern as she basted the thirty-pound turkey centered on her husband's well-being. In all the years she'd known Trey, she couldn't recall him ever taking a death so hard. He left the house every morning but she knew he didn't go to work since almost everyone from the dealership kept calling the house looking for him. Where he went every day was a mystery to her. He refused to talk about it and even the kids were feeling the brunt of his distant behavior. The one good thing that had come from this tragedy was it enabled Andrea to take her mind off her own demons as she tried to help Trey cope with his.

"Mom," Brittany said running into the kitchen, "is Daddy going to be happy today?"

Not too certain of that herself she half-heartedly assured her daughter that once everyone arrived to start the day's festivities, her father would be fine. "He's just dealing with the loss of a close friend."

"Hey Mom," Brett called out entering the kitchen, "is Uncle Mo coming?" Uncle Mo was Trey's mother's youngest brother and the resident family drunk. "I hope so cause he cracks me up."

"Behave yourself, boy," she laughed, secretly hoping he didn't show up.

"Owwww… that's the bell, someone's here already," Brittany excitedly announced like she was the only one who heard the door bell sound. She hopped down from the stool and ran to the front door.

"Girl, don't open that door without asking who it is," Andrea shouted after her. "Go with your sister and find out who it is before you open that door."

"Aww… Mom she got it,"

"Boy I said go."

Brett didn't have a chance to comply before Uncle Mo clouded the doorway riding a giggling Brittany on his broad shoulders. "Baby girl it sure smells good up in here," he said sniffing the air. "Look at how big you got in just a year, boy. Come give your ole uncle some love."

"Hello Uncle Mo," Andrea said stiffly.

"Happy Turkey Day to you," he responded placing Brittany down and picking up a wiggling Brett. "I know you think you to big to get picked up boy. I'm just showing you how strong I am."

Andrea dictated the usual mixture of Old Spice and cigarette smell on Uncle Mo as he pulled her into a tight embrace. One scent was missing from his normal aroma and it was the hint of whiskey on his breath. As if he read her mind he whispered in her ear, "Clean and sober for six weeks now."

"Really?" She didn't bother to hide her disbelief since going cold-turkey, no pun intended was something he did every two or three years. It usually didn't last longer than the next day that ended in the letter 'y'.

"Yep, this time niece by law, I'm officially on the wagon and fully intend to stay on for the entire ride."

"You ain't getting drunk today?" Brett asked, listening in.

"Boy you know better than to get up in grown-folk talk," Andrea scolded him. "Now run and tell your Father that Uncle Mo is here."

"Nah don't do that. I want to surprise him," he stopped Brett. "Besides my sister told me he ain't been right since his boss died."

"He's been dealing with it."

"They were that tight?"

"Apparently so."

"Where is he?"

"In the basement setting up some tables and chairs," she told him.

Playfully popping Brett upside the head he said, "Nephew, this year ole Uncle Mo ain't gonna get tore down and make of fool of himself, but don't you fret, some other member of this family will."

"Yeah but it won't be as funny as you."

"Boy you too much," Andrea said. "One of these days I'm going to pull out your tongue."

"Now that would be funny," Brittany snickered. "Hey Mom can you do that today?"

"Oh yeah, how 'bout I pull out yours." Brett ran after his squealing sister as Andrea's demand for quite fell on deaf ears.

"Now that's what makes life worth living," said Uncle Mo. "Damn if I didn't mess it up." For a moment it appeared as though he was going to cry. Instead he squared his shoulders and blew out a deep sigh. "I know you probably don't believe me and I guess you have no reason to but this time I'm really off the sauce for good."

"I hope so, Uncle Mo."

"Well baby girl, losing my wife and kids, more jobs than I can count and even the loss of my own folks couldn't stop me from drinking."

"What makes this time different?"

"Truthfully?"

"That would work."

"You probably going to think I've lost it."

"Try me."

"Okay. Well one night I'm lying up in bed with some ugly women, hell she look good at the bar."

"Uncle Mo, stay on topic."

"Allright, allright. I'm just laying the foundation. Anyway, this woman is besides me snoring like a truck motor and all of a sudden I saw my mother hovering over my bed."

"Grandma Natty?"

"One in the same and she was in her coffin."

"You were high," Andrea said as a way of explaining why he had had a vision.

"As a kite, but I'm not crazy."

"Go on."

"All of a sudden my mother, God rests her soul, sat up in the casket and started talking to me."

Totally wrapped up in the conversation Andrea stopped messing with the turkey and wiped her hands on a hand towel as she gestured for him to continue. "What she say?"

"She told me that she missed me and couldn't wait to see me again."

"And?"

"That she wasn't in a rush to see me." He stopped as his voice caught in his throat. "Then she told me that God told her that if I didn't stop drinking, I was living my last days."

"What happened after that?"

"I woke that ugly heifer up and kicked her butt out of my apartment and then I threw every drop of liquor I had down the toilet and flushed it. And I ain't had a drop since that night."

"Wow," was all Andrea could think to say. "Did you go to AA?"

"Nope. I carried my AA to church."

"Your aa?

"Alcoholic ass. Now let me go see my favorite nephew."

****

"Watch out der now," Uncle Mo shouted out borrowing the catch phrase of a popular radio personality. "How's my favorite nephew by default?"

Looking up from his task of arranging the tables and chairs that Andrea had insisted would be needed for dinner; he barely shrugged and gave his uncle a head nod. "Why by default?"

"You the only one who invites me to anything."

"Family is family and life is way too short and you never know when the last time you saw someone it could be the last time you saw them."

"You speaking truth there, nephew," he whole-heartedly agreed. "Your Moms tells me that you kind of living that right now." Uncle Mo grabbed one of the chairs to help Trey finish setting up.

"Yeah man," sighed Trey. "My boss and mentor just had a heart attack and flat out died on the spot. They tried to revive him on the way to the hospital and worked on him for close to an hour once they got him there. Doctor said he was really DOA but he believed in miracles."

"They do happen."

"Not this time and this was another time in my life it was needed."

"Sit down, son," he said feeling Trey's pain.

"I'm cool, Unc. Want a shot of bourbon?"

"Nah. I'm off the juice."

"Again?"

"This time it's for keeps."

"Good for you." Trey thought that pork had a better shot a being served at a Muslim rally than his uncle staying sober.

"I'm for real this time. Ask your wife what I told her when you get a chance," he said. Uncle Mo patted the cushion on the couch beside him.

Trey obeyed him this time as he flopped down. "Seriously, I'm cool."

"I know, I know. Humor an old man none the less. Talk to me."

"You ain't that old," declared Trey. "You just been drunk so much, you forgot your own age."

"Oh you got jokes."

"Sorry, that one was too easy to pass up."

"I know I ain't been the best example of how to live, but if my life can teach you anything— it's don't let outside forces control you."

"Nah now don't go getting all sensitive on me."

"Boy, you look like you lost your best friend, your dog and your woman."

"Just a mentor. And in about a few weeks a ton of money. And if my luck keeps going the way it has, maybe my wife and kids."

"Spill."

And spill he did. Trey told his uncle about putting down the non-refundable deposit without Andrea's knowledge that he'd forged her signature and how if the bank didn't approve the loan they stood to lose one-hundred thousand dollars. Then he told him about Taylor and how they almost slept together and that to complicate matters, his best friend Ian was currently dating her.

"Damn, yaw rolling like you even had a hundred G to lose?"

"Who said I can afford to lose that kind of money?"

"I'm just saying that's a lifetime of money."

"Why you acting like some country bumpkin with all the money you used to have?"

"Being sober makes a man's vision and his reality clearer."

"Well Uncle Clear-eyes, you got any words of wisdom for your favorite-nephew-by-default?"

"Yep. I got six words for you."

"I'm listening."

"Take it to the Lord in prayer."

"You made more sense when you drank ole man. And that was seven words."

Uncle Mo counted the number of words on his fingers as he followed Trey up the steps. Upon reaching the top landing both could hear the loud, boisterous sound of people talking and laughing. The gang was all here. Trey abruptly stopped and turned to his uncle. "Hey Unc, please keep that to yourself."

"I can hold my water, nephew."

"Not when you're drinking."

"Dammit, didn't I tell you I'm off the sauce. Now get out of the way. That bird is calling my name."

****

Across town as Trey and the gang happily gathered around the dining room table, a lone figure sat alone at his home and angrily pushed his half-eaten plate full of food so hard its contents hit the floor. Slamming his fist down on the kitchen table caused a can of pop to fall on its side spilling the lukewarm content all over the table. A trail of liquid began to drip down onto the floor joining the mix of dry overcooked bake chicken, soggy mashed potatoes and too-long steamed string beans.

Ian hopped up from the chair kicking it back so hard it bounced off the wall in the small interior. He couldn't care less that he'd just put a dent in the wall or that his floor was a gooey mess. All he felt like doing was ramming his fist into something. As he started to walk out of the kitchen his clean-freak gene kicked in and he simply had to grab the mop and clean out of the pantry.

After mopping up his messy tantrum and putting the chair back under the table he threw himself across the couch. But not before kicking off his shoes so as not to scuff or smudge the material. Andrea had invited him and Taylor to Thanksgiving dinner. But Taylor's sudden need to come clean derailed that idea. There was no way he could have gone over there and pretended like everything was still the same.

His cell phone rang twice and then his house phone sounded. Ian glared at the offending instruments. He almost threw one of the accent pillows to knock the phone off the end table then he decided that if he missed he would probably knock over his cactus plant. And make another mess he would have to clean up. Again his cell phone went off and almost as soon as the ringing stopped the house phone sounded as if in tandem. As far as he was concerned Taylor could dial his numbers until her fingers bled. He wasn't going to answer. Now more than ever he was glad he'd stopped using the old-fashioned answering machines and used the voice messaging system provided by the phone company. At least he didn't have to hear her plead with him to just listen to her as she made excuses for her inexcusable act of betrayal. Just the thought of her incensed him.

Here he had finally let his guard down and allowed a female into his life and the one time he had, she turned out to be a Jezebel of the highest order. Sinking further down into the soft comforting sofa Ian gave in to his flashback mental video.

Right after he and the band had torn the roof off the Blue Way nightclub during his personal showcase, Taylor had insisted that she meet the A&R reps alone to gauge their interest in signing him to a recording contract. While he attempted to remain calm in the downstairs dressing room, Ian had called to find out why Trey and Andrea hadn't been seated at the VIP table he'd reserved for them. That's when Andrea informed him of Trey's boss's passing. Truth be told, he felt sorry for the guy, but he couldn't help how slighted he felt by them not showing up for his once-in-a-lifetime shot. *Oh well. I'll get over it*; he decided chastising himself for being selfish.

After what seemed like eternity, one of the barmaids knocked on the door to let him know that Taylor wanted him to come upstairs. As he rounded the bar and stage area, he was shocked to see a familiar looking man sitting with Taylor.

"Ian, allow me to introduce you to D-Jay," she had said more excitedly than he had ever seen her.

"What up?" D-Jay head-nodded.

"Nothing much. Nice to meet you."
"Right," D-Jay stated.

Ian nervously sat down across from one of the biggest moguls in the music game. He admired how confident the man was and how his poise made him appear much older than his actual age. Not to mention the cat's wardrobe. Sean Johns from head to toe, the guy had it going on. "You like the show?"

"Like it?" Taylor responded instead. "Not only did he like it; his offer sent the other guys running out of here so fast they forgot to leave a tip."

Ian could hear his heart pounding inside his narrow chest so hard it made him look down to ensure it was still inside. "Offer…what offer?"

D-Jay shushed Taylor like he'd done it before. "I got this. Look here man. Your age bothers me and how exactly I'm gonna market you has me thinking I might have lost my mind. But brotha your voice is off-the-hook."

Ian took the little put-down in stride and figured he would concentrate on the compliment about his vocals instead. "Thanks. That means a lot coming from you. Especially after all that you've done in the business."

"Right…I was one of the youngest cats to ever own his own label and I sold it for a mint," he said boasted. "But my real skill was that I just straight up recognized talent."

"And he recognized yours."

"Taylor, could you let two men do business without a play-by-play?"

"I'm just saying."

"How 'bout you just don't."

Ian started to get a little heated hearing D-Jay speak to his woman so disrespectfully. In an attempt to lighten the mood he said, "Back to our regularly scheduled offer."

"Go on baby girl. I'll let you do the honors."

"Thank you so much; glad to know I have permission to speak."

"Just tell me, Taylor," Ian said.

"As you may or not know, D-Jay sold his record company a couple of years ago and since that time he's been semi-retired. That is until tonight."

"What happen tonight?"

"He heard you rip the roof off this joint. So he made me an offer we simply can't refuse."

"Which is?"

"Which is my brotha. I'm gonna start a new label and feature you as my number one act."

"I don't mean to sound ungrateful D-Jay, but I was hoping to sign with a major label."

"He is major," Taylor reminded him.

“Not anymore.”

“Ole dude, you trying to call me a has-been?”

“Never. I’m just stating fact. You must start up a label and that takes big cash.”

“Which I have.”

“Yeah but it will be an independent label none –the- less and I’ve been there and done that. Hello, that’s the reason for tonight, so a major label could see me and possibly sign me.”

“Tell him, Taylor.”

“They all passed on you,” she sadly informed Ian. “They all loved your voice and the show but none of them wanted to put big dough behind a forty-year old local dude.”

“They all passed?” He was floored. “Not one of them?” He asked, silently praying that she was only pulling his leg.

“Going out the door, Warner offered a one album deal without any options and no signing bonus.”

“I would have taken that.”

“Don’t be silly, my man,” D-Jay interjected. “That’s a sucker deal. There’s absolutely no marketing on a deal like that. And no marketing is the kiss of death for any artist.”

“Let me think about it,” Ian said. He walked out of the club on the biggest night of his life feeling like his was over.

Early the following morning before the sun had even made an appearance, Taylor was banging his door down. Opening the door, he noticed that she was wearing the same slinky pink dress from the previous night.

“Ian we have to talk.”

"I need some time to think, Taylor."

"I'm so sorry no one stepped up last night but at least D-Jay recognized your potential and is willing to bet the bank on your talent."

"Why you let him talk down to you like that?"

"Huh? Oh that was nothing, we go way back. You know we used to be together."

"Did he treat you like that then?"

"What?"

"You heard me."

"Forget all that for now. Let's talk about the deal."

"There is no deal."
"Don't be a baby."
"Don't talk to me like that."
"Ian, be for real. This is your last chance."
"Perhaps."
"Oh please! I've worked too hard and sacrificed too much to have you blow this for me."

"For you? Have you lost your mind? I'm the talent not you."

"You would still be singing for pennies all over this dirty-behind city if it wasn't for me."

"Oh so now the real you comes out."

"You're being silly. Come on baby this is a great opportunity for both of us."

"One that I need more time to think about."

"Look if you don't make up your mind before his plane leaves today, the offer is off the table."

"Why you still wearing the same dress you had on last night?" Ian asked, switching gears.

"Huh?"

"They do say that's one of the first things to go."

"What?"

"Your hearing."

"What about my hearing?"

"I asked…" Ian slowly spaced out his words, "why are you still wearing the same dress you had on last night?'

"Don't."

"Don't what? Ask my woman why she coming up in my house wearing the same clothes from the last time I saw her with some other dude that she used to be with."

"It's not what you think."

"I think you spent the night with D-Jay."

"Nothing happen." It sounded weak.

"Don't play me for a fool."

"It didn't mean anything."

"It did to me."

"In this game you have to give a little to get a little."

"I don't play games. You can let yourself out."

"Ian."

"Get out!"

"Ian, please."

"I said get out!"

"Allright be like that. Just remember this: we have a contract, so get over yourself because I own your butt. You are so lame, just like your boy Trey."

Getting up in her face he said through a tight jaw, "What about Trey?"

"Nothing."

"Then why you mention him?"

"Okay. I'll tell you. When it came time for him to seal the deal just like you he wasn't man enough to do so."

"What the hell does that mean?"

"Take your hands off me!"

Loosening his grip on her arm while still holding on he asked her again what she meant. "Before you and I got serious he hit on me and when it came time to get down, he caught a case of conscience and couldn't perform."

"You slept with Trey?"

"No, nothing happened. I'm not going to ask you again. Take your hands off me."

He did, once he threw her out of his house.

CHAPTER THIRTY-ONE

They entered the lobby of the impressive architectural structure, the latest fad with every developer trying to surpass The Donald— cloud scrapping and full of glass. A burly security guard called ahead to announce their arrival. The attractive couple loosely held hands as they made their way to the bank of elevators. On the ride up he tried to calm his nerves. "You okay?" she asked.

"I'm good," Trey responded straightening his tie. "Just a little nervous I guess."

"That's understandable. It's kind of weird coming to a will reading of someone who wasn't a family member."

"Yep."

The doors opened up way too fast. Andrea stepped out first with Trey on her heels as they walked up to the receptionist. "I'm Trey Edwards and this is my wife Andrea. We're here to see," he hesitated.

"Mr. Walker," Andrea picked up.

"Ah yes, Mr. Edwards, Mr. Walker is expecting you. Please have a seat and he'll be right with you."

The law firm office exuded wealth and power. From the highly polished oak wood walls to the over- the- top expensive art work that adorned the corridors there was no mistaking that this firm didn't chase ambulance.

Within five minutes an attractive woman approached and asked them to follow her. They walked two steps behind her as she led them down a long glass-polished hardwood floored corridor until they came to a stop in front of a ceiling-touching mahogany door.

"The others are inside the conference room. You may go in."

"Thank you," said Trey.

"You want me to wait out here?" Andrea asked.

"I'd rather have you with me."

She was touched. The gentleness of his voice almost caused her to lose it. Instead she squeezed his hand and motioned for him to open the door.

Four tight-faced people looked up expectedly and each one had a question mark on their forehead as they looked at Trey and then Andrea as they entered the vast conference room.

"Hey man, nice to see you." Dexter's brother extended his hand to Trey. "Really missed you down at the dealership."

"Yeah…umm…sorry 'bout your brother. He was a great guy."

Ryan introduced Trey to his parents. "Mom…Dad this is Trey Edwards, the top sales guy at the Philly location."

"Sir…Ma'am sorry for your loss. This is my wife Andrea," he said swallowing back the cotton in his mouth.

"My fault," said Ryan pointing at a tear-stained faced woman sitting at the end of the long conference table. "This is my ex sister-in-law, Eliza."

"We've met," she spoke softly.

"Yes, please accept my condolences for your loss as well," Trey said.

"Young man," Dexter's father said and hearing Dexter's voice coming from the older man practically floored Trey.

"I know. Pretty eerie isn't it?" quipped Ryan. "Not only do they look alike; they share the same voice."

"Yes sir?"

"Why are you here?"

The one question that everyone else wanted to ask was finally put on the table, "I received a letter from a Mr. Walker requesting my presence and other than that I really don't know, sir."

"Well take a seat son; we're all waiting for the lawyers to get in here."

They didn't have to wait long. Shortly after Trey and Andrea settled into butter-soft leather chairs an attorney straight out of central casting glided through the doors. His eye-blinding smile advertised his dental bill. "Good day folks. Sorry to keep you all waiting. I'm Chad Walker, the late Mr. Fortune's attorney."

"My son's not late, he's dead."

"Dad."

"Hell the man is stating the obvious."

For just a split second the attorney lost his slick but before that could happen he cleared his throat and marched around the room with the proper amount of sympathy on his face as he shook everyone's hand. "It appears that every one is in attendance. So we can begin."

"Before we do," senior Fortune interjected, "May I ask why he was invited?"

The older man's fingertips held fire as Trey stared down the length of the digit being directed at him. "I was kind of wondering the same thing," Trey said.

Mr. Walker sat down at the opposite end of the table from Dexter's ex-wife. "Mr. Edwards is mentioned in the will."

Trey looked down to avert the accusing eyes of Mr. Fortune. "I was? I mean, I am?"

"Yes. All will be explained once this proceeding gets underway."

"What are we waiting for exactly?"

"I'm waiting for my assistant to finalize one matter that must be cleared up."

"Pertaining to?"

"The will."

"What about it?"

"Dad, calm down."

Mr. Walker twirled around in his chair as the same attractive woman who escorted the Edwards earlier came into the room protectively grasping a folder. "Thank you Erin, "he said taking possession. Once the door closed, he turned back to face his audience. He opened the folder and examined the contents before speaking. "Okay, now we can proceed. I will read Mr. Dexter Fortune's last will and testament."

The room became so quiet that if an ant sneezed in the adjoining room it could have been heard. Trey felt Andrea pat his knee while Mr. Fortune cracked his knuckles and his wife remained meekly still and stoic all the while twisting a napkin into knots. Ryan was on the edge of his seat and at the end of the long table Eliza wiped her weeping eyes.

"I must explain that Mr. Dexter Fortune's will was revised two weeks prior to his untimely death," Mr. Walker said. "And that was the reason for the delay for which I do apologize. I needed to make certain that everything was in order and accordance with his wishes."

"What do you mean, revised?" Ryan spoke up before his father had a chance to comment.

"He made a change."

"What kind of change?"

“Mr. Fortune, your son left his Philadelphia location of Fortune Motors to,” he paused. “Mr. Trey Edwards.”

“What the hell you say?” Trey heard Mr. Fortune demand. The rest of the meeting was a blur.

CHAPTER THIRTY-TWO

"What the hell you say?" Jerry blurted out. "You pulling my leg ain't you?"

Inwardly Tony was cracking up watching Jerry lose his mind over hearing the news that his arch nemesis was now his boss— that is— if Trey even allowed him to stick around.

"Nah man, Paula pulled my coat first thing this morning."

"How did she find out?"

"Ryan told her."

"When?"

"All she told me was Trey was the new owner of the dealership and a formal announcement would be made shortly."

"This can't be happening," he muttered storming off.

Tony fully let out the laughter he'd been holding since the start of the conversation with Jerry. "Business is about to pick up."

****

"Mr. Edwards…what are you doing here?"

"This is a place where the lost can come when in need isn't it?"

"Of course," Pastor Douglas said. "I meant that I wasn't expecting you."

"The doors were open. I'm not bothering you am I?"

"Not at all, Mr. Edwards."
"Please call me Trey."

Swallowing hard Pastor Douglas motioned for Trey to take a seat. He walked over to his office door and closed it after poking his head out to ensure that his assistant had gone to lunch. Last thing he wanted was for Sister Allen's partner in gossip to hear anything juicy to report. He figured this day would come where he would have to answer for his deeds. He had hoped it would be much later rather than right now.

Twisting his body around like a dance move, he turned first his head then his shoulders and finally his entire body whipped around and faced Trey. For a tick Pastor Douglas thought about bolting out of the church and hitting I-95 faster than TD Jakes could sweat out a suit during a sermon. That route went only north and south, however, and going back south was definitely out. Stalling for time he offered Trey something to drink or eat. A man feeding his face couldn't hold a sandwich and a gun at the same time. Trey's polite decline flustered him. For a guy coming to inflict some damage he was being awfully calm.

"Can I confide in you Pastor?"

"In me?...Oh yeah, I guess." He stammered not to sure where this was leading. He thought it best to keep standing just in case. He wasn't much of a fighter but if he got in a quick shot and it landed flush then he could… Could what? He was a man of God, a man who made a mistake and just as his Heavenly Father had forgiven him, he would ask this man to forgive him as well. "Yes you can, Trey." Pastor Douglas found his strength. He walked around his desk and sat down. "But first I must ask for your forgiveness."

"Forgiveness? You haven't done anything to me."

"I haven't? I mean I know." Maybe it wasn't the Lord's will for him to confess his sin just yet. "I meant for not following up with you from your last visit."

"Well that's okay. It's not like I'm a regular around here. Not like my wife."

Pastor Douglas fixated his attention on a picture of the old leader of the church that hung on the wall behind Trey. Hearing Trey mention his wife made him nervous all over again. His eyes quickly darted over to two wing-backed chairs with a small round table situated between them. After his last unexpected visitor he had ordered the couch removed and replaced with chairs. Just in case. The image of Andrea's naked body across the couch popped into mind. He shook his head so hard he developed a headache.

"You allright, Pastor?"

"Yes…yes…of course. As you were saying?"

"Question for you."

"I'm listening," he replied hoping that this wasn't the moment of truth.

"Has God ever spoken to you?"

"Every day," he replied relieved.

"In your head or out loud?"

"Depends on how I need to hear from Him."

"How do you know it's the voice of God and not just your mind playing tricks on you?"

"God's voice always calls you forward while any other will keep you either in place or going backward." Now he was on comfortable ground "Has He spoken to you?"

"I think so."

"Go on."

"I really need to get this off of me."

Pastor Douglas remained quiet as he allowed Trey the breathing room to gather his thoughts. Whatever burden weighed Trey down, as a minister of the gospel he was inclined to put Trey's needs in front of his own fear of exposure. The man sitting in front of him hadn't come to do him harm; he came into the

House of the Lord seeking His presence. "Before you do, would you mind if we prayed so that He might join us."

"Who? Oh you mean…duh. Sure."

"Stand up," he said soothingly as he walked around the desk. As Trey stood to his feet Pastor Douglas guided Trey by the elbow and led him into the sanctuary. "I find that when I pray with someone seeking counsel, it's best to do so at the altar. You see, Trey, at the altar is where you can leave your burdens behind and walk away knowing He has taken them over. All problems, no matter the variety, can be solved at the altar. Do you believe that?"

"Pastor, I don't really know what I believe anymore."

"Do you believe in God?"

"Yes."

"Do you believe that He died for our sins?"

"Yes."

"Brother that's all you need. The Word says it's impossible to please Him unless you first believe, and since you do that's half the battle won already."

With his hand on Trey's shoulder they knelt down at the same time. For over forty minutes the two men were side by side sometimes praying silently and at times praying so loud it sounded like there were fifty of them.

Afterward they stood to their feet and Trey pulled the Pastor into a heartfelt embrace. The two men walked back into the office and Trey proceeded to unload all of the heavy weight he'd been carrying on his back for months.

"To make matters worse, my boss dies and blesses me with his most profitable dealership. How can God reward me after all that I've done wrong?"

"We all sin and fall short of the glory of the Lord. All that you've told me shows that you're a good man with an incredible spirit. Yes you did wrong by not telling your wife about the money but in my opinion that raises issues of control more than anything else. And yes you put yourself in harms way with that woman but brother don't negate the fact that you didn't have sex with her. That took you being more of a man than some others I've known." *Like me for one.* For an instant he almost confessed his own sins. Instead he continued to counsel Trey, while inwardly feeling overwhelmingly hypocritical.

"So I guess it's true that confession is good for the soul," said Trey.

"Indeed it is." His heart demanded he tell Trey what happened between him and his wife but self-preservation took over and he kept his mouth shut. Confession may be good for the soul but staying alive was good for life.

****

"Girl I've got to tell him."

"Andrea that would be the dumbest thing you've ever done."

"The guilt is killing me."

"Look you made a mistake. Learn from it, don't do it again and move on. Take it to the grave."

"Tina, that's not good advice."

"It's the best I got," said Tina reaching for another hot wing. "Girl these wings are the bomb."

****

The dealership was abuzz with the news. Everyone from the service department to the sales staff was talking about it. So much for Paula keeping it to herself.

Ryan sat at Dexter's desk contemplating his next move. His father had almost had his own heart attack during the reading of the will. As expected Dexter had left a nice chunk of change to his ex-wife, enough money for his parents to live out the rest of their lives comfortably as well as a sizable donation to his church. Just as he figured his brother had left him his business interest, but what no one expected him to do was leave the Philadelphia dealership to Trey Edwards. Never in any conversation had he given even the slightest impression that that was something he would do or had even thought about doing. As far as Ryan knew Trey was merely his protégé. Sure the guy could sell cars like nobody's business, but that didn't warrant leaving him the place. And to make that change in his will a couple of weeks before he dropped dead in his driveway made no sense. Did his big brother have an imtimation of his impeding death? Was this his way of showing that all that religious mumbo-jumbo was for real and not a fad as Ryan thought it was? Whatever it might be, no way was he willing to give up what should rightfully be his without a fight. *Hell I'm his brother, not no darn Trey Edwards.* As soon as he completed the thought he remembered his mother's words. "Son we might not like what Dexter has done, but as his family we need to respect his wishes. If he wanted the boy to have the dealership I'm sure he had his reasons."

Contemplation time over, he tapped the intercom. "Paula would you please ask Jerry to come into my…the office." From his previous discussions with Jerry, Ryan knew that he despised Trey, so he had no doubt that once he informed him of the ownership change, Trey's first order of business would be to find a new sales manager.

"Hey Jerry, take a seat. I assume you've heard the news," he said once Jerry walked into the office.

CHAPTER THIRTY-THREE

For the first time in a long while the family sat around the kitchen table ravaging the dinner Andrea prepared. She had fixed Trey's favorite meal, fried pork chops with garlic mashed potatoes, brown gravy and string beans. She threw in some cotton-soft cornbread to appease Brittany.

"Mommy this corn bread is soooo good," Brittany exclaimed chomping down on her third piece.

"I'm glad you like it, baby," Andrea said. She looked over at her silent husband. Normally he would've gone through three or four pork chops by now instead of barely touching his first one. "Everything okay with the meal, Trey?"

"Huh? Oh yeah, it's all good."

"Hey Dad, Mom put her foot in these chops didn't she?" Brett asked between bites.

"Yeah, she did."

"Daddy how long has this been your favorite meal?"

"Since I was younger than you, baby girl."

"This is my favorite meal too."

"Copy cat."

"Stop teasing your little sister," ordered Andrea. "And you put that tongue back in your mouth little girl."

"He started it."

"Did not."

"Did too."

"And now I'm finishing it. If you're finished take your plates over to the sink."

"Mom what's for dessert?"

"Later, let your dinner settle first."
"Okay," Brittany pouted, but she did as she was told. "Brett can you help me with my homework?"

"What is it?"

"Spelling words."

"Only if you take my plate to the sink."

"Boy, just help your sister." The sharpness in Trey's tone startled all three of them.

"I am Daddy. I was just kidding."

"Are you okay?" Andrea said once the kids had left the kitchen.

"Yeah, why?"

"Well you haven't really touched your food and you just seem I don't know, out of it."

"Tired I guess."

"That's understandable especially with everything that has been going on."

"I went to see the Pastor the other day?"

Andrea's expression of utter fear was lost on Trey since he didn't look up from his plate. She willed herself to keep it together as she stealthy moved the knife away from Trey's plate. The desire to crawl under the table and start digging a hole to China or beyond overwhelmed her senses. Fearing the worst she looked directly at Trey. He had sat back in the chair and his eyes revealed nothing. Going out on a limb she asked, "What Pastor?"

"Yours. I mean, ours. The new one who took over from one that married us."

"Okay."

"You probably won't believe this but that was the second time I'd spoken with him."

"It was?" She forced the words from her closed throat. "About what?"

"I had a lot on my mind and I don't know, for some reason I thought…I don't know."

Turmoil and despair was written all over her husband's face. His body sagged down in the chair and for the first time she noticed the dark circles that had formed under his sad eyes. Here he sat the brand-new owner of one of the largest automobile dealerships in the tri-state area and he looked like his world had fallen down on top of him. So how could she tell him how she'd betrayed him? It would be better hearing it from her than the man who stripped her of her dignity. "Trey…I'm so sorry..."

"Thanks. I can always count on you to be there for me. That's why this is so hard for me."

"I'm sorry Trey. It shouldn't happen."

"I know."

"Oh my God…please forgive me."

"Forgive you? Oh baby there wasn't anything you could have done."

"It was all my fault."

The puzzled look on Trey's face stopped Andrea from saying another word. *Oh my God he doesn't know!* She struggled with her conscience for a moment. Silently she prayed for strength.

"What's your fault?"

"Nothing."
"Are you okay?"

"I'm just worried about you."

"I'll be fine. I think I'll turn in early and get ready for tomorrow."

"So you're going into the dealership?"

"Yes," he answered standing up. "Drea…why do you think he left me the dealership?"

"A blessing from above."

"I need a little more time, but there's something I really need to talk to you about."

"Whenever you're ready."

"I love you Andrea."

Without any announcement the tears showed up and threatened to drown her eyeballs. "I love you too, Trey." She moved into his embrace as he lifted her up from the chair and wrapped his strong arms around her. Andrea held on as tight as she could.

"Let's do something we haven't done in a long time."
Nausea hit the pit of her stomach just thinking that she would have to fake it while making love to her husband. "Okay," she said hoping her voice didn't betray her true feelings.

Trey took her hand in his and led her from the kitchen into the living room. As she was preparing to go upstairs, he released her hand and walked over to the flat-screen CD player that sat on top of the mantle piece. She warily watched him sort through some disks before settling on one. Suddenly the room was filled with the velvet smooth vocals of Smokey Robinson singing about a quiet storm.

"May I have this dance, Mrs. Edwards?" He extended his hand toward her.

Andrea couldn't help but smile as she reflected on the sweet memory of Trey and Brittany dancing to this song every morning before she went off to school her first year.

"This is your and Brittany's song."

"She won't mind." Then he asked, "Do you want my arm to fall off?"

"Stealing from Billy Dee, huh?"

"Whatever works."

Husband and wife gazed into each others eyes, each one praying that the other couldn't see the hidden shame. Andrea took his offered hand and moved in close. She placed her head against his firm chest as they moved in sync with the music. Their bodies melted together as one.

Brett and Brittany quietly watched their parents dance from the middle of the staircase.

"See? I told you everything would be okay," Brett whispered.

As the music switched to another song, Trey and Andrea continued dancing, the kids continued watching and for that moment in time husband and wife reconnected in mind, body and spirit.

Outside the wind picked up and made sounds that sounded like wolves howling. Then the rain poured from the clouds. A loud clapping noise and bright sharp flashes of light lit up the night. After a roaring thunder clap, Brittany screamed and shot down the steps. Brett followed just as the power in the house went out.

"Rain check?" Trey asked in Andrea's ear.

"You betcha," she responded.

Trey scooped Brittany up in his arms and patted Brett on top of his head. "How 'bout that dessert?"

"In the dark?" Brittany whined.

"By candlelight," Andrea said.

After dishing up a big heaping of rocky road ice cream for everyone the family gathered in the middle of the living room floor and ate their dessert by the glow of the scented candles Andrea had lit.

Outside the house the storm raged so violently that both kids begged their parents to allow them to sleep with them. Even though Trey didn't care too much for waking up with Brett's feet in his face and Brittany's knees in his groin he gave in to their collective assault. The kids fell asleep lying between their parents on their king-size bed. Neither of them could recall the last time it had rained so hard and ferociously. They softly whispered back and forth although they could have started a band and the kids wouldn't have budged.

"Drea…we need to talk."

"Now?"

"Tomorrow. I have to tell you something."

"Me too."

"Goodnight."

"Night."

Andrea rolled over on her side. She wondered what Trey needed to tell her and if he already knew what she had to tell him.

Trey stared at the ceiling and wondered what Andrea wanted to talk about and if she already knew what he had to tell her.

****

At two o'clock in the wee hours of the morning the phone on Trey's side of the bed startled him awake. Moving Brett's limp body off of him he fumbled for the offensive interrupter of his dream where he had just told Andrea everything and she had forgiven him. And just when they were about to embrace, the piercing shrill of the phone on his night stand jolted him awake. "Hello," he grumbled his voice full of sleep-bass.

"Come outside," the familiar voice on the phone said.
"Ian, is this you?"

"Yeah, come outside."

Trey looked at the time on the alarm clock. "Man, do you know what time it is? Is everything okay?"

"Come outside. I'm sitting in my car." Click.

Placing the receiver back in its holder Trey gently pushed back the covers and swung his legs over the side of the bed. Looking over his shoulder he wasn't surprised that neither Andrea nor the kids had moved a muscle. He stepped into his slippers and pulled his bathrobe from the hook on the back of the door.

"Who was on the phone?"

"Sorry it woke you. It's Ian. He's outside."

"At this time of night? Is everything okay?"

"Who knows? It's Ian. Go back to sleep."
Trey sluggishly walked down the steps. He was happy the power outage had been short-lived. Punching in the four-digit security code he waited for the deactivation button to light up. Once it did he opened the front door and stepped outside.

Ian barely acknowledged his presence as he opened the car door and sank into the tan leather interior of the Cadillac Seville that Trey had put him in three years ago.

“What up?” Trey asked, reaching out his hand. Instead of shaking it Ian ignored the gesture. Swiveling around in the passenger seat he studied his best friend’s solemn- looking face. “Ian, are you allright?”

“Why you do it?”

“Do what?” He already knew the answer. Finally one of his darkest secrets had been exposed to the light. “She told you?”

“Yep.”

“Man, I messed up and it was before you got with her.”

“What about your marriage?”

“I’m going to have to tell Andrea.”
“Don’t do that.”

“Huh? I have to.”

“Tell her what? That you almost slept with another woman.”

“I punked out at the last second. But damn man. I wanted to hit it bad.”

“I wish you had told me.”

“You mad at me?”

“I was…but man we go back too far to have a chick come between us.” And just like that the matter was cast into the sea of forgetfulness.

They finally shook hands. Ian turned around to face Trey. “I couldn’t sleep.”

“I wasn’t having that problem.”

“I owe you one.”

"It's all good. Talk to me."

"Sorry about Dexter. But from what Andrea told me, you made out."

"Thanks. After everything I've done, I get blessed like that— man it blows me away."

"Stop beating yourself up. Everybody makes mistakes."

"I won't be okay until I get this junk off my chest."

"You think everything needs to come off?"

"Yeah, it's tearing me apart."

"I got your back."

"Sorry I missed your show," Trey said sincerely. "So am I best friends with a new recording artist?"

"Not quite."

"What happened?"

"Taylor's old boyfriend came to the show and made me an offer." He bought Trey up to date on D-Jay's offer and Taylors demand that he accept it or she would ruin his chances of signing with anyone else. "Hell man, I'm forty years old, still chasing the dream. This could very well be my last chance."

"She threatened you?"

"Said she owns me."

"Does she?"

"According to the lawyer she does, for the next seven years."

"Dang…what you gonna do?"

"I really wanted to sign with a major label. Being realistic I guess I don't have a choice but to sign with D-Jay."

"Maybe it won't be all bad."

"I have my suspicions that the guy couldn't care less about me; what he's really after is her."

"You in love with her?"

"Not really. You know me and women."

"I must admit I was a little surprised you had hooked up but she is fine as hell."

"And deadly as a snake."

"Thank God all I did was rub the apple."

"Yeah but rubbing cost you something," Ian said.

"What you mean?" Trey inquired. "You talking about Andrea?"

"That and did you give her a big break on the car she brought?"

"Yeah, I cut the price so low I only made a hundred bucks on the deal."

Ian laughed and shook his head. "I guess we both got screwed."

The sun came up on the two old friends chatting away in the car helping each other with their separate issues. Trey was able to help Ian see the possibilities of signing with D-Jay's new label and Ian convinced Trey to think it through before confessing. As far as Ian was concerned since it hadn't actually happened there was no reason to ruin his marriage over nothing. "Tell her about the money and forging her signature, take the whupping for that, and move on."

"True dat." They touched their fists together and Trey stepped out of the car. "Give me a holler later today."

Ian drove off leaving Trey standing on the sidewalk in his bathrobe and slippers.

CHAPTER THIRTY-FOUR

Lincoln Drive was crowded with cars driven by barely awake coffee drinkers and make-up applicators controlling their steering wheels with one hand or one knee as they held onto hot cardboard cups or eye- lash curlers. Trey was right in the middle of the pack maneuvering his Benz by mental reflex as his mind played three to four different versions of what he had to look forward to once he arrived at the dealership. His initial intention was to show up before everyone else to have the upper hand, but since he didn't have a key to open the front door that thought went out the sunroof.

So he settled on Ian's suggestion. Simply come in his regular time acting like it was just another day at the salt mines. Only this time he wasn't just the leading miner; he actually owned the salt, the mines and all the equipment.

As he kissed Andrea and the kids good-bye this morning he couldn't help but think that although his life and theirs were about to change, it might not be for the best. Door number one may have contained the grand prize, but when he opened door number two later this evening the booby prize surely awaited him. Trey had decided that despite Ian's sound advice about keeping his trap shut, he was going to confess everything to Andrea. He prayed that fourteen years of marriage, two kids and all that they had gone through stood for something. Infidelity had destroyed Andrea's parents' marriage and it was a wound that hadn't healed inside of her to this day. So telling her he had almost given into temptation scared him far more than his other crimes against the sanctity of their martial vows. He couldn't begin to explain to her why Taylor had gotten to him the way that she had. It wasn't simply her Halle Berry looks or Jennifer Lopez bottom, though that didn't help the cause. There was something else about her. Even Ian had fallen under her spell. Trey prided himself on always being in control. So many fine women came into the dealership on a daily bases and let it be known by words and actions that they found him attractive. He never gave in. Sure he flirted, but that was all in fun or to get the business. It was part of the game. But actually going for a test drive and winding up in a hotel room. Never. It wouldn't be so bad if that was all that happened.

His replayed him and Taylor banging into the hotel room kissing and tearing at each other's clothes. He had stripped her down to her undergarment and thrown her across the bed. For the life of him he couldn't understand why he'd stopped. All he knew was that something gripped his heart in a vise-like grip and his hard-on deflated as if Taylor transformed from the most beautiful woman he'd ever been with to the least desirable person on the planet. And he got out of there fast enough to make Carl Lewis look slow.

To makes matter worse, Dexter's untimely demise and subsequence gift from the grave only served to intensify his already guilt-ridden brain. Why would God see fit to pull his bacon out of the frying pan? Why did a man have to die for that to happen? Didn't everybody preach that sin had a cost? What payment would he be called on to make? Is this the beginning of an unfunny joke, one where he would see his vision come to past only to see his dream-family blown to smithereens? That question plagued his mind as he pulled into the parking lot of Fortune Motors.

Trey stepped out of his car with a hint of hesitation. Looking around the area where the employees parked he smiled at Tony's BMW still occupying the coveted top producers spot. With the events of the past few weeks weighing heavily, competing with Tony was the last item on his agenda. He winced as he spotted Jerry's apple- red Corvette. Having to deal with Jerry thrilled him as much as getting root canal. An unfamiliar Rolls Royce sat parked in Dexter's old space. *That's probably Dex's brother's car*, he assumed. Merely thinking about Dexter set pangs of sorrow through his system.

The cold December breeze left no doubt that winter had arrived with a vengeance. The usually incorrect weatherman had predicted that Philadelphia would experience its first snowstorm before Christmas. Trey made a mental note to remind Paula to contact the guy who plowed the dealership's parking area every winter so he would be prepared. Inwardly Trey gave himself props for thinking like an owner already. With his emotions in an uproar he slid his arms into his cashmere overcoat, straightened his perfectly knotted tie and grabbed his briefcase from the back seat.

The neon sign commanded his attention. One of the bulbs had blown out leaving the sign to advertise, "For une Motors." Blown bulbs were one of Dexter's pet peeves; if he were still alive and saw the sign he would've blown a gasket. Another note went into the mental log.

The early morning time at the dealership prior to any customers or tire-kickers storming the lot was Trey's favorite time of the work day. He loved arriving in the morning and going into his office to review his "to do list" before getting started. By habit he would look at his desk calendar to track his progress in achieving his written sales goals for the month. There wasn't a need to do that today. Having been out of work for the past two weeks he knew that he was way behind Tony and probably every other salesperson on staff. Nothing wrong with that, he reckoned. The boss didn't have to be the number one sales guy anyway.

Trey took a moment to survey his newly won kingdom. Over the weekend, as usual, every car on the lot had been washed so they were gleaming brightly under the early morning sun. Knowing the inventory better than anyone, (except Dexter) he knew simply from looking around the front potion of the lot that the new shipment of automobiles hadn't arrived. As a rule Dexter insisted the count never fall below one hundred cars on display and Trey fully intended to use every lesson he'd learned to maintain and even surpass the success that Dexter had enjoyed. *God rest his soul!*

****

One of the guys from the service department spotted Trey as he rounded the corner of the building and ran into the dealership to alert everyone. "He's here," he shouted.

"Okay everybody, take your places," Paula ordered. "Tony, make certain the CD is set."

"I got it," Tony fired back.

****

Jerry angrily shuffled the papers on his desk. He refused to participate in their foolish butt-kissing ritual. He figured that his last day at the dealership was certain— the day Ryan called him into the office. What a difference a day made. One day he was on the fast track to becoming the general manager and the next he was on the chopping block. After all the animosity between him and Trey, there didn't stand a snowball's chance in a flame of Trey keeping him, let alone him keeping his position as sales manager. Jerry picked up the box beside his desk and starting packing up his belongings.

****

"Welcome back!" they screamed in unison as Trey walked through the double glass doors. Paula was the first to reach him and wrapped her arms around his neck before he knew what was happening. He gladly accepted her hug as he returned one just as tight.

"Congratulations. Although the circumstances suck, this is still a great thing," she exclaimed.

"Thanks," he responded uncomfortably. "What's going on?"

"I got this one." he heard Tony shout. "On behalf of all of us…the sales guys and everyone from the service department, admin and oh hell…everybody, we welcome you back and say that we look forward to working for you." Tony approached Trey and he also grabbed him up in a huge bear hug. "Sorry about Dexter, man. But you know what they say; the Lord works in mysterious ways."

"Thanks, man," Trey said.

Paula had arranged streamers all over the showroom and a large banner hung from the rafters. It read, "From Good to Great under the new management of Trey Edwards."

It took twenty minutes for everyone gathered to come up to Trey and either shake his hand or give him a hug as they paraded past him extending their condolences and congratulations. Trey fought back the tears and thanked everyone for their kindness.

"Speech, speech," Tony hollered, throwing back one of the doughnuts Paula had placed out as refreshments.

Trey walked over to stand beside Tony on wobbly legs. Someone had placed a podium and a wireless microphone in the center of the showroom. Clearing his throat he handed Tony his overcoat and briefcase. Looking at the expectant faces of his inherited employees filled him with more pride than he had felt since the birth of his children.

"Thank you all for your support and for maintaining everything in my absence." He stopped short.

"Take your time, man," whispered Tony.

"The loss of Dexter Fortune will be felt by all of us for many years to come. To be honest with you I don't know why he left me the dealership."

"You deserve it," Tony said.

"But I don't take his trust in me lightly. I'm sure all of you might be wondering what the future holds for this location. I can only say to you that we are still going to do business the way that Dexter Fortune did…the right way."

Everyone broke out in applause. He waited for them to stop and in the interim he gathered his thoughts. "Since this is new for me I ask that you be patient and allow me time to get my feet firmly under me. But I assure you that no one is going to lose their jobs and any arrangements that were in place before Dexter passed I will honor."

"Oh yeah," Jerry said out of nowhere. "And what about me? I'm not losing my job?"

"We'll talk later Jerry," Trey said, with a poker face. "Okay, I see Paula put out a nice spread, so eat up and let's go do what we do better than anybody else."

On cue they all shouted loudly, "Outperform the competition."

"You setting up shop in Dexter's office?" Paula asked as she took his coat and briefcase from Tony.

"Nah, I'm going to my office," he answered. "Where's his brother?"

"In Dexter's office."

"Jerry," Trey called out. "May I see you for a moment?"

"Yes sir, big man. I'm on your heels."

Trey stared coldly at Jerry not bothering to hide his disgust. "Can that junk. Walk with me," he said leaving no doubt he meant it.

People tried to pretend they weren't staring at Trey and Jerry. Some of them had created a betting pool on how long it would take for Trey to can Jerry. If he got fired today before noon, Tony stood to win the whole seven- hundred dollar pot.

"That was so unprofessional of you," Trey said through clenched teeth when Jerry came up to him.

"Come on. Who we kidding? We both know I'm out of here."

"You quitting?"

"Like you gonna keep me as your…" he said the word "your" like it caused him pain, "sales manager."

"I haven't made any decisions about anything yet. Maybe you kind of noticed I just got here." Then just for spite he added, "Could you grab me an orange juice and meet me in Dexter's office? Appreciate it." He half expected Jerry to curse him. Instead the man looked baffled and walked away. Then he got an even bigger surprise. Jerry actually grabbed two bottles of orange juice and some napkins.

"Here you go boss…I mean Trey." No sense messing up a good severance package.

"Thanks. Let's go see Ryan."

"I want to warn you, he's not too pleased with this turn of events."

"Would you be?"

"You got a point there," Jerry said shrugging his shoulders.

****

"Look Dad," said Ryan into the receiver, "it's like the lawyer said. Whether we like it or not, Dexter's will is binding and all we would be doing is wasting our time and money to fight it." Ryan shook his head as he listened to his father rant and rave over the phone line. It had taken him a while to come to grips with Dexter leaving a piece of his business to an outsider. Then he realized the one truth that he hadn't wanted to face. He couldn't care less about the auto industry. His life was in the "ATL" and doing his thing and not having to live under the enormous shadow of his big brother's many accomplishments. All he really wanted to do was sell the other two dealerships, take the money and hightail it back down 95 in time to catch the Lakers come take it to the Hawks as he chilled with the fellows in his front- row season- ticket seats. They didn't call Atlanta "Hot Lanta" for nothing. Ryan got off on owning his own business. He also appreciated the bevy of beautiful women who out-numbered the men somewhere in the neighborhood of four-one. So if Dexter wanted Trey to become his successor, so be it. For all he cared if Trey had the financial means to do so he could get first right of refusal on the other two lots. His mind was made up; his father would simply have to get over it. His big brother would get his last request partially honored. Trey would get the Philly dealership and whoever came with the best offer would get the other two.

Tilting his head skyward Ryan said, "Big Bro…I know you wanted me to take over for you, but I hope you understand…I have to live my life my way and blaze my own trail. I promise you I won't do a garage sale on your business. I'll do right by you."

****

Trey felt awkward knocking on the office door. He turned the knob and walked in the room that for the past five year always gave him a thrill. This time the thrill was replaced by emptiness. Ryan sat behind Dexter's desk and to Trey's astonishment he didn't fit the bill, and that made him wonder if he even could.

"Trey. Good to see ya, man," said Ryan rising up from the high-backed leather chair and coming around the desk to greet him.

"How's it going, Ryan?" said Trey. "Again, my condolences."

"Thanks and I guess the same to you. Over the past few years you and my brother got pretty close."

"Closer than I knew, from what has happened."

Jerry cleared his throat to announce his presence. They both turned to face him, which made him shuffle his feet like a scolded child.

"Sit guys, sit," Ryan said walking back around the desk. With his hands on the arms of the chair and his butt in mid-air he stopped before sitting fully. "I almost forgot, Trey. This is your seat."

"Nah…nah you go head." Trey wasn't ready to take the throne just yet.

"Well," he hesitated, "the lawyer will be here today at." Ryan stole a glance at his gold Rolex… "at noon to finalize everything."

All of this was too much for Trey to really handle at once. Overwhelming emotions erupted inside of him. He didn't know whether to be ecstatic or scared stiff. Yes he was now the owner of an automobile dealership, but in less than two days he still stood to lose one-hundred thousand dollars of his and Andrea's retirement money. Whoa…hold the door. What was he thinking? He didn't have to lose anything. Given the fact that he had inherited this dealership there stood a greater chance that the bank would give him the loan and he would own two dealerships. Suddenly all his problems were solved. Talk about when one door closes…

"What you think about that, Trey?"

"Huh? Oh yeah."

"You didn't hear a word I said did you?"

"Sorry, man. My mind drifted for a moment," he apologized.

"Kind of overwhelming, huh?" asked Ryan.

"To say the least." Trey faced Jerry. "Ryan could you give me and Jerry a moment please?"

"No problem."

Trey waited until the door closed behind Ryan before speaking. "Are you going to cause me a problem?"

"What do you mean?"

"I mean that if I keep you in place, are you going to try and undermine my efforts."

Not expecting to hear those words Jerry was caught totally off-guard. He had his farewell to the troops speech already rehearsed to go along with his to-hell-with-you words for Trey.

"Look, before Dexter died I was working on opening up my own car lot," Trey explained, leaving out the small details. "So I definitely wasn't expecting him to leave me this dealership. But since he saw fit to do so I'm going to need to keep things running smoothly. Though you and I never got along that well, I do respect the job you've done as the sales manager."

"You for real?"

"Yeah, you just kept power-tripping on me."

"I thought you didn't respect me."

"Maybe sometimes I didn't, but if you can put that behind us, I would like for you to stay on."

"Hell yeah."

"Cool." He patted Jerry on the shoulder. "Grab Ryan for me and go do what you do."
"Hey…Trey…thanks."

"It's all good."

Trey waited until Jerry had exited the office then he slowly approached the desk and ran his fingers across its top. Then the newly crowned auto king took his throne.

****

"The greatest feat I've ever accomplished is making people believe that I don't exist. They go about their daily lives truly thinking that they are in control. Little do they know that the battle for their souls has been waged since long before they came into existence. I'm really no different than the one they call "The Almighty." I simply deal with the nature of man while HE wastes time trying to deal with their hearts. Give any man power and it will corrupt them absolutely. Let a man think that he has gotten away with an offence and he will do it again thinking that he is immune to its consequences. Consequences, now that's where I do my best work. Let's see how much faith this couple truly has when they have to deal with the consequences of their actions. HIS people curse him in more ways than just by their tongues. When the going gets rough, they turn away and some never go back to HIM. True with some it takes more than a little rain; sometimes I must send the thunder."

CHAPTER THIRTY-FIVE

"Good morning, Andrea."

"Oh hi Kathy," Andrea replied looking up from her cluttered desk.

"I haven't seen you in church lately."

"Huh?"

"Your church. I've visited the past two Sundays and you haven't been there."

Andrea busied her hands with moving paper around on her desk. Ever since her promotion her work load had practically doubled; and she couldn't remember the last time she and Kathy had gone to lunch or indulged in their favorite pastime, shoe shopping. She felt the hot eye of accusation coming from Kathy as she made herself comfortable in one of the chairs situated in front of her desk. Thinking fast she told her that the family had been visiting other churches the past couple of weeks.

"You looking for a new home church?"

"Not really, just a change of pace." She struggled to maintain her composure.

"I tell you that pastor you got can preach his you- know- what off," said Kathy not picking up on Andrea's discomfort.

"Ah…ah."

"You missed a good sermon this past Sunday." She rambled on about how Pastor Douglas was on fire for the Lord and how his inspired words made her run to the altar during altar call. "I'm telling you if there was a devil in the house he got up out of there. That man brought the fire."

"That's good."

"You okay? You seem a little distracted?"

"Just busy as all get down."

"Well you know what they say busy means."

"What?"

"Being under Satan's yoke," explained Kathy. "Well let me get out of here so you can get back at it. Oh by the way the partners are very pleased with your performance. Keep up the good work; you're making me look good."

Andrea gave her a tight smile and lowered her head, hoping that she got the message that she was politely attempting to convey: get out of my office.

Kathy did her patented model-walk to the door and on her way out said, "It takes courage to have faith and maintain faith in the face of adversity."

"Say what?" Andrea looked up.

"That's what he preached about, having and maintaining faith."

"And?"

"So you be encouraged to keep the faith." She left Andrea alone.

Where had that come from, Andrea wondered? Maybe it was nothing, it wasn't like she and Kathy hadn't spoken about their spiritual lives many times in the past. Did it show on her that her faith was severely shaken? What did faith have to do with what she had allowed to happen? Then again, had she allowed it? Tina spoke of date rape with so much conviction that Andrea wanted to believe that's exactly what happened. If that was the case then she wasn't to blame for what transpired between her and Pastor Douglas. But still she had given the man signals that she was interested in him. Sneaking around talking on the phone late at night and early in the morning behind Trey's back surely didn't exonerate her completely. And although she loathed herself for admitting it, their attraction for one another was mutual. However the mere thought of being taken on a couch inside a church made her sick to her stomach and the image crossed her mind more often than she cared to remember.

Never in her life had she done anything so vile and disgusting. To commit adultery was one thing, but to do so with a Shepard of the Lord… *Oh my God I'm going straight to hell.* Why in the world had this man, of all the men she'd encountered, gotten to her so much? Were things that bad in her marriage where she needed to seek outside stimulation? It's not like Trey wasn't very attentive to her sexual needs— well his needs. The words of her grandmother's favorite scripture played in her subconscious: "If ye shall ask any thing in my name, I will do it." Her grandmother used to tell her that all the time. She taught Andrea that the devil was always looking for an invite and if you didn't stay mindful of temptation and keep your spiritual eyes open, he would find a way in and set up shop before you knew it.

"Father God, I have not been able to come to you in prayer and ask for your forgiveness," she found herself saying out loud. "But today Oh Lord I pray that you forgive me for my sins of omission and commission as well as my sin of adultery. I know that I degraded your house with my actions and I'll probably never forgive myself for that, but God I don't want to lose my husband over this, so if you see fit to forgive me and it says in your word that you will, please oh please place forgiveness in Trey's heart. Amen."

When she opened her eyes she was startled to find Kathy standing over her desk. "You know Sister Allen from the church?"
"Of course."

"We got to talking after church and she let it slip— I think on purpose— that you haven't been coming lately because you and the pastor had some kind of a falling out."

Straightening her back Andrea's eyes became narrow slits as she hissed, "I think that you and that nosy old lady need to find better things to talk about. Now if you will excuse me I have work to do."

"I'm here if you need to talk."

"Whatever. If I do I know where to find you."

The walls of deception were closing in on her. It panicked her to hear from Trey that he and the Pastor had spoken. And now Sister Allen was running off at the mouth. If the Man above was still taking her request then tonight would be the night of reckoning because she had no other choice than to come clean to Trey before he found out from somewhere or someone else and pray that he would find it in his heart to forgive her. *Lord hear my plea!*

Little did Andrea know that while tonight might not be the night, the reckoning was forthcoming and like a twin-bladed sword she and Trey would both draw blood.

****

Ryan popped the cork off a bottle of sparkling grape juice. "This will have to do I don't drink the hard stuff."

"Neither do I."

"So Dexter converted you too?"

Trey shook his head and accepted the overflowing glass from Ryan. "Not exactly, I just never acquired the taste."

"Good for you, wish I could say the same. One of these days we'll have to get together and I'll share my story."

"Anytime," Trey said, already aware of his past alcohol problems.

They touched glasses and just as Trey was about to take a sip Ryan halted him by saying, "I want to say a few words as a toast."

"For whatever reason my brother saw fit to entrust you with this location. And at first I must admit it pissed me off." He noticed Trey squirm. "Nah don't get me wrong, it had more to do with my hurt feelings than anything else. Then I gave it a lot of thought and my Moms kept saying that since it was Dexter's desire and his right to leave whatever he had to who ever he chose, there wasn't any better way to honor his memory than to respect his wishes. And you know how Moms normally are. She was right. Besides it's not like he didn't look out for us."

Trey attempted to interject some humor to cover up his discomfort. “This is a long toast.”

“I know. I’m getting there,” Ryan promised. “To be totally honest with you I’m relieved.”

“With what?”

“That he left you the dealership. You see when I left Philly and stopped working here; it caused a riff between me and Dexter.”

“I didn’t know that.”

“Yeah, he felt like I was abandoning him. But then you came along and starting selling cars like nobody’s business and he thought that you were more than capable of taking my place. Shoot you broke every record I set in your first year on the floor. He did want you to become the sales manager though.”

“I just wanted to sell and not have the responsibility of the job.”

“That’s understandable. Well now my man, you have an even greater responsibility. Now you are the new owner of this dealership. As I raise my glass to you allow me to congratulate you on that. I wish you the very best and may God continue to bless you in all your endeavors. Cheers.”

“Cheers,” said Trey as he sipped the lukewarm liquid. “I give you and your family my word that I’ll run this business with the same high degree of honesty and integrity that Dexter did.”

“I have no doubt. Why are we standing?”

Trey started to take his usual spot, the chair on the left in front of the huge hand-made desk until he looked over and saw Ryan shrugging his shoulders. “Get used to the chair. It’s yours.”

Reluctantly Trey did just that. He didn’t mind deferring to Ryan, but he did have a point the chair, the desk and the office he’d admired for the past five years belonged to him lock, stock and barrel. Gingerly he picked up the signed papers and took a moment to reflect on their meaning.

During the official signing over of the dealership, the lawyer had informed Trey that he was receiving Fortune Motors totally debt-free. Dexter had paid off the land three years ago and the facilities were also owned out-right. Unbeknownst to anyone beforehand there was a small strip mall located next to the dealership that sat on land attached to it that was also part of the ownership package. So not only would Trey derive income from the car lot alone, there were seven businesses that leased space in the mall which provided monthly rental income as well. For whatever reason, he'd hit the jackpot and didn't even have to buy a ticket. It was like opening up your e-mail and learning you'd won a fake lottery you'd never entered. But, this time it was real, not a scam that played on greed and a lack of common sense. Overnight, Trey Edwards had gone from scared out of his mind to wealthy and successful business owner— at least on paper. And all it took was a death. His feelings of elation quickly dissipated. Getting comfortable with all that he'd inherited was going to take time. Every time he got excited, his past transgressions and Dexter's death would take away his TGF (temporary good feeling). Was it asking too much for the bank to call and give him the loan? If that happened maybe he wouldn't feel so… guilty, selfish, sneaky, and slimy. Darn the list kept growing.

Ryan interrupted his free-fall on the emotional elevator ride. "I wanted to throw something by you."

"What's that?"

"As you know I got my own thing happening down in Atlanta."
"Yeah, Dex said you were doing big things down there in real estate."

"Business is good and the other perks are… well you know."

He did. Atlanta was known for more than just peaches. "I hear that. It must be a single man's playpen."

"Don't get it twisted; married guys too. Anyway what I wanted to throw at you was an opportunity."

"Go on," he said going back up on the ride.

"I'm going to sell the other two locations and I wanted to give you first shot at refusal."

"Say what?" Trey stammered not wanting to believe that he would actually commit such a crime against Dexter's last wishes. "Why would you do that? Your brother built his empire from scratch, man."

"That's just it, Trey. This is Dexter's world, not mine. I can live my life being his little brother and become a second-rate Dexter Fortune or I can do my own thing and be a first-rate Ryan Fortune."

"Dang man, you hit a brotha in the gut with that one."
"But you understand don't you?"

The pleas in his voice made Trey want to understand even if he didn't. "I guess so."

"So if you got the dough or can get financing you can have all three locations."

"Your father know about your plans?"

"Nope not yet."

"Man, he darn near burst a vein in his neck at the attorney's office when he heard Dexter's will. Now you about to hit him with selling. I hope you too big to get spanked."

Ryan's laugh was a mix of giggling and snorting. "You ain't said nothing but a word, good brotha. My Dad is crazy enough to pull off his belt, but Moms would stop him like she would when we were kids. I have to do this, Trey. When I left the business I left for two reasons."

"I'm listening," Trey said still trying to wrap his head around Ryan selling out and the possibility of him owning four locations. His eyes were bigger than his stomach but he knew that dreaming didn't cost anyone a thing.
"Selling cars was a means to an end for me. I did it for the money and at the time I was content to be in Dexter's shadow. My folks didn't expect big things from me like they did Dexter."

"Why's that?"

"I was always a screw-up. I got by in high school and college because I could hoop. I just knew I was going to the NBA, then I got hurt and my real dream was gone forever. So I started drinking and doing drugs. Dexter put me in rehab and gave me a job here. For the first time in my life my folks started to be proud of me. But living in his huge shadow started to get to me— so I moved down south and started to find my own way— which I did."

"And you don't want to give that up?"

"You got it. I'm now more than a little brother. I'm a grown man."

"So running the business would take you away from your own path."

"And put me back on his."

"Owning the whole kit and caboodle would be the bomb, but man I'm in no position to pull something like that off. Shoot to be real with you. I was about to lose a hundred grand on a car lot up in the Northeast I was trying to buy. The bank hasn't approved my loan." Trey threw up a Hail Mary. "You wouldn't carry the note would you?"

"I really would prefer to be free and clear and just to let you know whomever I sell to will not use the name. Oh by the way have you given any thought to that?"

"To be honest with you I haven't. Everything has happened so fast, although I do want to honor his memory in some way."

"Whatever you decide, I'll back your play with my folks."

Trey escorted Ryan to the door and asked him for his other reason for leaving the business. "I hated selling cars. Peace out top dog."

CHAPTER THIRTY-SIX

"You've made a wise decision. You'll see your career is about to blow up."

"Yeah," Ian said feeling like he'd sold his soul to the devil at the crossroads. A devil in a thong. "So do I at least get to pick the producer?"

"We'll see," Taylor said. "Let's ink the deal first."

"Isn't that part and parcel of a solid deal?"

"Honey let's not forget this isn't my first rodeo."

"Yeah, I'm sure you've been ridden many times," Ian shot back.

"Cute. I'll see you in LA in two weeks." Taylor spun around on her hooker-heels and without a glance backward walked out of Ian's apartment.

Ian grabbed one of the folded boxes he'd picked up from U-Haul. He had exactly two weeks to pack up his belongings, get out of his lease and head off to the land of sunshine, silicone and shattered dreams. Well as his grand-mother used to say— God willing and the creek don't rise— his dream wouldn't become one of the shattered. As he cleared the cabinets of canned goods to take to the homeless shelter, he laughed finding it funny that as an adult he repeated more and more the sayings that he heard as a child. Life sure did have a way of repeating itself no matter the generation. Times change, fashions might change, but good old- fashioned advice always withstood the test of time.

Twelve hours and ten trash bags full of throwaways and thirty-five boxes later he completed his task. The only items that remained undone were selling his furniture and his car and sweet-talk his landlord into letting him out of his lease two years before its end date. Out of every thing, the latter would be look pulling teeth from a snigger-tooth tiger.

Ian threw himself across his queen-sized bed that had lost its cover during his packing frenzy. The cover now sat neatly folded in the bedding box. *That was stupid*, he fussed to himself. *It's not like I'm out of here tomorrow.* He rolled off the bed and used the cutting knife to remove the tape from the box so he could retrieve his sheets and blanket. Methodically he remade his bed like it would get inspected in the morning. First he laid the fitted sheet and pulled it as tight as it would go, then he placed the second sheet and put hospital corners on each end, then he laid the blanket over the sheets folding the top of the blanket back equally on both sides. Finally he fluffed and stuffed his soft pillows into the matching pillow cases. Ian took two deep breaths which he held to the mental count of three and then released it with a sigh. He gave his mind permission to relax and wished that his body would obey the command as well.

After over twenty years of hoping to catch a break and more disappointment than he cared to remember (like he would ever forget), and as much as he hated to admit it— especially since his opinion of Taylor had changed drastically— she had come through in the end. The recording contract wasn't necessarily with a major label like he would have liked. But, at least he was with a label that would have national distribution and money to market their product. If D-Jay lived up to his word and gave him everything he'd promised — such as solid material and allowing him to record some of the songs he'd written as well as getting him radio play, which was a must for a recording artist— then he had no doubt that he could become a platinum- selling hit. Music lovers were hungry for music that made sense and talked about finding and keeping love and not just making love in a jeep. That was the void he wished to fill. Realistically the odds were very much stacked against him. Forty-year old singers didn't burst on the music scene everyday. He would be competing with the Ushers and Chris Browns of the industry who appealed to younger demographics. Finding his audience would be the obstacle he faced. But it was a challenge he looked forward to. He'd waited too long to not give it his very best. So no matter what happened in LA and with this opportunity, he could one day sit on the porch and reflect back and say, "I gave it everything I had and here are the results."

Purposely Ian had put one other task out of his mind. He decided that procrastination wasn't going make things any less painful. He picked up the phone to make the call he'd been putting off making. "Hey, Trey," he said when he came on the line. "Let's meet up at the Lasagna Warehouse for dinner about seven tonight." Trey agreed and he hung up the phone a mere second before the floodgate broke loose. He and Trey had been "boys" since elementary school— more like brothers than best friends—so the thought of moving across country away from his closet friend in the world filled him with a searing pain he hadn't felt since his father passed away.

Sitting in the middle of his living room floor, song lyrics kept bouncing around in his head. They demanded to be released so much so he felt strongly compelled to get up and grab his writing pad off the top of one of the packed boxes.

Without knowing it in less than twenty minutes, Ian wrote the tune that would go on to become a smash hit on his debut album defying the critics, skeptics and even D-Jay and Taylor.

****

The dust that had accumulated over the years in the storage room that housed old papers and documents from governments of the past had Tina and her co-worker sneezing and their eyes blood-shot red.

"This is some flat out bull," her co-worker shouted. "You mean to tell me that in this day and time they can't put this stuff on a computer."

"Girl," Tina cautioned, "lower your voice before she hears you complaining." The "she" Tina was referring to was their overbearing, obnoxious supervisor who ran the file clerk department with an iron-fist and an if-you-don't-like-it-quit mentality.

"Look if we stand up to her things would have to change around here."

"Okay, Norma Rae. You do your thing. I'll keep my job."

Through another bout of sneezing and wheezing her co-worker rolled her bug-eyes at Tina and muttered under her breath. Through all that she continued putting papers into folders and putting the folders back into labeled boxes that felt like they contained baby elephants.

"Tina," the slave-driver called out from the doorway of the storage room. "At my desk in ten minutes."

“Don’t dilly-dally now; master has beckoned you to the big house.”

“If you hate the job so much, why you been here five years?” Tina fired back.

“Shoot girl. You know darn well I got mouths to feed.”

“Yeah just what I thought,” she laughed, playfully nudging her complaining co-worker.
“I wonder why she wants to see me.”

“You get tested yet?”

“Tested?”

“Urine test.”

“Yeah I’m good,” Tina responded suddenly feeling light-headed. Rubbing her hands together nervously she did a dead-man-walk to the ladies room to run some water over her face. Standing over top of the sink she concentrated on slowing her breathing. She didn’t want to panic, but the longer she stood in front of the mirror looking at the disheveled image looking back at her only served to make her more nervous. *Get it together, girl. Think positive.* This is one test she definitely prayed before God she hadn’t failed.

The walk from the restroom to her supervisor’s desk reminded her of every movie she’d ever seen where the prisoner was being led down a dark hallway as he or she tried to keep their composure as their knees buckled and right before they entered the gas chamber they started to freak out. The only thing that prevented Tina from going absolutely bonkers was the fact that there were two other people surrounding her boss’s desk and her curiosity took over.

“Oh Tina there you are,” the normally salty woman said sweetly.

“You wanted to see me?”

“Yes my dear. Tina this is City Councilwoman Randle and Mr. Randle.”

The expensively clad woman extended her manicured hand with an amused smile plastered on her handsome face. "Hello Tina."

Tina almost bowed at the waist, "Hello." She didn't want to stare or appear like a country-bumpkin coming to the big city for the first time, but the woman standing in front of her had an imposing bearing. She had it going on from her designer two-piece pant suit and her salon-styled hair. It seemed to Tina that Miss Randle had taken a page straight out of the how-to-be-fabulous guide written by the Queen herself, Miss Oprah.

"This is my husband, Jonathan." They shook hands.

"Now as I told you, Councilwoman Randle, Tina here is one of my hardest workers. She is always on time, never complains and does every task assigned to her effectively and efficiently."

Tina smiled tightly wondering how much she would fetch on the auction block. Besides in the two months she'd been employed at City Hall all her tasks consisted of was filing papers, copying papers and filing the copied papers. To hear her boss give her such a glowing report only served to fuel the flame of panic inside of her.

"Well Tina," the councilwoman said. "I guess you are wondering what this is all about."

"Yes ma'am," she said in a soft voice.

"As you may know or maybe you don't I worked closely with the Mayor in getting this work program underway."

Tina recalled reading in the papers that some of the city council strongly opposed the program, calling it a drain on the city's already strapped budget. And if memory served her correctly it was the woman in front of her who was most vocal in opposition. But wisely she said, "Thank you so much for doing so."

"Yes, you're welcome. Anyway the reason for this little meeting is I'm in need of an assistant and you came very highly recommended to me."

"I did?"

"They asked me who I thought would do the best job and I recommended you," her supervisor proudly stated.

"Would you like the job?" Councilwoman Randle asked.

"Hell…I mean yes I would."

"Fabulous, here's my card I'll see you next Monday morning seven-thirty sharp. And dear, the dress is business attire."

As she and her silent husband walked away Tina didn't hear her say, "So you think this will soften my image and get my approval ratings up?"

Even if she had heard, Tina wouldn't have cared. All she cared about centered on getting as far away from that dusty, moldy file room as she possibly could get.

"Can I take the rest of the day off to try and find an outfit for Monday?"

"Have you lost your mind? Get back to work; you still belong to me until then." The wicked witch of City Hall had re-emerged.

****

The privately-owned Cessna approached the landing with a wide-eyed Taylor onboard. Experience had taught her many lessons over the years. The first time she came to LA on a bus she'd had only a broken-handled suitcase with enough clothes to be considered empty. Now Taylor Daniels was returning, like an exiled Queen ready to reclaim her throne. By time the plane landed and the chauffeur-driven limo took her back to the mansion she and D-Jay used to share, the heifer who had taken her space for the past two years should have vacated the premises. She'd come too far to not go all the way. If he wanted her to be his wife, so be it. If a girl had to get locked down it might as well be with a lot of perks. No pre-nuptial agreement for her. Fifty-fifty, just like California martial laws stated.

The plane might have been descending from the clouds, but Taylor's head was still in the sky.

Meanwhile as one bird was coming back to the coop another was being set free. "Open this door! Let me in. I live here," the blonde woman hollered at the top of her lungs.

"Please go away, Miss Suzette," D-Jay's housekeeper said through the intercom. "My orders were to not let you in. The locks have been changed and all of your possessions are waiting for you at the hotel in Crenshaw. Mr. D-Jay said you would know the one."

What a slap in the face. Not only had she been kicked out of the mansion she'd called home for the past two years; he had the cruel audacity to send her back to the same fleabag dump she swore she would never set foot in again. Attempting to save a small measure of her dignity she shouted, "Well tell that loser I'm keeping the Corvette."

"I was told to tell you that you could keep the car. And if you look in the glove box you will find a check for your severance pay."

Suzette kicked the front door three times, breaking a heel in the process, before limping off. She refused to shed one tear over being humiliated and treated like…like…a Hollywood booty call that got to stay over until the caller wanted to switch over to the other line. There wasn't any proof that her nemesis Taylor had decided to return to reclaim her spot, but D-Jay's cowardly actions surely gave evidence. Letting her keep a used car and giving her a check resembled throwing a bone to a dog. The nerve of him, having his illegal alien housekeeper stand guard at the door and speak to her through a box. Then to give her a check called, "severance," something an employer gave to a fired worker, not to someone who shared your home and bed for two years.

Suzette stomped around the large stoned-circular driveway until the final blow to her dignity showed up. A police car pulled into the driveway. The officer on the passenger side rolled down the window once the car came to a stop beside her. "Miss we just received a complaint that you are trespassing on the premise. You need to vacate these premises now." He spoke with full authority and the tone in his voice left no room to doubt that he was serious.

"I live here," she said weakly.

"Not anymore."

****

"Is she gone?"

"Yes, Mr. D-Jay the police just came and she's driving off."

D-Jay clapped his hands together gleefully. "Maria happy days are here again, my baby is coming back home!" He picked her up and spun her around before he ran up the spiral staircase taking two steps at a time.

Maria watched her employer run up the stairs. Never had she seen him in such great spirits. However after working for two washed-up movie stars prior to coming to work for D-Jay, she'd seen it all. These people fell in and out of love quicker than a dollar was lost at the slot machines. That reminded her, she could go to Vegas with her girlfriends after all. He'd given her a nice bonus for doing his dirty work.

CHAPTER THIRTY-SEVEN

The Lasagna Warehouse was a little- known bistro frequented by true lovers of old-world Italian food— owned for over seventy-five years by the same family— passed down from one generation to the next. The interior of the restaurant remained dimly lit regardless of the time of day, allowing one to eat in peace. Besides the finger-sucking great food, one of the main reasons celebrities and public figures often came was to eat dinner served on real china, sterling silverware and the biggest heaping of pasta served anywhere in the city.

Ian had stumbled across the place ten years ago while performing in a bar down the street from the restaurant and had wandered in looking to get a late night snack. One bite of the lasagna and he became a regular customer. The owner's daughter heard him sing and became a fan. Now his signed picture hung on the wall alongside Tony Bennett and Nat King Cole. That was an honor that still resonated in his heart eight years later. Every time he entered the place his eyes searched the wall to ensure that the picture still hung.

"Ian, my boy. How yaw been?" The elderly owner greeted him at the door. Although he'd been born in Philadelphia he spoke with a deep Italian accent like he'd just arrived from Sicily. "Itsa been a long time."

They greeted each other with a hug and peeks on both cheeks. "Itsa still there." He said noticing Ian's eye travel to the wall.

As he showed Ian to a private booth they caught up on each other's lives. He listened with pride to Ian's great news about finally realizing his dream. He was sad to hear that he had to leave the city to do so. "So your paesano is coming?"

"Yes he'll be here shortly," said Ian.

"I'll get yaw some fresh bread and a bottle of my finest vino, on the house."

Fifteen minutes later a plump waitress led Trey over to Ian. "I see your picture is still up."

"Hey man." Ian exclaimed, "'Bout time you got here. I already went through two baskets of bread." The two old friends warmly embraced and Ian held on a tad longer than usual.

"First day in charge of the salt mines," Trey said snatching up the last piece of garlic bread much to Ian's dismay.

"So how did that go?"

"Much better than I thought it would."

"How are things at the ole homestead?" Ian inquired. "Please tell me you didn't tell Andrea everything."

"We haven't had a chance to talk yet," said Trey. "I was planning on telling her tonight."

"Think that one through, man. I'm not saying I condone what happened but honesty isn't always the best policy."

"I'm torn. On one hand I agree with you and on the other and I don't know why, it's kicking my butt."

"Maybe it's just an accumulation of everything and not just that one," said Ian.

"Could be, but since I don't know for certain…"

Ian interrupted, "Do like the Marines and don't ask, don't tell."
"Army."

"What?"

"I was in the Army. It's also the Army's policy of don't ask don't tell."

"Whatever. You do the same thing."

The aroma of garlic-tinged tomato sauce hit their nostrils as the plump waitress approached their table with two heaping plates of three-cheese lasagna— the house special. Conversation ceased as they dug into the food. Ian went through two platters and was working on his third while Trey struggled to finish his first.

"You know one of these days you're going to get fat eating like that," Trey assured him.

"I have the metabolism of a teenager."

"Man, if I ate like that I would blow up."

"I come from a long line of skinny folks," said Ian. "Don't hate on the genes."

Finally over a shared slice of New York style cheese cake, Ian dropped his good news/bad news bomb. He confided that the main reason he decided to sign with D-Jay's label had more to do with his fear of this really being his last chance than any of Taylor's weak threats.

"Bro, I seriously believe she would eat her first born," said Ian. "But I would rather have her on my side than on the other team."

"For sure," agreed Trey. "You know you have to give her credit though. Since you met your career has taken off."

"Although I don't want to I have to concur. The girl is a whiz at getting things done and making that cheddar. You know man, for my last gig at the Blue Way I was paid five grand?"

"For the showcase?"

"Yep. She worked it that I got a piece of the gate and a percentage of the bar over whatever she and the old man agreed."

"Is that common?"

"Not unheard of, but I haven't ever pulled anything off like that. And to be honest I never gave it any thought."

"Well the girl is obviously a good businesswoman."

They both knew they were simply having cocktail conversation to avoid talking about the impeding separation. Since the first day of school during the second grade the two of them had been practically inseparable. Even when Trey joined the Army and went to basic training at Fort Dix, they still managed to see each other on weekends. And during his three months of job training at Fort Lee, Ian was performing as the house band for a nightclub just a few towns away. Andrea often joked that when the preacher asked the question about anyone having cause to stop the wedding, she swore she saw Ian raise his hand. So to think that in less than two weeks there would be over 2300 miles between them, both men suddenly felt like little boys going off alone to summer camp for the first time.

Trey broke the silence. "You realize we haven't gone more than a week or so without seeing each other since we met?"

Hard-headed tears dampened Ian's eyes. "I was thinking the same thing. Even when you went into the Marines we still hung out. And I have to admit, I really thought you getting married and having kids would make a difference but it didn't."

"Army. I was in the Army," Trey corrected him for the hundredth time. "We're more than friends, man— we brothers— I love you, man."

"I love you too. Hey let's go to our other spot for old-time's sake."

"They tore Richards down," Trey reminded him talking about the little corner bar on Mt. Airy Avenue they used to frequent.

"Not there."

"Where?"

"Rock Creek Park. Remember how we used to hang out there as kids and drink water from that little creek?"

“Man, I ain’t drinking water from that creek; you know how many years ago that was?”

“Not for the water, the memories.”

“What the hey. Let me give Drea a shout and tell her I’ll be a little late.”

As Trey called home, Ian signaled for the check. The plump waitress waddled over and whispered in Ian’s ear, “Mario said it’s on the house.”

CHAPTER THIRTY-EIGHT

There's an old song that children sing that talks about the wheels on a bus going round and round, and for some reason that little ditty played in his head as he imagined getting run over by that bus. First his past came to visit and hold him accountable for previous deeds. Then the husband of his current backslide came to him for help. Of all people. Now his present was threatening to destroy his future.

"Look here, Pastor," Deacon Allen said. "My wife may be a meddlesome woman and sometimes she can get up into everybody's business."

Pastor Douglas waited impatiently for him to get to the point. It wasn't simple intuition that told him that Deacon Allen was about to drop a bomb on him— it was plain old street-sense. When he received the deacon's phone call at his apartment insisting that they meet at the church, he knew the time had come for him to pay up.

"As you know, she believes that something is either going on or went on between you and Sister Edwards."

"I was under the impression that that matter was explained and resolved."

"Not quite."

"Why not?"

"Have you noticed that Sister Edwards hasn't been in attendance the past few weeks?"

"Well, neither has her husband, if I recall. Maybe they are visiting other churches."

"Her husband hasn't been a regular since he was a kid, but Sister Edwards has attended this same church since she her family moved to Philly."

"I'm sure there's nothing to worry about."

"Boy, I'm going to ask you straight. Enough of this dilly-dallying around." Deacon Allen spoke with a sharpness that froze Pastor Douglas in his seat. "Are you sleeping with a married woman?"

The air in the office became a little thick. He suddenly lost the ability to breathe. From everything Pastor Douglas could tell about the man who sat across from him, he was not one to mince his words. And with his responsibility as head deacon, he held a lot of clout. If Deacon Allen told the congregation it was going to rain on Saturday, most of them would buy an umbrella on Friday. The man carried enough weight as one of the founding fathers of the church to have him removed with a single phone call to the other weak-kneed members. That had been his major concern since accepting the pastoral position at a church controlled by a deacon board. Once he got out of this mess, he would have to work on changing some of the by-laws of the church. The flock followed the Shepard, not the other way around.

"With all due respect, Deacon I will not dignify that question with a response." *That's it take the moral high ground.* "As I said, this matter has been addressed and laid to rest."

"Well son, I'm resurrecting it."

"Why?"

"People are starting to talk."

"People? Don't you mean a person, namely your big-mouth wife?"

"Watch it now. The woman might talk too much, but don't you forget she is still my wife."

"I'm sorry," back-pedaled Pastor Douglas. "This is getting us nowhere."

Deacon Allen softened his tone and leaned forward, placing both elbows on the desk. "Son, believe it or not I was once young myself." He raised his hand to silence the Pastor. "In my seventy-odd years on this here earth I've seen and done my share of dirt. And I'm sad to report that most of that was in the church. People of God are a peculiar brand of folk. We despise the devil and yet we get caught up in his mess. Now son, you wouldn't be the first man who sat in that there chair and made a mistake. And when you make a mistake, and come out and confess that mistake, those same peculiar folks who judge you will ultimately acquit you. But if they catch you in a lie that you keep telling, they will sentence you. Now you don't have to confess to me, but as a leader of God's peculiar folks, I'm here to tell you that you of all people know who to confess to."

"And lose everything."

"No man walks this earth without making mistakes. We just hoped that the ones you made down South stayed there."

Pastor Douglas' breath got caught up again. He swallowed hard and couldn't stop his eyes from blinking rapidly. "You know about that?"

"Son we knew what we were getting when we hired you. This is a church. Where else can a person come to receive a second chance if not the House of the Lord?"

"But why did I get the job?"

"Because you received the call of the Lord to preach His word. Now as I said you ain't the first man to sit in that same chair and make mistakes. So if you plan on staying in that seat. I strongly suggest you be as strong and righteous a man as your predecessor and get it right. You can start by leaving that woman alone and if you can't be like the Apostle Paul, I also strongly suggest you get a wife of your own."

"Deacon Allen there's one thing I still don't understand," said Pastor Douglas clearly confused.

"What's that?"

"Actually a couple of things, first off does the entire board know about Georgia and secondly are you going to tell your wife?"

"No and are you crazy? Son, only I and the last man who sat where you now sit know. And if you give your solemn word right here and right now—we can move on and continue doing the work that God sent you here to do."

"My word on what?"

"Number one, that whatever happened between you and Sister Edwards is over. And two, that if you can't keep it in your pants you can resign right now. I'll give you a glowing recommendation."

Pastor Douglas rose humbly to his feet and extended his hand to the wiser older man. "Sir you have my word as a Man of God that what transpired between Sister Edwards and me is over and will never happen again and I mean with no one."

"That's good enough for me. Now son, don't go having no Jimmy Swaggart moment. Keep it out of your next sermon. Take it to the Lord in prayer, ask for his forgiveness and sin no more.

"Yes sir."

Deacon Allen pulled him around the desk to accept his embrace. As he turned to leave he stopped short and said, "Pastor Douglas when a man accepts the call from Jesus to become a solider in the army of the Lord he puts himself on the front line of the spiritual battle. That man can either become a warrior or a casualty. You decide. My last piece of sage advice to you is this; get into your prayer closet and don't come out until you know that He's given you the strength and ability to resist the pull of the flesh. You do that and as a witness to HIS prayer- answering mercy, I tell you. He will do it."

And once Pastor Raymond Douglas was alone, that's just what he did.

****

Trey entered the house through the garage half-expecting his family to be up waiting for him. A glance at his Rolex quickly dispelled that illusion. It was one-thirty in the morning. Time had flown by so fast after he and Ian left the bistro and drove down East River Drive to get to Rock Creek Park. Once they pulled up in separate cars Ian had hopped into Trey's Benz and insisted that they find a bar to pick up a bottle of wine like back in the day. They drove over to Ridge Avenue and grabbed a pint of cheap wine that if mishandled could take the paint off a car. Since neither of them really drank liquor it didn't make sense to Trey. But Ian's insistence on re-creating a moment from the past won out. Back at the park —which was really just a small section of Fairmount Park— they sat on a boulder and poured out half the bottle in memory of the others who either were no longer above ground or those who were currently trying to dig their way out of a hole called prison. "You know, man, back in the day if we had poured out this much wine in honor of the brothas that ain't with us, we would have caught a bullet," Ian had joked.

For hours the two best friends sat on that rock passing the bottle back and forth and pretending to sip on the paint-thinner and reminisced about growing up in North Philly. They argued about how they first met and all the trouble they had gotten into over the years. Surprisingly it was Trey that broke down first. Ian held it together for as long as he could but once he noticed Trey sniffling and blinking his eye dam broke loose as well. If anyone had happened to past by they would have witnessed two forty-year old men hugging and balling like they were the last two passengers left off the lifeboats of the Titanic.

Then before they could digress any further in time, the two old friends walked arm in arm back to the parking lot and drove off with tears of happiness for each others recent good fortunes. And they were consumed with sadness that 2300 miles of highway would do what time, age, marriage, kids and careers hadn't done before— separate them.

CHAPTER THIRTY-NINE

Timing is often said to mean everything. If only someone had reminded Trey. Sitting in his newly acquired office he felt pretty confident that he could find a way out of his minor dilemma. So thinking positive thoughts he picked up the phone determined to solve one problem at a time. And with that telephone call his timing was off by twenty minutes. It became one the most costly calls of his life. "Good day sir, this is Trey Edwards," he announced full of bravado. It was short-lived. "No sir I haven't finalized the finances as of yet. However if you aren't aware, I recently became the new owner of Fortune Motors and if you just give me a few more days I'm certain…"

The person on the other end of the line spoke very loud causing Trey to hold the phone away from his ear and even then he was still able to hear the man clearly. "Mr. Edwards that is not acceptable to me. I have given you ample time to get your finances in order. You aren't the only party interested in obtaining my dealership."

"Yes, yes," Trey said feeling less confident by the moment. "But maybe you didn't hear me. I'm the new owner of Fortune Motors and once I go to the bank I'm certain they will approve the loan. So all I'm asking for is a little more time, just a day or so."

"Young man, I would really like to help you, but I'm sorry. If I don't have a check by close of business today, you will simply forfeit your deposit per our agreement. Business is business." He hung up.

Dumbfounded he replaced the receiver. No longer did he feel so sure of himself. There was still a slight glimmer of hope though. Trey dialed the bank and waited while the annoying robotic voice instructed him through the many channels of delay that accompanies calling any business in today's hands-off, impersonal way of taking calls. Finally after two minutes of going through the prompts an operator came on the line to direct his call. Mr. Davis, the loan officer handling Trey's application, answered on the third ring. "Mr. Davis, this is Trey Edwards," he announced.

"Good morning Mr. Edwards how may I assist you?"

"Well for starters you can tell me my loan has been approved."

"I'm sorry it hasn't."

"I didn't think so." Trey wanted to scream. "Look I recently inherited Fortune Motors if that would help my case."

"Under normal circumstances it might have, but in today's uncertain economic climate it's getting harder and harder for small businesses to get capital without strong established credit and collateral."

"I have good credit," protested Trey.

"Yes you do. But that's personal, not business. Mr. Edwards you don't have a track record as a business owner. But if you reapply six months to a year down the line we would probably look more favorably at your request."

"Damn man," he shouted into the phone. "Don't you understand? I don't have six months. I need the money today or I stand to lose one hundred thousand dollars."

"I'm truly sorry Mr. Edwards."

"Wait you mentioned collateral. I own this business out-right."

"A word of advice?"

"Go 'head."

"Have you ever run a car dealership before?"

"That sounded like a question."

"It was," said Mr. Davis.

"No," answered Trey.

"Just playing devil's advocate here, what if the car industry takes a greater hit than it has recently and your dealership doesn't sell as many cars as it has?"

"What's your point?"

"My point and advice is this, don't bite off more than you can chew."

"I can't swallow losing one hundred grand," Trey exclaimed.

"I'm not a tax advisor but since you are now a business owner, write it off as an expense and a lesson learned."

"Easy for you to say it's not your money."

"Mr. Edwards are you really ready to run two dealerships in two separate locations?"

"I don't know," he answered honestly.

"Don't lose the house trying to save the barn as my granddaddy used to say."

Trey disconnected the call, totally oblivious to the fact that if he had called the bank first the owner of the car lot would have called him and wanted out of the deal.

At five thirty in the afternoon, Trey's attorney called to inform him that since the time had expired on the written agreement for the dealership and he couldn't finalize the purchase, the money currently held in escrow would be paid out to the owner as the agreement stipulated.

Not even a business owner for an entire week and Trey had already lost money.

****

Andrea had made up her mind. Tonight would be the night that all dirty laundry got cleaned. She left work early and picked the kids up from school and dropped them off to spend the night with her mother. They protested and her mother mildly complained but she put her foot down with all three and drove home to set the stage for what she prayed wouldn't become a modern-day OK Corral. Earlier in the day she had called Trey to find out what time he would arrive home. He sounded distracted, but she chalked that up to stress and his getting settled with all his new responsibilities. Despite all of her worries over the years and fearing that he would one day make another sole decision that affected the entire family without her knowledge— she had to give credit where due. By the grace of God they'd managed to survive and thrive and much to her surprise he had taking to selling cars like he was born to it. Her largest concern with him simply quitting his insurance career at the time centered on money and the security that came from knowing where your next dollar was coming from. Not to mention that in all the time they'd been together he had never uttered one word of interest about being in the car business, let alone selling automobiles for a living.

But now everything had worked off for the best. And since forgiveness started within, she pledged to forgive Trey just as she surely needed his forgiveness. As soon as she made a full-bodied decision to forgive her husband for making a career change— without consulting her first— she felt a tremendous weight lifted off of her spirit. Andrea instantly realized that part of the wedge that existed between her and her husband had to do with her losing trust in him and how his making that call on his own made her feel powerless. For years she'd harbored feelings of resentment toward Trey and never wanted to admit that she did. Maybe he was right all along that she punished him through sex and if that was the case, intimacy suffered in their marriage as a result. Well as of tonight, no more punishment, no more resentment, and no more dirty laundry. *As if it was that easy.* She truly hoped so.

Andrea looked at the clock on the nightstand as she undressed. She had better kick it up a notch; Trey would be home in ninety minutes if he stayed on course. Knowing his affinity for scented candles Andrea quickly threw on her robe and ran downstairs to light some in the living room. She placed one on the dining room table so they could eat the meal she had prepared by candlelight. Since he didn't seem to enjoy his favorite meal the last time she fixed it— she went back to an oldie but goodie— fried pork chops, string beans and garlic mashed potatoes. Sorting through the drawers in the kitchen she couldn't find a single match. Looking at the kitchen clock hastened her search. Andrea looked in every conceivable place she could think of in the lower level of the house. Then she remembered that Trey always kept a candle lighter in his nightstand.

Andrea checked the time again and ran back upstairs to retrieve the lighter. Pulling open the nightstand drawer she reached in and grabbed hold of the lighter and pulled it out. As she attempted to close the drawer a large folder prevented the drawer from closing completely. Pulling the folder out to rearrange its contents a slip of paper fell to the carpeted floor. Andrea reached down to pick it up. Everything had to be back in its proper place since Trey got angry anytime he thought she had been snooping in his nightstand, ever since she found that men's magazine with the half-naked women. She rolled her eyes when he argued that the articles were the only reason he'd bought it. Laughing at the memory, Andrea sat on the bed to rearrange the paperwork. As she was putting everything back in order she spotted a statement from their joint retirement account. That was strange. He never kept any financial papers in his nightstand. It was her job to keep track of their money. Something else was even stranger. If her eyes weren't deceiving her the total at the bottom of the second page stated that their balance had taken a huge drop since the last quarterly statement. Well that explained why he had the file. He was probably on top of the matter.

But then again, better safe than sorry. Andrea picked up the phone and called the 800 number listed for Savings and Trust. After ten long minutes of listening to the worst elevator music version of "Endless Love" she had ever heard, a disinterested voice asked her for the purpose of her call. "I'm calling to speak with someone in regard to my last quarterly statement. I believe a mistake has been made."

"Please hold," the lifeless voice said. Within seconds another voice came on the line and asked the purpose of her call. Andrea repeated herself and waited on hold; this time the torture song was "Celebration" by Kool and the Gang.

"Thank you for holding, Mrs. Edwards. Our records indicate that a request was granted for a withdrawal for one hundred thousand dollars."

"That's impossible," Andrea blurted out. "We never made any such request and I know I didn't authorize a withdrawal for that amount of money."

"Ma'am, I'm looking at the file and both your and your husband's signatures are on the request and withdrawal paperwork. You should have a copy of both."

Flabbergasted Andrea hung up while the voice was still rambling on. She riffled through the folder and sure enough there it was— a request form and at the bottom of the page was her signature. Only she hadn't signed it, nor had she signed the withdrawal paperwork in the folder. In fact she'd never seen either document before.

Andrea lay back across the bed to counter the spinning of the room. It was happening all over again. The feelings of mistrust, lack of power and resentment came back just as quickly as she'd released them. He had done it again!

CHAPTER FORTY

She met him at the door with a fury that rivaled a fresh kill in a wolf pack. Totally taken aback he grabbed the flailing hands that were beating him across his chest and narrowly missing his face. "Take your hands off me!" Andrea shouted at the top of her lungs.

"What's your problem?" Trey asked, refusing to let go. "Why are you swinging on me like you lost your mind?" Inwardly he suspected he already knew the answer.

Calming down just enough to convince him she wasn't going to cold-cock him. She snatched away and stormed into the living room. Andrea sat down on the couch, tucking her legs underneath her buttocks. She looked up at him with fire shooting from her darkened brown eyes. "Why?"

That one word felt like she had taken a pair of pliers and ripped his heart clean out of his chest. He searched her face for just the slightest sign of compassion. None existed, but if he was looking for contempt, every fiber in her body let him know he'd found it.

"It's not what you think," he said timidly. "Just let me explain."

"Explain," she huffed. "Let you explain how you have disrespected me."

"Baby…"

"Don't baby me!" she snapped. He was so lucky that the candleholder sat on the mantelpiece and not on the coffee table as it normally had before she'd moved it earlier. Andrea wanted to throw something at him so badly. "You are so selfish."

Trey slowly approached the couch and when she didn't protest he sat down as close to the opposite edge as he could without sitting on the arm of the couch. "It meant nothing."

"It did to me."

"I'm so sorry; it was a moment of weakness. I promise you it will never happen again."

"So you took money from our retirement account and forged my name all in a moment of weakness?"

Trey felt like he'd dodged a bullet and in his elated state he opened wide and put both feet into his mouth. "Oh that. I thought you were upset about Taylor."

Andrea sat up straight and looked him in square in the eye. "What about Taylor?"

"Huh?"

"You heard me. Why would I be upset about Taylor?"

"Nothing…nothing," He attempted to recover. "Look I'm sorry about the …."

"Stop Trey! I want to know why you mentioned Ian's girlfriend and why you thought I was upset about her."

"I thought that she told you about the account."

"You're lying," she said.

"Huh?"

"You're biting your top lip. Every time you lie. You bite your top lip."

What a time to find out how she always knew when he wasn't being completely honest. Now the real moment of truth had arrived for him. No matter how he tossed it around, he couldn't find a way out. He'd blown his best shot with the weakest explanation he could come up with on the spur of the moment. Trey stood up and moved over to the recliner chair that sat next to the fireplace. He wanted to be as far away from her as possible when he confessed. "Taylor came into the dealership to buy a car." He forced himself to look at Andrea and saw her beckon him to continue. "We went for a test drive and stopped to get a bite to eat."

"Stop," said Andrea so softly she almost didn't hear her own voice. "Stop talking," she said a little louder.

"Drea," Trey said. "Let me finish."

"This can't be happening," she said. "I need some air."

Trey jumped out of the recliner and raced to the center of the room to reach out for her. Andrea held up her hands and backed away. She knocked over the flower vase on the side coffee table as she grabbed her car keys. Turning to face Trey she whispered, "Two wrongs don't make a right, but you got me beat." Then she left the house.

But no sooner as the front door slammed shut, than Trey heard the alarm beep announcing the door was opened. Andrea walked back into the living room and walked up to Trey. She put her arms around his neck and pulled his head down onto her shoulders. Andrea slid her arms from his neck and kissed him softly on his lips. Taking his hands in hers she led Trey over to the couch.

"I didn't sleep with her," he said not bothering to wipe his wet face.

"I had sex with someone," she said wiping his face.

Trey saw her mouth moving, but his brain didn't fully register the words. He looked at her as if he was seeing her for the first time. He gazed into her moist eyes hoping to read another story other than the one he was about to hear.

Andrea told him everything not leaving out a single detail. She spoke as if each word weighed a ton. She took a deep breath on almost every syllable. She made no excuses for her actions and during the entire reciting of her misdeed she held onto his hands.

"Never in my wildest imagination would I believed I would be capable of doing such a horrible thing," she said. "I was so afraid to tell you and so ashamed of what I'd done that for the longest time I couldn't even pray and ask God to forgive me."

"You had sex with a preacher?" His shock was so evident that she couldn't help but wonder if that was what was keeping him so calm.

"Yes."

"And I went to that guy with my troubles and he sat right there knowing what he had done."

"I can't speak for him but he probably wanted to confess to you himself."

"Why didn't he?"

"I guess he was like me. He was also afraid of the consequences." She felt him tighten the grip on her hand making her flinch in pain. "I believe you that you didn't sleep with Taylor."

"Earlier that might have meant something to me," he said releasing her hand and standing up. "All this time you've made me beg you to make love to me and you were lusting after another man."

"I guess I deserve that."

"I want to kill somebody right now," Trey said matter-of-factly. He balled his left hand into a fist and punched his right palm. "I'm numb. I'm actually numb. What am I supposed to say to you? What am I suppose to do?"

"Forgive me."

"Are you for real? When I walked up in here you were throwing haymakers at me for forging your name on some paperwork and then you drop this on me and ask me to forgive you?"

"I overreacted, but your doing that made me relive the horror I went through when you up and sold the insurance agency without talking to me first."

"Is that why you slept with another man? Because I changed careers? Do you know how weak that sounds?"

"That's not it at all. I resented you for making me feel powerless. And yes, your doing that rocked my security level."

Trey raised his voice for the first time. "Andrea I am the man, the head of this household and never have I done anything to destroy my family. Can you say the same?"

She sank back against the couch, speechless. His question didn't hurt her as much as the disgust in his tone had. For weeks she had flip-flopped between feeling guilt and shame, to excusing herself and placing full blame on Pastor Douglas, to trying to pretend it had never happened. Now after confessing her sins to her husband and having it out in the open, she couldn't understand why she felt relieved. Her marriage was in great peril, possibly on the verge of total destruction but she felt relieved.

"No I can't," she finally answered. "I was wrong. I had no business putting myself in that position in the first place as a married woman and as a Christian woman."

"You not going to play the Christian card are you?"
"You know me Trey; you know I don't do that."

"Do I know you? The woman I fell in love with and married, the mother of my children she would never become a common whore." He regretted saying it as soon as the words passed his tongue. Even in anger, hurting her was unthinkable. She was the woman he adored more than life itself.

He couldn't have slapped her with his hands and inflicted as much pain. "You know what Trey? That's the one word I kept trying not to call myself, although that's exactly what I feel like."

"You're not a whore," he tenderly said. "I'm sorry. I'm just hurting now that the numbness has passed."

"I'm so sorry for inflicting that pain on you."

"And I'm sorry for doing what I did."

"May I ask you a question?"

"Sure," he responded.

"Now that I know about the money and Taylor do you feel a sense of relief?"

"Kind of. Why did you ask that?"

"Because I feel relieved that I told you. It's almost a sense of peace."

"Why is that?"

"Corny as it may sound, I guess there is truth to the saying that the truth will set you free."

"They should add, it might set you free— but get ready for the cost to your heart."

"Can we move on from this?" Andrea asked prepared to beg if she had to.

Trey found himself spinning the solid gold band on the ring finger of his left ring finger. For fourteen years he'd worn that ring with a sense of pride, commitment and an absolute sureness that nothing and no one could break their bond. But it had been broken. And they both shared the blame. Trey knew in his heart that if Taylor hadn't mistakenly called out the name that his wife called him, he would have had sex with her. And then he would have been no better or different than Andrea. Trey walked back over to the couch and sat closely beside her. "Do you love him?" he asked.

"Oh, Trey! Heavens no! I love you and I always will."

"I don't know what tomorrow may bring, but I do know that tonight I don't want my marriage to end."

"I don't ever want our marriage to end," she cried out.

Husband and wife fell into each other's arms and rocked back and forth as they released bottled up tears of pain, sorrow, regret, and relief. Together, as if their souls spoke one to the other at the same time, they got down on their knees in front of the couch and feverishly called on the Great I AM to enter into their hearts as they confessed their collective sins and prayed for forgiveness, renewal and His will and purpose for their lives.

AMEN!

****

Now faith is the substance of things hoped for, the evidence of things not seen.

But without faith it is impossible to please him; for he that comes to GOD must believe that he is and that he rewards those that diligently seek him.

That is the true blessing of choice and it's called: free will.